Beyond Religious Borders

JEWISH CULTURE AND CONTEXTS

Published in association with the Herbert D. Katz Center for Advanced Judaic Studies of the University of Pennsylvania

A complete list of books in the series is available from the publisher.

Beyond Religious Borders

Interaction and Intellectual Exchange in the Medieval Islamic World

Edited by

David M. Freidenreich
and Miriam Goldstein

PENN

UNIVERSITY OF PENNSYLVANIA PRESS

PHILADELPHIA

Publication of this volume was assisted by a grant from the Martin D. Gruss Endowment Fund of the Herbert D. Katz Center for Advanced Judaic Studies of the University of Pennsylvania Press.

Published by
University of Pennsylvania Press
Philadelphia, Pennsylvania 19104-4112
www.upenn.edu/pennpress
Printed in the United States of America on acid-free paper

10 9 8 7 6 5 4 3 2 1

Library of Congress Cataloging-in-Publication Data
Beyond religious borders : interaction and intellectual exchange in the medieval Islamic world / edited by David M. Freidenreich and Miriam Goldstein. — 1st ed.
p. cm. — (Jewish culture and contexts)
Includes bibliographical references and index.
ISBN 978-0-8122-4374-1 (hardcover : alk. paper)
1. Jews—Islamic Empire—Civilization. 2. Islamic Empire—Civilization. 3. Islamic Empire—Ethnic relations. I. Freidenreich, David M., 1977– II. Goldstein, Miriam Bayla. III. Series: Jewish culture and contexts.
DS135.L4B49 2012
305.60956'0902—dc23

2011023217

CONTENTS

Introduction

MIRIAM GOLDSTEIN

The individuals and communities that lived in the Arabo-Islamic world speak through their many and diverse literary creations with a variety of voices. Distinguishing among these voices and evaluating their interaction is a challenging and often elusive task. For this reason, students of this interaction have conceived of it in various ways, in terms that reveal their differing perspectives and approaches. Terms like "influence" and "reception" emphasize the agency of the "donor culture"; "appropriation" and "accommodation" emphasize the agency of the "adoptive" group or culture; biological metaphors such as "cross-pollination" and "symbiosis" emphasize mutual aspects of exchange; and terms like "diffusion" avoid specifying the means of transfer.[1]

All of these concepts, as well as the phrase "beyond religious borders," assume the existence of virtual "border lines" that establish the boundaries of identity between communities—their members, their compositions, and their ideas. In his book *Border Lines*, Daniel Boyarin compares cross-cultural exchange to a border patrolled by customs inspectors, who monitor and selectively control the crossing of merchandise. Boyarin explains how the border space serves as "a crossing point for people and religious practices," despite the control mechanisms set up by definitions of identity and belonging. He cites an anecdote about a man who crossed the Mexico-U.S. border daily with a wheelbarrow full of dirt. Despite assiduous searches by a customs inspector in the dirt being transported, nothing illegal could be unearthed until on the day of the inspector's retirement it was revealed that the man had spent his life successfully smuggling wheelbarrows. Boyarin's anecdote is an example of the contrived and even humorous nature of such imposed partitionings. The anecdote further demonstrates that cultural goods crossed borders, and did so in unexpected ways, despite the efforts of customs inspectors or other such guards to create sealed boundaries based on considerations of identity. Indeed, Boyarin goes on to claim that the inspectors themselves in certain cases became prominent and unwitting agents of this interchange.[2]

Boyarin's work focuses on the border between Judaism and Christianity in the early centuries of their coexistence, when lines of identity were vague and unclear—and heresiographers were hell-bent on defining them once and for all. In contrast, during the period of Islamic rule, there is little question of who is a Jew, a Christian, a Muslim, a Zoroastrian, a Manichaean, and so on.[3] The borders of group identity, at least between religions, are significantly clearer and for the most part not subject to debate.

Yet despite the relatively clear-cut nature of the individual's religious identity during the Islamic period, the religious identity of ideas and customs remained far from clear. Cultural boundaries were somewhere between semi-permeable and nonexistent; for this reason, the analysis of religious borders is yet relevant in analyzing the relationships between religious groups living under Islamic rule. Numerous lines of affinity linked these groups. The religions of the Near East draw on a lengthy and complex common past and, furthermore, communities of a variety of religions dwelled side by side in various periods. This combination of diachronic kinship and synchronic contiguity led to a complex interrelationship, one in which it is quite difficult to identify and describe the interactions between religions, let alone trace the origins of particular institutions, customs, or scholarly approaches.

Many of the specific questions raised by Boyarin's discussion of identity in the early centuries of the Christian era remain relevant in the Islamic milieu. One area of inquiry relates to the nature of the goods transferred and the reformulation of ideas, customs, or institutions as they traveled along and through communal borders. In what ways were boundaries permeable, and in what ways were they impermeable? In what ways did locally or temporally specific factors affect the nature of such interactions? Other questions relate to the individuals involved in the transfer: To what extent was the process of cultural exchange across communal boundaries conscious? That is, to what extent were members of communities aware that such exchange was taking place, and what was their evaluation of that activity? Furthermore, how did individuals involved in these interactions understand or choose to represent their own identity and that of ideas or institutions that originated on the foreign side of the border?

Marshall G. S. Hodgson, implicitly responding to such questions of identity, proposed a view of the history of the civilization marked by Islamic rule that effectively removes such cultural borders or communal boundaries from consideration.[4] Hodgson explained that non-Muslim groups formed an integral part of the social and intellectual systems that developed in areas of Islamic rule, and he coined the adjective "Islamicate" to replace "Islamic" or "Muslim" in describing these groups and systems. The word "Islamicate" could describe the creations of both orthodox Muslims and non-Muslims in addition to—as Hodgson put it—the decidedly "un-Islamic" creations of certain Muslims. This term, Hodgson argued, could more accurately characterize the variety of elements that contributed to the common civilization of the Near East and Mediterranean during the medieval period.

It was Hodgson's broad perspective—geographic, religious, and chronological—that led him to remove the border lines between religious and ethnic groups alike by speaking instead of an Islamicate civilization. Hodgson viewed this civilization as an Irano-Semitic one dating as far back as Sumerian times yet evolving and developing thanks to overlays from later cultures. For this reason, Hodgson opposed labeling ideas as belonging to one religion or another; he saw them as part of the shared framework native to some degree or another to all the religions of the East and the Mediterranean.

Hodgson's perspective leads to important conclusions regarding interactions across community lines. According to Hodgson's model, parallel ideas proposed by thinkers of different religions are a natural and even predictable occurrence. This predictability, however, does not preclude examination of the parallels. Even while acknowledging a common source for ideas and institutions, the student of such concepts may nevertheless examine their differing contexts and evaluate their transformation in each one, as did Hodgson in his work. Hodgson's model of interreligious relations was part of his more comprehensive aspiration to contextualize Islamic history in the broader framework of world history, and despite criticism of some of his terminological innovations,[5] his broad vision of Islamic civilization was adopted and employed by many later historians.[6]

Shlomo D. Goitein, the great historian of the Cairo Genizah, affirmed like Hodgson that the religions of the Near East were shaped by a common origin, including a shared regional culture and intellectual tradition. Indeed, he called his study of the Jewish society that produced and preserved the documents of the Genizah *A Mediterranean Society*, emphasizing the organic establishment of these Jewish communities in surrounding cultures.[7] In his studies of religious communities, however, Goitein nonetheless portrayed the impact of longstanding and internally transmitted tradition as more significant than that of adopted concepts or institutions.[8] For him, the common origin of distinct religious communities was part of a distant and secondarily relevant past that could account only for a limited and definable number of similarities. Goitein viewed the traditional customs and methods of social organization transmitted over the years within each particular group as the most influential factor in shaping culture and creation.

Despite his belief in the superior weight of internal tradition in shaping culture over and above contemporaneous interactions, Goitein is well-known, and perhaps best known, for the metaphor he coined to describe just this contemporaneous interaction in areas under Islamic rule: the metaphor of biological symbiosis. A similar term—the Romance cognate of symbiosis, "convivencia"—had already been adopted by certain scholars of the Andalusian context who chose to emphasize similar characteristics of the society they studied.[9] In symbiosis or convivencia, two organisms coexist, each preserving its own identity, in a relationship that is either mutualistic or parasitic. This concept in and of itself emphasizes the existence of border lines between communities and the exchange across them. Goitein emphasized the mutual nature of such exchange and viewed the various phases of the relationship between Islam and Judaism with the broad lens—chronologically, in particular—that enabled him to adopt this approach. During the early development of Islam, importation was carried out from Judaism into Islam, while in later centuries, once Islam had become the ruling religion and the majority religion in many areas, the direction was reversed.

The symbiosis metaphor was widely adopted in scholarship following Goitein's usage.[10] Goitein's irenic vision of symbiosis did not present the details of how contact along and across communal borders worked in practice, and later scholars suggested new terminology to characterize its varied aspects and shadings. They used terms such as "accommodation" and "appropriation" to emphasize the agency of adopting cultures in choosing which ideas cross the border, as well as in adapting these ideas to their own cultures. This view was proposed by A. I. Sabra regarding the Arab appropriation—his term—of the scientific heritage of late antiquity, and the same approach underlies studies by Dimitri Gutas.[11] According to this view, adopting cultures make an active choice to accommodate ideas deriving from another culture, via translation or incorporation of these ideas in scholarship, which results in an original act of creation. Modern anthropological studies promote this view as well and emphasize the importance of examining the trajectory of the idea or object that is transmitted rather than tracing its earliest origins.[12]

Goitein's emphasis on symbiosis minimizes consideration of power imbalances, largely due to its broad chronological view of cultural exchange. In contrast, postcolonial studies, which focus specifically on the exchange between colonizer and colonized, highlight the power imbalances in such interactions and the impact of such imbalances on both groups. According to the concept of hybridity, cross-cultural products are created in two ways. Colonized subjects appropriate the language and other cultural forms of the colonizer, often in subversive ways, while in parallel, the colonizer appropriates those of the colonized subject, often with political motives.[13] While this analysis was originally applied to the modern colonial situation, its discussion of the cross-cultural products created in zones of contact can be relevant to the study of minority populations in medieval times, as in Ivan Marcus's consideration of medieval Ashkenaz.[14] Marcus proposes that Jews in northern Europe were attuned to trends in majority Christian culture but that their appropriation of Christian motifs reflects a polemically directed acculturation of inverted or revolutionary imitations. Such acculturation contrasts, in Marcus's analysis, with the symbiotic elite acculturation of Spain or of the Islamic East and creates just the subversive products highlighted in modern studies of colonialism. Viewed in light of revisions of symbiosis such as those proposed by Sabra, Gutas, and others, hybridity further emphasizes the agency of the minority or weaker group carrying out the act of accommodation as well as the political realities that constrain and shape such agency.

The essays in this volume explore the nature of border lines in the Islamic Middle Ages and consider from a variety of vantage points the individuals and cultural products that interacted along and across these lines. They examine the contexts of such encounters and the ways in which they occurred in the early Islamic period; they analyze specific ideas that crossed the borders between groups to find new yet organic settings in others, as well as the mechanisms that motivated such border crossings; and they evaluate how the players in such cultural exchange viewed their own actions. While focused geographically and chronologically on the Islamic Middle East and its mosaic of religious communities, this collection also contains essays that touch on pre-Islamic late antiquity and Christian Europe.

Contexts of Interreligious Interaction

In Part I, our authors consider the cultural contexts of the interaction and exchange that occurred in various locations under Islamic rule. Haggai Ben-Shammai's essay discusses the linguistic changes that were the basis for interaction between communities of Jews and Muslims. Ben-Shammai argues that Jewish material of the sort found in the Qur'an and other early Islamic sources was already available in Arabic as early as the late sixth or early seventh century. This argument sets the beginning of Judeo-Arabic literature and culture significantly earlier than previously thought, shedding light on a period from which few sources survive. The suggestion that Jews were using Arabic in contexts of learning and education, as well as in everyday interaction, even prior to the rise of Islam, confirms the *longue durée* as well as the broad-ranging roots of the shared culture discussed by Goitein and Hodgson.

Milka Levy-Rubin's essay, like Ben-Shammai's, is a reevaluation of well-known evidence and widely accepted assumptions. Levy-Rubin examines the treatment of *ahl al-dhimma*, protected non-Muslim communities, under Islam and presents the asymmetrical nature of Goitein's "symbiosis." Muslims and non-Muslims indeed lived together and shared ideas, but because Muslims were governing, underlying this interaction was a relationship of dominance and subordinance ordained by the Qur'an and detailed in Islamic religious law. These laws imposed particular restrictions on non-Muslim communities that were implemented in varying ways and degrees of severity during the early period of Muslim rule. According to earlier assumptions, these laws were only sporadically issued and were rarely enforced even when they were issued. Levy-Rubin makes the case for the opposite, drawing on both Islamic sources and an often overlooked Samaritan source. Her essay demonstrates that beginning as early as the second Islamic century, caliphs and other rulers regularly promulgated—and enforced—a well-established and familiar set of rules and that they were actively applied well into the Mamluk period and beyond.

Sarah Stroumsa's chapter focuses on the foundations of the Iberian philosophical tradition, emphasizing the practical relevance of analysis of the interactions between cultures. Stroumsa proposes that significant gaps in the understanding of the development of the Iberian tradition of philosophy among Muslims can be resolved by means of consideration of the Jewish role in Andalusian philosophy as a whole. Stroumsa's view, like Hodgson's, suggests that borders are an artificial construction and, at worst, can obfuscate necessary conclusions. The comprehensive analysis that she proposes is, moreover, encouraged by the sources themselves, in which authors of all religions repeatedly refer to Andalusia and Andalusians as possessing a unique local character. Stroumsa's essay concretely demonstrates how the examination of sources from Jewish, Muslim, and Christian traditions as comprising a single intellectual tradition can provide a fuller picture where it is needed. Her work is also an introduction to a broader methodological approach that encourages us to ignore borders, constructed or real, when warranted—indeed, at times demanded—by the subject material.

Adopting and Accommodating the Foreign

Following these essays examining the possibilities of cultural exchange and important limiting factors, the authors in Part II examine the impact of such exchange on ideas that did cross communal boundaries. Sagit Butbul examines a particular example of the products of symbiosis as described by Goitein. Her study spans the pre-Islamic and Islamic periods and focuses on approaches to exegesis that cross the Jewish-Christian border. Butbul suggests both microscopic and macroscopic lines of parallel between Jewish and Christian methods of Bible translation by examining early translations of the Bible into Judeo-Arabic and comparing them with translations into Syriac. She suggests that Jewish translators of the Bible interpreted individual words against the backdrop of a Christian Aramaic translation tradition. Butbul further proposes that approaches to translation in both traditions followed parallel tracks of development in which literal translations replaced an earlier body of paraphrastic translations. Butbul's analysis contributes to a growing body of evidence that suggests the existence of scholarly interchange regarding the Bible between Jews and Christians during the early Islamic period.

The products of symbiosis as described by Goitein emerge from specific and unique contexts: particular periods of time and locations in which particular communities interacted. Such creations are by definition context dependent. In her essay, Talya Fishman examines what happens to such context-dependent elements when they are embedded in a composition that gains canonical status and is transmitted within a religious tradition into a different cultural context. Fishman focuses on the tenth-century Aramaic *Epistle* of Sherira Gaon, in which the Gaon responded to questions regarding the genesis of the Rabbinic tradition. Fishman points out that while Sherira's *Epistle* became the canonical narrative of the origins of tradition, two of Sherira's claims regarding the Mishna had "an inconsistent afterlife" in later adoptions and adaptations of his narrative. She demonstrates that these are precisely the aspects of the composition that were native to Sherira's broader context, the Islamic world, and indeed, would have been familiar to the Gaon as central themes of discourse in contemporaneous Muslim theology. Sherira's assertion that Rabbi Judah the Patriarch personally established the precise language of the Mishna and that he did so as the human agent of a divinely guided process reflects his internalization of Islamic ideas regarding the inimitability of the Qur'an as well as his response to Karaite and Muslim polemics against a written "oral law." While the *Epistle* as a whole became the prism through which Rabbinic tradition was viewed in later and non-Islamic contexts, these two culturally specific ideas disappeared from such accounts. Fishman's analysis points out an important way in which Sherira's view of the Mishna is shaped by the Arabic-speaking environment around him. Furthermore, she demonstrates that intellectual goods do not always cross the border as organic wholes; features that are irrelevant or incomprehensible to readers in later contexts can be and are jettisoned in a surprisingly directed and accurate process of choice.

Charles H. Manekin examines Maimonides' importation of concepts found in the Arabic philosophical and scientific tradition in his discussion of the knowledge we can and cannot have concerning the heavens and their causes. In the *Guide of the Perplexed* (completed c. 1190) and other writings, Maimonides selectively appropriates elements of these "cross-border" discussions in order to justify philosophically what he considers to be the correct interpretation of the Law of his own religion. The symbiosis of the world in which he lived allowed Maimonides to cross not only religious boundaries but also philosophical ones, appropriating arguments and claims from divergent traditions in order to construct his own doctrine.

Part II concludes with a case study of an individual who overcame the limitations of geographic, communal, and religious borders: between Iberia and North Africa; Judaism, Islam, and Christianity; and Arabic and Hebrew. Indeed, the mingling of cultures, languages, and religions in Iberia makes it an ideal location for examination of a life and a career created in a symbiotic society of the type described by Goitein. Jonathan P. Decter's essay is the first study of the diplomat, poet, and patron of Hebrew letters, Abū Isḥāq Ibrāhīm Ibn al-Fakhkhār, an Iberian Jew who moved with ease between Islamic and Christian political and cultural domains. Al-Fakhkhār was active as a diplomat during a key period of Christian strength in Iberia, the late twelfth and early thirteenth centuries, and served as ambassador between the Christian king of Castile and the Almohads of North Africa, crossing borders frequently both literally and in his poetry. In the Islamicate civilization described by Hodgson and a symbiotic society such as that described by Goitein, men like al-Fakhkhār could achieve posts of rank, going so far beyond the concept of borders as to figuratively and boldly perch right on them, as in the poem cited by Decter in which the Jewish poet employs the Qur'an's description of a biblical figure—in Arabic—to praise his Christian king and patron.

Agents of Interaction and Exchange

Part III examines the agents of cultural exchange: the motivating factors and limitations governing not only why and when exchange occurs but also what is exchanged.

In Part II, Charles H. Manekin's analysis of the intermingling of the foreign and the traditional in Maimonides' philosophy is one example of the longstanding interest regarding the exchange of ideas within Jewish philosophy. Daniel J. Lasker considers the intercommunal factors that shaped the growth of particular topics in medieval philosophical works by Jews. He queries why philosophers imported certain ideas but not others and proposes that answers to this question may be found in a heretofore overlooked genre of literature: polemics between Jews, Christians, and Muslims. As Lasker points out, the same author frequently composed both polemical literature and philosophical works; for this reason, it is not surprising that such authors frequently considered many of the same issues within both genres. Lasker's examination suggests that the polemical context frequently and silently dictated the topics chosen in philosophical works. He reminds us that the antagonistic aspects of symbiosis led to results ranging far beyond polemical literature strictly defined. As Hava Lazarus-Yafeh has pointed out regarding the impact of polemical considerations on Judeo-Arabic literature as a whole: "We should, however, consider a great part of Judaeo-Arabic medieval literature . . . to be both explicit and implicit attempts to refute Islam."[15] Lasker suggests that the same is true of the philosophical oeuvre.

Gad Freudenthal takes up an example of the transfer of ideas between two Jewish communities and examines the circumstances that motivated the transfer. The question he addresses is similar to that posed by A. I. Sabra regarding the "forceful and . . . unexpected act of appropriation" of Greek sciences by Muslims.[16] Freudenthal considers the factors that motivated the enthusiastic and sudden adoption of philosophical-rational material by the Jewish scholarly community of southern France during the second half of the twelfth century, following decades of disdain and even animosity toward it. The community imported this material "over the border" with the neighboring and quite distinct Jewish community of Iberia, which had cultivated such subjects for centuries. Freudenthal, like Lasker, identifies the requirements of polemic as one motivating factor in this cultural transfer and suggests a direct variation between the polemical environment and the importation of such material. In areas where polemical exchange between Jews and Christians was rational and relatively free, as in southern France, philosophy and logic were eagerly developed as tools in such exchange. The Jewish community in northern France, in contrast, viewed such tools as unnecessary because Christian polemics in that region were largely vituperative rather than based on rational argumentation. Consequently, these Jews refrained from adopting Jewish philosophical-rational material even when it was available. Freudenthal demonstrates that the nature of symbiotic interactions with their non-Jewish host societies—whether irenic or antagonistic—shaped mechanisms of border crossings between different Jewish communities.

David M. Freidenreich offers another answer to Lasker's question regarding the factors governing the transfer of ideas. He examines how two scholars, both of whom were philosophers as well as legists, subjectively understood their own roles in the transfer of ideas. In the process, Freidenreich complicates Hodgson's conception of an effectively borderless "Islamicate" civilization. Freidenreich examines restrictions governing food associated with adherents of foreign religions in the legal codes of Gregorius Barhebraeus and Moses Maimonides. These jurists incorporate elements derived from the surrounding Islamic milieu into their presentation of restrictions that are inherently parochial in nature because they do not perceive these specific ideas as "Islamic." Freidenreich suggests that religious authorities in the Islamic world were very much aware of borders that demarcate "Jewish," "Christian," and "Islamic" ideas but labeled them not on the basis of origins but on the basis of compatibility with the receiving community's intellectual tradition. He thus offers an interpretation of the exchange of ideas within the Islamic world that blends Hodgson's conception of an Islamicate civilization and Goitein's focus on dynamics internal to particular religious communities. This essay is a fitting conclusion to our volume, in that it is an epitome of the porous nature of intellectual and confessional borders based on a focused inquiry of individual thinkers, yet at the same time it is an encapsulation of the larger issues involved.

In their essays, our authors reexamine well-worn assumptions and throw new light on old questions, treating the subject of interaction and exchange between neighboring cultures from a variety of vantage points. While the chapters treat diverse subjects, they combine to form a unified whole that addresses many of the issues fundamental to intellectual exchange, including the underlying prerequisites and motivations for such exchange and the details of such exchange in practice. In their topical, geographical, and chronological breadth, they model diverse approaches. It is our hope that this variety of approaches to the same fundamental issues can serve a similarly diverse audience of readers.

PART I

Contexts of Interreligious Interaction

CHAPTER I

Observations on the Beginnings of Judeo-Arabic Civilization

HAGGAI BEN-SHAMMAI

An appropriate definition of Judeo-Arabic civilization would be the following: the sum total of all communications, or documents, as well as other written materials, in which Arabic-speaking Jews have expressed their spiritual and material needs, occupations, aspirations, and achievements. The focus of this definition is no doubt linguistic and will continue to be the focus in the present study, which is based on the premise that language is a major expression of the uniqueness or particularity of any culture. The definition applies to communications that incorporate certain Jewish elements, including the Hebrew script, a considerably large, or at least discernible, body of Hebrew vocabulary, and a distinct presence of references to Jewish topics and sources.

It could be argued that the term "culture" suits the present study better than "civilization," but I have chosen the latter because the written materials under discussion relate to all aspects of the lives of Arabic-speaking Jewish individuals and communities, including intellectual and theoretical creativity and literature; political, legal, and religious institutions; socioeconomic activities; and everyday private matters. Furthermore, if it were only for isolated poems whose Jewish connection is confined to the alleged Jewish origin of their author (e.g., *Lāmiyyat al-Samawʾal*, whose author is said to have lived in Western Arabia in the sixth century CE),[1] or to philosophical[2] or medical works of a general nature whose authors happen to be of Jewish origin, there would be little justification for the use of the term "Judeo-Arabic civilization" or "Judeo-Arabic literature." Such materials would merely testify to the extent to which Jews adjusted to or assimilated into the civilization in which they lived. Furthermore, such works would not become part of the cultural legacy of Judaism, at least not without particular adjustments to Jewish characteristics.

Usually the concept of medieval Judeo-Arabic civilization is understood, considering the absence of living witnesses or recordings and the meager quantity of art works, to cover written materials specifically. The oldest such materials are believed to have survived from the ninth century (or perhaps even earlier) in small quantities and from the tenth century onward in ever-increasing quantities.[3]

The last statement may be put more dramatically. Scholars used to marvel at the literary accomplishments of Saadya Gaon (882–942), especially considering the poor achievements of Judeo-Arabic literature in general, and Bible translations in particular, before Saadya's time. The research of Blau and Hopkins in recent years and, in particular, their findings of fragments of Arabic translations of biblical and Geonic works (see below), which clearly predate Saadya by a century or so, put Saadya's works into a different historical perspective. Considering the chances of survival of papyrus and parchment writings for twelve centuries, the volume of the materials that Blau and Hopkins have accumulated so far is impressive indeed.

It is thus widely believed today that the starting point for the history of Judeo-Arabic civilization is the ninth century. It is true that Geonic literature even at that period of time was written mostly in Aramaic (or a mixture of Aramaic and Hebrew). However, the process of the adoption of Arabic by Jews—the Arabization, so to speak, of eastern Mediterranean Judaism—could have started earlier. A. S. Halkin, in his comprehensive essay on Judeo-Arabic literature, states that the beginnings of such literature probably go back to the ninth century; he then hints that some earlier activity in this field is quite possible but does not elaborate on that possibility.[4]

Arabic was introduced as the administrative language of the Arab state by ʿAbd al-Malik at the end of the seventh century. There are official inscriptions that date from the time of Muʿāwiya (r. 660–81), several decades earlier.[5] In fact, there are some inscriptions in northern Arabic that date from pre-Islamic times,[6] but according to current research on Judeo-Arabic civilization, Jews are believed to have been rather slow in their adjustment to the new cultural order in the eastern Mediterranean.

Jewish materials in the Qurʾān might provide additional information or even hints regarding when Jews began to use Arabic extensively, for it is widely accepted that the Qurʾān contains Jewish (as well as Christian)[7] materials.

However, scholars who have dealt with this phenomenon referred largely to the biblical or Rabbinic sources that are written in Hebrew or Aramaic rather than sources in Arabic. Furthermore, it should be emphasized that the term "Jewish materials" is used here only with reference to such materials that may be traced in Jewish sources and have no parallels in Christian or other sources.

Muslim traditions that are perhaps, but not necessarily, contemporaneous with the Qurʾān also contain Jewish elements (designated by the Muslims with the Arabic term *isrāʾīliyyāt*). The Jewish origin of many of these Arabic materials is sometimes identifiable on the basis of some degree of verbal similarity with their Hebrew or Aramaic counterparts or origins. The period in which such textual shifts are said to have taken place is believed to be the seventh through the ninth centuries.

The Jewish materials in the Qurʾān are quite well-known and perhaps do not need special introduction. It would be useful, however, to mention a few examples.

One of the most interesting features in Qurʾānic stories about biblical personalities is that these stories are often restructured on the basis of midrashic models and do not represent even approximate translations of the biblical text. This can be demonstrated in several such stories. Take for example the Qurʾānic version of the story of Noah (Ar. Nūḥ). In the biblical story Noah is virtually mute: he does not pray or preach, nor does he say a word to any member of his family. In fact, Noah's only recorded utterances in the Bible are the curse and blessings he bestows upon his offspring.[8] In the Qurʾānic story the figure of Noah underwent a radical change and was restructured after the motif of the public preacher and polemicist who is involved in constant verbal and other conflicts with his contemporaries.[9] This motif echoes what can be found amply in midrashic sources,[10] as well as in Christian sources,[11] and becomes a central theme in several versions of the story in the Qurʾān.[12] This absorption of midrashic themes is also apparent in details of legal matters and in other stories, such as the story that Pharaoh was saved from drowning, left alive as a reminder for subsequent generations.[13]

One may also quote in this context the passages from the Qurʾān[14] dealing with divorce that are formulated in what Schacht called magical language:[15] "you are for me as untouchable as the back of my mother." Although early commentators[16] ascribe this custom to the Jāhiliyya, one should consider very close parallels in the Mishna[17] and in the Palestinian Talmud,[18] where the language "You are forbidden for me like my mother" is already found. An early Palestinian source (in Hebrew) from the Geonic period (or probably late Byzantine period in Palestine) stipulates a penalty of flogging for the husband in such a case and declares the divorce null and void.[19] The Qurʾān likewise stipulates a penalty for men who commit such a transgression, though of a different kind.

The Jewish materials in Islamic tradition (*ḥadīth*), in different genres, have been the subject of important scholarly studies by Goldziher, Vajda,[20] Goitein, and others. Norman Calder has analyzed the story of the sacrifice of Abraham in early Islamic tradition which, according to his definition, includes the Qurʾān.[21] In fact, he argues that materials contained in the *ḥadīth* literature may be older than the Qurʾān. Calder arrives at the conclusion that all the Arabic versions of the story, rearranged or restructured or reformulated as they may be, originate in Rabbinic (or midrashic) literature. The midrashic stories may have been translated at some point, as a result of a new demand for old stories (see below).

Calder's study applies to the case in which the same story appears in various Islamic sources and genres, one of which is the Qurʾān. There are many other cases in which *ḥadīth* literature contains Jewish elements independent of the Islamic scripture. The extent to which even minute details of Rabbinic literature are found in Arab sources may be indeed amazing. Thus we find in a local chronography of Damascus (to be sure, it is an abridged version of the work) the story of the sun that did not set for Joshua (cf. Josh. 10:13) because it was Friday and Joshua was afraid that the sun would set and the Sabbath would commence before he had won his battle against the Canaanites.[22] This version is a word-for-word parallel to a Rabbinic homily, which is admittedly somewhat late (probably from the early Islamic period).[23]

Another type of Rabbinic element may be exemplified by the parable about the tongue which is the best and the worst among the organs of the human body. In Rabbinic sources the scriptural verse that occasions the parable is Proverbs 18:21 ("Death and life are in the power of the tongue") and a story is told about Ṭabe, the servant of Rabban Gamliel.[24] In the *ḥadīth* literature the discussion is often prompted by Qurʾān 31:12 ("Indeed we gave Luqmān wisdom"), and then a similar story is told about Luqmān, who was an Ethiopic slave.[25]

An interesting case is discussed by Goldziher,[26] namely an exegetical tradition of Mujāhid that relates the story told in Numbers 20:7–13. According to Mujāhid, Moses told the Israelites: "Drink, ye asses [*ḥamīr*]." Goldziher opined that Mujāhid misunderstood or was misinformed regarding the meaning of Hebrew *ha-morim* ("the rebellious"). It seems to me that a preferable understanding of the tradition is that, considering the midrashic comments that interpret the Hebrew word according to Greek *mōros* ("fool"),[27] somebody (Jewish) could have created a similar pun but in Arabic.

A similar case in point, regarding the relationship between Rabbinic sources, the Qur'ān, and early tradition is found in exegetical traditions (*tafsīr*) on Sura 32:5. The verse reads: "He directs the affair [*amr*] from heaven to earth, then it goes up to Him in one day, whose measure is a thousand years of your counting." Al-Ṭabarī quotes a whole range of opinions and traditions concerning this verse.[28] The main ideas are that the "affair" is identified with angels and that the descent and ascent of the angels who carry out divine command last one thousand years, five hundred for each direction. However, some traditions link this specifically to the days of Creation that are mentioned in the previous verse,[29] saying that each day of the Creation lasted for one thousand years "of our counting." Other traditions (notably on the authority of Mujāhid) maintain that each mission of the angels connected to the governance of the world lasts one thousand years, and such missions recur ad infinitum (*thumma ka-dhālika abadan*).[30]

Speyer has discussed the relationship between Jewish sources and the Qur'ān,[31] noting the relationship between *amr* in 32:5 and Jewish (Targumic) sources; Talmudic and midrashic sources for the idea that the distance between the earth and heaven is five hundred years;[32] the biblical parallel to the idea that one day in God's counting equals one thousand years; and a parallel from the New Testament, namely 2 Peter 3:8ff.[33] An additional interesting parallel not mentioned by Speyer is a midrashic source[34] concerning the connection between the Creation and the "thousand-year days," and the distances between earth and heaven. The parallel between such specific Jewish and Islamic traditions cannot be a coincidence.

Even when traditions reflect Rabbinic sources with blatant inaccuracies or distortions, they can attest to the existence of Jewish sources that had been available to the exegetes, who could then adapt them according to their needs or understanding. On Sura 37:97, al-Ṭabarī adduces[35] a tradition on the authority of Sulaymān b. Ṣurad,[36] in the course of which Qur'ān 21:69 is quoted. This verse describes how God saved Abraham from the fire in Nimrod's furnace. Al-Ṭabarī continues with a short story recounting the subsequent death of Lot's son or nephew by that same fire as a consequence of his pride in ascribing Abraham's salvation to himself. This story is a clear reflection of a midrashic motif found in Rabbinic literature,[37] the Targum Neophyti on Genesis 11:28,[38] and the printed edition of Pseudo-Jonathan on the same verse.

Certain Rabbinic traditions are reflected in an Islamic tradition after having undergone a fundamental change in meaning. The Islamic tradition becomes understandable only in the context of the earlier midrashic tradition. As a result, one has to assume the existence of a Judeo-Arabic version of the Rabbinic tradition. In a recent study[39] I trace the origin of a saying ascribed to Muḥammad according to which "the Qurʾān has been brought down in seven modes of articulation."[40] This saying served as a basis for several early Muslim scholars who recognized the legitimacy of a number of competing variant readings of the Qurʾān. It seems, however, that the origin of the saying is a similar Rabbinic tradition that formed the basis for the recognition of the legitimacy of alternative interpretations of scriptural verses, which they defined as "seven voices."[41] It seems inconceivable that this parallel is incidental. The two cultures drew on the same tradition, applying it to their particular circumstances and needs.

Another topic of possible connection between Judaic and Islamic materials through Judeo-Arabic channels is the concept of *ism allah al-aʿẓam*, the glorious, supreme name of God, which clearly parallels a similar Jewish notion, namely the Name (perhaps the Tetragrammaton) explicitly pronounced (*ha-shem ha-meforash*).[42] Note that in a rather late midrashic source[43] it is said that in the beginning of the world there existed nothing except for God and his Great Name (*shemo ha-gadol*). More interesting are some peculiarities, such as the name of seventy-two letters, for which documentation is found in quite early Jewish sources as well as in Islamic traditions.[44] This is especially important, because the concept of the divine name is probably a specifically Jewish motif.[45]

Rabbinic parallels with Islamic literature are not necessarily limited to sources considered typically Rabbinic.[46] They may include liturgical poems, which quite often reflect clearly midrashic interpretations and homilies, as well as distinct genres, such as Hekhalot literature and the like.

An interesting example from liturgical poetry is the following. Sura 112 reads:

> Say: "He is God, One,
> God, the Everlasting Refuge,
> who has not begotten, and has not been begotten,
> and equal to him is not anyone."[47]

The famous and prolific Hebrew liturgical poet (*payyeṭan*) Yannai was likely active in the Land of Israel during the latter part of Byzantine rule, that is, prior to the advent of Islam. Yannai begins his *piyyuṭ* on the Torah reading that includes Leviticus 12, which deals with laws pertaining to childbirth, with the following line in praise of God:

> "No father has begotten You, / nor have You begotten any son, /
> but You it is who causes every child born to be born."[48]

The effort to distance the Divine from even the remotest association with any procreative activity (as opposed to polytheist traditions) is in no way unique to the texts quoted here; indeed, it is well-known in monotheist confessions from ancient times. What is most striking is how similar the two polemical statements are in both poetic style and content. Yannai's words are explicitly intended for liturgical recitation, while the liturgical element in Sura 112 can only be surmised from the style.[49]

Let us turn now to an interesting example related to the Hekhalot literature.

In his discussion of Qur'ān 17:85 ("They will question thee concerning the Spirit"), the exegete al-Ṭabarī quotes a tradition: "ʿAlī—ʿAbd Allāh b. Ṣāliḥ—Abū Marwān Yazīd b. Samura *Ṣāḥib Qaysariyya* [the governor of Caesarea]—anon.—ʿAlī b. Abī Ṭālib: [the Spirit] is an angel who has seventy thousand faces, each face having seventy thousand tongues, each tongue has [speaks] seventy thousand languages. The angel praises God with all those languages. From each praise God creates an angel who hovers [*yaṭīr*] with the angels until the day of resurrection."[50] It seems that this angel somehow reflects Metatron and that this is an "inflated numbers version" of a Hekhalot-type homily.[51]

It is widely accepted that important Judeo-Arabic works in various fields dating from the ninth century onward were influenced by, or at least reflect, Islamic culture. One may mention works in the fields of Bible exegesis, religious philosophy, linguistics, and even folk stories about prophets (*qiṣaṣ al-anbiyāʾ*)[52] and the like. Arabic names are even found in midrashic Hebrew and Aramaic materials (Targum, *Pirkei de-Rabbi Eliezer*). One may also mention that in such works Jews adopted typical Islamic concepts and terminology.[53]

It is evident that these influences, or repercussions, may be best explained by the fact that the Judeo-Arabic culture, by its very definition, represents the total adoption by Jews of the Arabic language for all their religious needs except liturgical poetry.[54] As noted above, such adoption is documented as early as the ninth century and perhaps even the late eighth. To the best of my knowledge, no linguistic explanation of this kind has been suggested for the earlier phenomenon surveyed above, namely the influence of Judaism on nascent Islam.[55]

In other words, there is no satisfactory answer to the question: Who was responsible for the translation of all the Jewish, mainly midrashic, materials found in Arabic-language Islamic sources from Hebrew or Judeo-Aramaic into Arabic?

To be sure, the question has indeed been asked with respect to the Qurʾān alone,[56] on the assumption that the Qurʾān constitutes a separate entity, that it reflects the spiritual history of the person of Muḥammad. The answer some scholars have given with respect to the Qurʾān as such was that the Jewish elements in the Qurʾān may be ascribed to the Jews of Medina (or, as some authors would have it, "Arabian Jews"), who would occasionally translate sections from the Bible "into the language of the land."[57] According to the same explanation these casual translators would also intertwine into their renderings haggadic materials, which their Arab neighbors accepted to be part of the Torah, that is, Jewish scripture. According to such theories this is how the term *tawrāh* came to mean "Jewish lore."[58] Deviations from biblical or Rabbinic texts were explained by Western scholars as misunderstandings on Muḥammad's part. The discrepancies between different versions of the same story were easily explained away as reflecting different periods or stages in the development of the personality of Muḥammad. The importance of suggestions such as Speyer's lies in the fact that they recognize that the initial effort of translation must be made by persons who regard the translated text as an integral part of their cultural heritage.

There are two possible answers to the question of who translated Jewish materials into Arabic.[59]

1. Muḥammad and his Companions and their followers in subsequent generations, or whoever authored the biblical and midrashic stories in the Qurʾān and Muslim traditions (*ḥadīth*), took upon themselves to choose the relevant materials from Hebrew or Judeo-Aramaic sources and to translate them into Arabic. The same persons also chose materials from Christian sources that they deemed fit for inclusion by translating them from various Christian-Aramaic (perhaps also Greek) dialects into Arabic. This proposition would involve the assumption that all those engaged in the translations acquired adequate knowledge of the languages concerned and good command of the Jewish and Christian sources so as to enable them to choose the appropriate materials from the various sources. One would have to accept that those translators had acted in a way quite atypical for the ancient and medieval world, namely, they had become well versed in a culture that was not their own.

2. Those who included the Jewish (and Christian) materials in the Qur'ān and Muslim tradition had these materials at their disposal in Arabic versions. These versions were authored by Jews who acquired sufficient knowledge of Arabic to translate from Hebrew and Aramaic into Arabic. These versions consisted of either written or oral paraphrases of biblical[60] and midrashic passages and were composed for the needs of their authors and their communities or for "missionary" purposes (e.g., in the Yemen). This proposition would involve the assumption that Jews adopted Arabic, or at least gained sufficient knowledge of that language, at a much earlier date than hitherto thought. Furthermore, one may argue that since Jews had sufficient knowledge of Arabic at a very early stage of the development of Islam, they could have taken an active part in the early development of Islam.

A decision in favor of the second alternative may be supported by the following argument: In the world of antiquity and the Middle Ages, texts were translated from one language to another for religious—or, more generally, ideological—purposes or to satisfy communal needs. For example, when a certain community came in close contact with, or under the influence of, a new culture or language, there arose a need to translate the community's scripture(s) into that new language. The Aramaic and Greek translations of the Hebrew Scripture are classic examples. Other examples that may be even more relevant to the present discussion are the Arabic Bible translations by both Jews and Christians. Missionary purposes could constitute an additional incentive for such translations. In contrast, translations of sacred texts were not made for the sake of knowledge or academic scholarship.

In addition to the above-mentioned ideological communal motives, translations were also made for practical purposes, for example, scientific texts on medicine, optics, zoology, pharmacology, and the like. In any case, the translators of all of the above-mentioned genres had to be well acquainted with both languages, that is, the source language and the target language. Normally the translated text constituted an integral part of the cultural heritage of the translator, who could thus master the entire corpus of texts out of which he intended to translate and was thus able to make the right choice from that corpus. So one finds that the majority of the translators of philosophical and scientific texts into Arabic, from the beginning of the ninth century onward, were Christians,[61] for whom either Greek or Syriac, or both, were not just tools of academic work but part of their culture, in fact of their religious tradition. When we learn that al-Fārābī may have learned a limited number of Greek words during his visits to Asia Minor,[62] this is the single outstanding exception. Al-Kindī provided editorial assistance[63] to the Christians in translations of works by Aristotle, but he had no knowledge of Greek whatsoever.

Another translator may be considered here, namely Ḥunayn b. Isḥāq. He came from a Nestorian family; that is, he probably grew up and was educated in a bilingual Arabic-Syriac milieu. When he wanted to study Greek he is said to have gone to Byzantium, stayed there for a few years, and then returned to Baghdad, having mastered that language.[64] Even though Greek was neither his mother tongue nor his language of prayer, he had enough in common with his Byzantine co-religionists (otherwise possible religious adversaries), or could have felt sufficiently comfortable among them, in order to be able to transform Greek to be part of his culture. No Muslim could have felt the same.

To sum up this point: In late antiquity and the early Middle Ages, sacred texts and other literary or scientific works that constituted the religious or cultural tradition of a certain community were translated into another language when that community underwent a linguistic transformation, taking on a new language. The translators had to be members of that community, well versed in its tradition and knowledgeable in its new language. Once these translations had become available in the public domain all the speakers of that language could benefit from them.

Let us turn now to some early Islamic traditions that reflect the attitude of Muslims toward the adoption or adaptation of Jewish materials. M. J. Kister, in his highly stimulating and learned study "Ḥaddithū ʿan Banū Isrāʾīl,"[65] discusses at length the attitudes of several Muslim authors toward the transmission of *Isrāʾīliyyāt*. Kister translates the Arabic formula of his article's title as "transmit stories about the Children of Israel"[66] rather than "from the Children of Israel." This translation is problematic, for it seems that much of this material relates to transmission, adoption, or adaptation by Muslims of materials Jews already possessed in Arabic versions, whether oral or written. Kister, like many modern scholars, tends to make Jewish (and indeed Christian) converts to Islam responsible for the translations into Arabic of Jewish elements in *ḥadīth* literature (in addition to the contribution of Medinan Jews to the Jewish elements in the Qurʾān).[67] However, this proposition views the process of such translations as a rather mechanical one, as though by conversion to another religion one may acquire the ability to translate texts into a language that prior to his conversion was personally and culturally foreign to him.

I would like to suggest a more comprehensive explanation of the Jewish elements in early Islamic literature that I have traced above, that is, in the Qurʾān and *ḥadīth* alike, and to propose that these elements are the earliest testimonies to the beginnings of Judeo-Arabic civilization. This contribution of Judeo-Arabic civilization to the emergence of Islam had been made possible by a constant process of Arabization of large sections of the population in areas such as Sasanian Iraq (mainly in the southern part) and perhaps in southern Syria. In Iraq Arabic was spreading in speech and writing (even on an official level) quite rapidly in the sixth century, especially around al-Ḥīra, where the Arabs probably constituted a majority in some localities, but also in other parts that had large Arab populations, both nomadic and sedentary.[68] In some of these areas, for example, between Pumbedita[69] and Nippur in southern Iraq, there were Jewish communities of considerable size.[70] A similar situation, probably on a smaller scale, but not smaller than that of Arabia,[71] may have existed in southern Syria, around the area of Ghassān, and in the Syrian desert in the area of Tadmor (Palmyra). There, too, some considerable Jewish communities could be found alongside a constantly increasing Arab population.

It may be relevant to mention very briefly at this point the presence of Arabs in Rabbinic sources. In Babylonian sources (mainly the Babylonian Talmud) they are termed mostly, though not exclusively, *ṭayyāʿā* (pl. *ṭayyāʿey*), representing the Judeo-Aramaic spelling for the name of a member of the Arab tribe Ṭayyiʾ, which before Islam had already expanded its pastures and settlements as far as the northern parts of present-day Iraq and Syria.[72] In Rabbinic sources of Palestinian and Babylonian provenance the terms *ʿArabya, ʿArbayya* indicate mainly a territory,[73] but the latter may also indicate Arab(s).

Some segments of the Jewish population in all those communities may have forged social contacts with the Arab, or Arabicizing, population, especially the sedentary element of it. Such contacts would have brought those Jews closer to Arabic language and Arab culture.[74] In these circumstances a certain number of Jews may have felt a need for an Arabic translation of parts of the Hebrew scripture, at least the Pentateuch, together with hermeneutical/midrashic material relevant to those parts. In fact, the Targumic literature could have constituted a very appropriate model for such paraphrases, combining proper biblical materials with midrashic elements, of the type represented later in the paraphrases of Wahb b. Munabbih. Such translations may have served the personal needs of members of certain communities and may have provided aid to the initiatives of Judaizing Arab neighbors (in the Yemen or perhaps on the banks of the Euphrates) on the part of other members of the same communities. Even if it is true that Jewish converts to Islam (such as ʿAbd Allāh b. Salām, Kaʿb al-Aḥbār, Abū Mālik, or Wahb b. Munabbih,[75] to whom written works are ascribed)[76] were responsible for the absorption of a large part of the Jewish materials in Islamic tradition (including the Qurʾān), it does not necessarily follow that they personally had to do all the translation from the start.[77] They could have used materials that had already been in use for some time, either in writing or more probably in oral transmission.

Consequently, *ḥaddithū ʿan Banū Isrāʾīl* should be translated "transmit from/in the name of/on behalf of the Israelites," that is, from the actual Jews of Muḥammad's time, rather than "about" the actual Jews or "about" the historical Children of Israel.

In the story quoted by Kister, ʿUmar hears of the contents of the Book of Daniel and orders a translation of it. This story makes much more sense when reversed, namely, it was an oral Arabic paraphrase of Daniel that was circulating and so greatly impressed an early, or the early, Islamic ruler. In the case of the Book of Daniel, Jews and Christians had probably similar interests in spreading their respective particular exposition of the biblical text, and therefore a number of competing Arabic paraphrases may have existed.[78]

A remark on the usage of the term *Banū Isrāʾīl* in the tradition just mentioned is in order, in light of the reinterpretation of Kister's traditions. Josef Horovitz argues[79] that the form Isrāʾīl corresponds exactly to the Syriac Christian form.[80] He further argues that in the Qurʾān the term *Banū Isrāʾīl* normally denotes the people of biblical history, in contradistinction to Jews contemporary with Muḥammad who are designated by the term *Yahūd*. Horovitz himself admits, however, that there are some verses in the Qurʾān that are exceptions to this rule, that is, verses in which the term *Banū Isrāʾīl* indicates the actual Jews of Muḥammad's time. These verses are 27:76,[81] 2:47,[82] 2:122 (where, according to Horovitz, Muḥammad speaks of the descendants of the historical Banū Isrāʾīl but has in mind the actual Jews of his time), and 17:101 (where Muḥammad is ordered to ask Banū Isrāʾīl). It may be understood from Horovitz's remarks that there may be additional references in the Qurʾān in which the term *Banū Isrāʾīl* indicates Muḥammad's actual Jewish contemporaries. According to Horovitz this usage of the term by Muḥammad resulted from the latter's view that the Jews inherited the Law from the biblical people of Israel.

The term *Yahūd,* according to Horovitz,[83] originated from non-Jewish usage, mainly Christian, and is typical of the sections of the Qurʾān he characterizes as "Medinan."[84] Thus, when it says in the Qurʾān (3:67) that Ibrāhīm was not *Yahūdī*, it may mean that he is not a certain type of Jew, a type that is comparable to the Naṣrānī (Christian) that is also negated with relation to Ibrāhīm.[85]

However, to my mind the usage of *Isrā'īl, Banū Isrā'īl,* designates both the biblical Israelites as well the Jews of late antiquity or the early Middle Ages. This usage is clearly present in the Qur'ān and originated in the Rabbinic and midrashic literature, where the term *Yisra'el* normally denotes, both in Haggadic (homiletic) and Halakhic (legal) contexts, the members of the nascent Israelite nation of biblical times as well as Jews of the Talmudic period. Several scholars in recent times have opined that the use of the term "Jew" (*yehudi*) in early Rabbinic sources is very rare.[86] The question is then what exactly is meant by "early."[87] For the purpose of the present discussion this assessment may be qualified in the following way.

In Rabbinic literature of late antiquity, down to the sixth century (with the exclusion of all texts related to the Book of Esther, where the use of "Jews" is called for by the context of the biblical text), the Jews identify themselves in internal contexts as Israel. In the context of their relationship with non-Jews (whatever the circumstances) they are identified as Jews.[88] The latter thus seems to denote them as a distinct, separate social entity, whereas the term "Israelite" does not bear this connotation. It also seems that the same distinctions can be applied to the Qur'ān and early *ḥadīth* literature.

The Daniel tradition discussed at length by Kister may be connected to another interesting tradition found in al-Bukhārī's *Ṣaḥīḥ,* describing the Jews at the time of Muḥammad reading the Torah in Hebrew and translating it into Arabic for the "people of Islam" (*ahl al-islām*).[89] This tradition is certainly meant to relate to circumstances in Medina at the time of the advent of Islam. Whatever one may think of its historical reliability,[90] it may very well reflect memories of an early stage during which nascent Islam was in the process of receiving Jewish materials from representatives of the nascent Judeo-Arabic civilization. What is perhaps more significant historically is the following consideration: While al-Bukhārī compiled his collection from existing sources, it is well-known that he shaped the collection personally by adding titles, *tarājim* (sing. *tarjuma*), to each section (*bāb*). These gave the old traditions, whose meaning very often could be quite vague already in al-Bukhārī's time,[91] a concrete, practical, and generalized meaning, beyond the specific conditions of Muḥammad's time and place. They were nicknamed *fiqh al-Bukhārī,* that is, the legal system or school of al-Bukhārī,[92] and relate accordingly to the actual historical circumstances in al-Bukhārī's time. The *tarjuma* of the tradition in question reads as follows:

> Section on what is admissible (*yajūz*) of the translation/interpretation of the Torah and other books of God in Arabic and other (languages), because of God's statement: "Bring you the Torah now, and recite it, if you are truthful" [Qur'ān 3:93]. Also, Ibn ʿAbbās said: Abū Sufyān b. Ḥarb related to me that Heraclios called his interpreter, then he ordered the letter of the Prophet and he [i.e., his interpreter] read it: "In the name of God, the compassionate the merciful, from Muḥammad, the servant of God and His messenger, to Heraclios," and "People of the Book! Come now to a word common between us and you etc." [Qur'ān 3:64].

In the tradition itself Muḥammad responds to the fact that the Jews were reading the Torah in Hebrew and translating it into Arabic for the "people of Islam" by quoting Qur'ān 2:136. This quotation is probably meant to legitimize the use of the scriptures of Jews and Christians as a source of knowledge and an object of reverence, even if such use is acquired through translations by members of these communities, regardless of their status or credibility. The tradition itself apparently reflects the circumstances of the seventh century. This is the practical position of al-Bukhārī, with regard to his own environment, and it accords with the tradition *ḥaddithū ʿan Banū Isrāʾīl*. It also recognizes the reality in which the Jews are the natural candidates, as it were, to make an accurate translation of their own scripture.

A corroboration of this situation from the Jewish side may be gleaned from a responsum ascribed to Rav Naṭronai Gaon from the middle of the ninth century (i.e., roughly an older contemporary of al-Bukhārī), in which he prohibited giving up the recitation of the traditional Aramaic translation of the Torah (*targum didan*) in favor of a translation "in our language or the language which the public understands" as part of the ritual in the synagogue.[93] This is no doubt a clear allusion to an existing Arabic translation. The Jewish Gaon may have had in mind exactly the same translations that al-Bukhārī mentioned in his compilation. In the middle of the ninth century in some places Arabic Pentateuch translations reached the status of being admitted into the synagogue ritual, which permits us to assume a process that should take a few generations to be accomplished from its inception in oral local traditions.

An interesting source for knowledge about early Bible translations into Arabic is Muḥammad b. Mūsā al-Khʷārizmī's description of the Jewish calendar, which cites extensively from the Bible in Arabic.[94] The author's information is drawn from Jewish sources; it is likely his Arabic quotations from the Bible are as well. Al-Khʷārizmī was employed by al-Maʾmūn in the Dār al-Ḥikma and died in 846 CE.[95] This again provides us with evidence of (written?) Jewish Bible translations in the beginning of the ninth century.

There is special importance to the findings of Blau and Hopkins mentioned earlier in this essay. They may illustrate the stages of the gradual development of Judeo-Arabic civilization. It seems quite clear that Arabic translations (or homiletic paraphrases) of sections of the Bible, mainly the Pentateuch but also other sections that could be useful for instructional purposes, such as the Book of Proverbs,[96] would accommodate the needs of comparatively low sections in Jewish society, such as farmers or craftsmen. It stands to reason that their religio-intellectual interests were confined to the biblical text, transmitted orally or in writing. They had close contacts with Arabs (see below) and were therefore the first candidates to become influenced by the process of Arabization and, consequently, the first to feel a need for Arabic versions of biblical texts. The fragments of translations of Geonic Halakhic works (*Halakhot pesuqot*)[97] testify to a further expansion of the Arabization into higher echelons of Jewish society, perhaps local judges in rural areas[98] or provincial towns for whom the Aramaic codes may have become less and less accessible (linguistically) and who would thus feel more comfortable having the text of such codes accompanied by a running Arabic translation. At the same time, in the Babylonian Academies Aramaic (or Hebraeo-Aramaic, such as the style of Pirqoi b. Baboi) would be retained for another century or two as the main means of communication.

I would like to adduce here another case that may be an instructive indication of the extent of Arabization among Jews (or at least one Jewish group) in the ninth century. As I have shown elsewhere,[99] Ananite Arabic literature had probably reached a very advanced stage by the middle of the ninth century. This may be concluded from the fact that it is certain that the Aramaic version of Anan's Code was not available in Babylonia (Iraq) at that time and from the many quotations by al-Qirqisānī (around 930) from Ananite works in Arabic, which must have come into existence as a substitute for the original text of the most basic source of Ananite legislation. It should be noted that the Ananite Arabic texts reflect not only the adoption of the Arabic language as well as initiating an Arabic version or paraphrases of Anan's Code but a further stage of adaptation of technical language, mainly terms of legal theory (*uṣūl al-fiqh*). These quotations may thus reflect texts that in their contents served purposes similar to those aimed at by the Rabbanite translations from *Halakhot pesuqot* but linguistically were much more "advanced," that is, the register used by the Ananite authors was closer to standard Arabic (if the texts were not reedited in al-Qirqisānī's time).

In the early tenth century, Saadya undertook to standardize and canonize a translation of the Bible. Notice should be taken that even an author as learned as Saadya, who certainly addressed, for the most part, an audience that was quite well educated in Jewish lore, still quite often prefers to quote biblical as well as midrashic materials in Arabic paraphrase.[100] Saadya adopted this approach for a number of reasons, one of which was that many of his readers likely read Arabic more easily than Hebrew or Aramaic.

In conclusion, if it is accepted that the beginnings of Judeo-Arabic civilization are earlier than has been hitherto thought, that in the early seventh century literary expressions of this civilization were evolving in several localities in which ancient Jewish communities were seated, then the meaning of Judeo-Arabic civilization gains an additional dimension of depth in terms of time and substance. This additional dimension should affect our understanding of the part Jews and Judaism may have played in the emergence of Islam and the evolution of its various facets, as well as the place the Judeo-Arabic component occupied in the complex framework of Arab civilization. A different understanding, of the kind that I have ventured to suggest here, may also lead to reconsideration of the somewhat crude portrayal of Islam as heavily borrowing from Judaism in its initial stages or of Jewish thought as considerably influenced by Islam. Common language makes an important difference in shaping intercultural relations. Consequently, the study of such relations should apply more subtle and complex criteria.

Thus, the departure point for the study of the relationship between Judaism and early Islam should not be the question "What did Muḥammad take over from Judaism?" ("Was hat Mohammed aus dem Judenthum aufgenommen?"), as Abraham Geiger put it more than a century and a half ago.[101] This question, in its various formulations or presentations, and also when applied to extra-Qurʾānic materials, envisages a mechanical process of borrowing across confessional demarcation lines. The question should rather be: What was the environment that enabled intercultural relations between Jews and Arabs from the earliest stages of Islam and perhaps even prior to that? When and where did this environment exist? According to the thesis suggested here, that environment was a rapidly expanding Arabic civilization, which at some time around the beginning of the seventh century already comprised certain sections of the Jewish society in Iraq and possibly in southern Syria and Arabia. It has long been recognized that Christians were part of this process;

this point need not be elaborated here. The parts played by Jews, Christians, and early Muslims have been described in very pertinent terms with regard to the development of the concept of early Islamic law by the late Norman Calder:

> The question of when this cluster of Arabic terms emerged as part of the self-expression of Jews and Christians is unclear. But, whatever model is adopted for the emergence and early development of Islam, it is necessary to acknowledge the co-existence or prior existence of Arabic-speaking Jewish and Christian communities. The development of an Arabic vocabulary for the expression of concepts and ideas integral to the prophetic religions of the Middle East is perhaps best understood as the common achievement of several communities engaged in polemical encounter throughout the 7th to the 9th centuries A.D.[102]

In such a sociocultural environment the free flow (not necessarily borrowing!) of religious ideas and literary motifs between various groups seems almost inevitable.

CHAPTER 2

Shurūṭ ʿUmar

From Early Harbingers to Systematic Enforcement

MILKA LEVY-RUBIN

It has been the prevalent view of scholars concerned with the treatment of *ahl al-dhimma*, non-Muslim "protected people," that various sets of restrictions enjoined upon *dhimmīs* in the early period of Muslim rule (known as *shurūṭ ʿUmar*) were irregular and sporadic, and, when issued, often were not enforced or fell quickly into disuse. Two famous episodes—the imposition of restrictions by the caliph al-Mutawakkil (r. 847–61) and those of al-Ḥākim (r. 998–1021), both of which are well-known and widely documented—are seen as exceptions rather than the rule. Thus Antoine Fattal, in his still relevant work, *Le statut légal des non-musulmans en pays d'Islam*, is of the opinion that "Les édits de Mutawakkil tombèrent vite en désuétude. Muqtadir (908–32) en Irak, et Muḥammad al-Ikhshīd (934) en Egypte, essayèrent *en vain* de les faire revivre."[1] S. D. Goitein states, "The *bizarre* edict on the attire of Christians and Jews promulgated by the caliph al-Ḥākim in a spasmodic fit of religious zeal (or political expediency) proves only that *no such discrimination had been customary before.*" He goes on to say that on other occasions, when the authorities did enforce restrictions concerning *dhimmī* attire, this was done only to extort money from the *dhimmīs.* At the end of this discussion, however, Goitein states that toward the end of the twelfth century "the wearing of distinctive marks by non-Muslims was already generally accepted and the stern warning was addressed only to a few transgressors, presumably of the upper class."[2]

Moshe Gil believes that even the restrictions of al-Mutawakkil were issued de jure but were not enforced de facto, at least not systematically: "They were imposed by the rulers in Palestine as well, but to the best of my knowledge there is nothing in the sources indicating their particular application in Palestine. Except that here, as elsewhere in the caliphate, they were not rigorously observed, which is the only explanation for the fact that they had to be renewed from time to time."[3]

It seems that the view common among prominent scholars is that the restrictions were in most periods a dead letter. According to this view, these restrictions were applied only sporadically and were largely viewed as an opportunity for extortion of the *dhimmī* communities. The restrictions were repeatedly issued without really having any long-lasting effect on *dhimmī* communities. Yet somehow, and surprisingly so, by the end of the twelfth century they came to be rigorously enforced, a rule ignored by only a rebellious few, presumably from the upper class.

In this essay, I will argue against the common view. While during the first century of Islam one cannot speak of a consistent policy adopted by Muslim authorities toward the *dhimmīs* and enforced upon them, this situation changed considerably starting in the second century and especially from the third century of Islam onward. During this period, Muslim authorities promulgated a crystallized set of rules that, in contrast to the above opinions, was uniformly enforced by various caliphs and rulers.

The Code of Restrictions Regarding Non-Muslims

It is not within the scope of this essay to trace the formation of the codes regarding non-Muslims. I will present here only a succinct summary of the conclusions of a broader discussion wherein I present evidence regarding the process of codification of *shurūṭ ʿUmar*. *Shurūṭ ʿUmar*, usually translated as "The Pact of ʿUmar," is the document regarding the position of non-Muslims under Muslim rule. It most probably became canonical during the first half of the ninth century. According to Islamic tradition, the concept of *ghiyār*, or distinguishing marks, which forms a central part of *shurūṭ ʿUmar*, was established formally in an edict promulgated by the caliph ʿUmar b. ʿAbd al-ʿAzīz (r. 717–20 CE).[4] This edict was the first stage of a process of codification of a set of regulations regarding the *dhimmīs*. The concept of *ghiyār* was embedded in the ideology promoted by ʿUmar b. ʿAbd al-ʿAzīz regarding the exaltation of Islam over other religions.[5]

The process of canonization of a comprehensive legal document containing rules and regulations regarding the non-Muslims, which began with the formulation of the *ghiyār*, came to its completion in the well-known *shurūṭ ʿUmar*. The *shurūṭ* reflects a rigorous approach, one that seems to have become prevalent beginning in the second half of the ninth century. Yet prior to its canonization, the *shurūṭ* was one of several competing documents. At least two other versions of such a document in existence ca. 800 reflect a more lenient approach toward *dhimmīs*.[6] The canonization of the text accepted finally as *shurūṭ ʿUmar*, therefore, was a victory for its supporters over the promoters of alternative views.

This victory is attested in the edict that was promulgated and (as shall be presently demonstrated) strictly applied by al-Mutawakkil, which reflects in most of its clauses the regulations contained in *shurūṭ ʿUmar*.[7] I will attempt to demonstrate here that from this time onward, this code of regulations was applied by several rulers and, by the second half of the ninth century, had become the norm with regard to the treatment of the *dhimmīs* rather than the exception, as has traditionally been claimed. This does not mean that it was always strictly enforced; there are many situations throughout the reign of Islam in the Middle Ages where many of these regulations were disregarded.[8] The question, therefore, is how established was the Pact of ʿUmar and the regulations that emanated from it? Was their enforcement a passing fit of zealous rulers, as claimed, or the upholding of an established set of accepted regulations? I hold that the latter was the case.

Restrictions upon the *Dhimmīs* Prior to al-Mutawakkil

The regulations and restrictions ordained upon the *dhimmīs* have been a subject of exhaustive research by scholars since the publication of A. S. Tritton's *Caliphs and Their Non-Muslim Subjects*.[9] I will present here a brief survey of regulations and restrictions up to the days of al-Mutawakkil to demonstrate the gradual development of a systematic code that was enforced in practice upon non-Muslims.

Dionysius of Tell-Maḥrē, the Jacobite patriarch in the first half of the ninth century, reports that as early as the days of the caliph ʿUthmān (644–56) the governor of Damascus ordered the destruction of crosses and forbade the public exhibition of the cross on Christian festivals and days of supplication.[10] It is reported that ʿAbd al-Malik b. Marwān (685–705) ordered the slaughter of all the pigs in the caliphate and the removal of all crosses.[11] His decree regarding the Arabization of the *diwāns* seems to have also entailed the attempt to curtail the employment of non-Muslims in the administration.[12] Sometime during the end of the seventh century or the beginning of the eighth, rulers in Egypt started demanding payment of the *jizya* from monks, who had until then been exempt from this payment.[13]

As noted above, the first caliph to have issued an edict containing a set of regulations regarding the *dhimmīs* was ʿUmar b. ʿAbd al-ʿAzīz. The main part of this corpus of regulations focused on the *ghiyār*; the corpus also included an order for the dismissal of non-Muslims from public service, either as a clause in the same edict or as a separate edict. This is, in fact, the earliest evidence of the enforcement of the principle of *khilāf* or *ghiyār*.

The sources that cite ʿUmar b. ʿAbd al-ʿAzīz's edict are quite consistent regarding its rules about *ghiyār*.[14] The edict seems to have been composed of two parts. The first relates to riding and forbade non-Muslims, men and women alike, from using saddles or sitting astride their horses, prescribing that they ride side-saddle on pack-saddles instead. The second part of the edict includes specific regulations regarding attire and appearance, including the obligation to cut the forelocks and to wear a (leather) girdle (*zunnār*) and the prohibition against wearing a special gown, the *qabāʾ*, or a turban (*ʿimāma* or *ʿaṣb*).

Several sources mention the fact that ʿUmar b. ʿAbd al-ʿAzīz also promulgated orders regarding the exhibition of crosses in public[15] and the use of the *nāqūs*, the clapper used for calling Christians to prayer.[16] Michael the Syrian also mentions a prohibition against raising voices in prayer.[17] There are conflicting reports in Muslim sources concerning ʿUmar's attitude toward *dhimmī* prayer-houses. Some sources report that he issued an order prohibiting the destruction of existing churches and the building of new ones.[18] On the other hand, ʿAbd al-Razzāq al-Ṣanʿānī, the well-known Yemeni scholar and traditionist (744–827), insists in more than one place that ʿUmar ordered the destruction of ancient as well as newly built churches in "Muslim cities" (*amṣār al-muslimīn*) or those that were taken *ʿanwatan* ("by force").[19] Nevertheless, there is information concerning the building of several new churches in the days of ʿUmar b. ʿAbd al-ʿAzīz.[20] There is also conflicting evidence deriving from the time of ʿUmar b. ʿAbd al-ʿAzīz regarding the question of the right to bequeath to the church.[21]

Although it has been claimed (without due evidence) that some of these prohibitions may have been ascribed to ʿUmar b. ʿAbd al-ʿAzīz anachronistically, it seems quite unmistakable that the regulations of the *ghiyār* were a product of his policy and ideology.[22] The following tradition adduced by Abū Yūsuf Yaʿqūb (d. 798) in his *Kitāb al-kharāj* regarding the *ghiyār* emphasizes the significance attributed by ʿUmar b. ʿAbd al-ʿAzīz to the enforcement of these regulations. It is transmitted by ʿAbd al-Raḥmān b. Thābit b. Thūbān, a well-known Damascene transmitter,[23] who heard it from his father:[24]

> ʿUmar b. ʿAbd al-ʿAzīz wrote to one of his governors:
>
> "Regarding the matter at hand: you shall not permit a cross to be manifested, that is not smashed and effaced; a Jew or a Christian shall not ride on a saddle (*sirj*), but shall ride on a pack-saddle (*ikāf*); their women shall not ride on leather saddles (*riḥāla*), they shall ride on a pack-saddle (*ikāf*). Order this expressly, and prevent those who are under your authority (from letting) a Christian wear a *qabāʾ*, a silk garment, or a turban (*ʿaṣb*).
>
> I have been told that many of the Christians under your authority have returned to wearing turbans (*ʿamāʾim*), have given up wearing the girdles (*manāṭiq*)[25] on their waists, and have begun to wear their hair long and to neglect cutting it [i.e., their forelocks]. I swear that if anyone under your authority does so, this attests to your weakness, inability, and flattery, and when they go back to this [i.e., their former costumes and habits], they know what you are. Look out for everything which I have prohibited and prevent it from being carried out. Goodbye."

The fact that ʿUmar b. ʿAbd al-ʿAzīz claims that the governors have allowed matters to deteriorate could be taken to mean that the rules predated his reign, but he may equally well be referring to an edict that he himself had published in the past.

It seems, therefore, that the idea of *ghiyār* struck deep roots in the Muslim domain as early as the second/eighth century and, by the end of the eighth century CE, when Abū Yūsuf was writing his *Kitāb al-Kharāj*, had become an accepted concept. While the *ghiyār* was not always rigorously enforced, it was nevertheless considered an official code of dress and appearance, one to which non-Muslims were required to adhere.[26] The gradual progression of the enforcement of the concept of *ghiyār* specifically, and other restrictions in general (see below), may thus be traced to the eighth century CE.

Between the time of ʿUmar b. ʿAbd al-ʿAzīz and al-Mutawakkil there are several mentions of restrictions and regulations, most of which reappear later in the *shurūṭ*. Thus, several restrictions were prescribed by the caliph al-Manṣūr (754–75) in the beginning of the ʿAbbāsid period. These include prohibitions on the employment of Christians in public office, on holding vigils for liturgical purposes, and on teaching in Arabic.[27] Al-Manṣūr also removed the crosses from the tops of the churches,[28] ordered that the palms of the *dhimmīs* be marked (a statement apparently not attested elsewhere),[29] and imposed the *jizya* on the monks, who had been exempt from it up to that time.[30] The order to remove the crosses existed prior to ʿUmar b. ʿAbd al-ʿAzīz, and dates to the seventh century,[31] while the first systematic attempt to oust non-Muslims from public office was carried out by ʿAbd al-Malik (685–705)[32] and the second by ʿUmar b. ʿAbd al-ʿAzīz. Such restrictive policies were also applied around the same time in Egypt: Ṣāliḥ b. ʿAlī, the governor of Egypt (750–51, 753–55), prohibited public theological debates between Christians and Muslims, the exhibition of crosses in public, and the building of new churches.[33]

Hārūn al-Rashīd (r. 786–809) ordered that churches in the frontier areas be razed, an order that no doubt had to do with the security situation along the border. As already noted above, particular instructions concerning *dhimmī* appearance, a clear development of ʿUmar b. ʿAbd al-ʿAzīz's edict, were articulated by al-Rashīd's legal advisor, Abū Yūsuf Yaʿqūb (d. 789). Al-Ṭabarī mentions that al-Rashīd ordered that the *dhimmīs* in Baghdad change their appearance so that they would look different from Muslims.[34] However, Abū Yūsuf's edict is a general one and applies to all non-Muslims; there is thus good reason to presume that at the very least it was enforced wherever there was a significant Muslim presence.[35] Between Hārūn al-Rashīd's time and that of al-Mutawakkil there is a report concerning the caliph al-Wāthiq (r. 842–47), who prohibited the use of the *nāqūs* in churches.[36]

The evidence presented thus far seems to indicate that although there was no single document nor a single consistent, accepted, and comprehensive set of regulations regarding non-Muslims, many of the regulations themselves were starting to take shape and were enforced at least, but not only, in the above-mentioned cases that were recorded by historians. *Shurūṭ ʿUmar* (and its competing documentary accounts) therefore constituted an attempt to give one formalized and uniform expression to a host of variegated regulations that were applied sporadically under different rulers.

The Restrictions Issued by al-Mutawakkil

The first established and comprehensive set of restrictions known to us is that which was promulgated by al-Mutawakkil. For the first time, the caliph issued an organized set of restrictions—rather than individual, sporadic, ad hoc regulations—to be applied to the *dhimmīs*. These included not only detailed instructions concerning *dhimmī* appearance in public, in the spirit of the *ghiyār* regulations promulgated by ʿUmar b. ʿAbd al-ʿAzīz, but also the destruction of renovated places of worship and their confiscation; a demeaning marking of *dhimmī* houses; a prohibition on the employment of *dhimmīs* in government offices and on the education of *dhimmī* children in Muslim schools; a total prohibition on religious processions, including on Palm Sunday; and the leveling of *dhimmī* graves to a height lower than that of Muslim graves.[37] Contrary to the arguments by scholars that this was an isolated case, I will demonstrate that such comprehensive sets of restrictions were repeatedly issued in the following period. In fact, once clearly established, this set of regulations seems to have become a paradigm for later caliphs and rulers to follow.

The sources mention several caliphs who issued similar edicts. Al-Muqtadir (r. 908–32) is reported to have issued a set of regulations concerning the employment of *dhimmīs* in public service, the requirement that *dhimmīs* wear distinctive honey-colored attire, and other *ghiyār*.[38] Al-Maqrīzī reports that the *wazīr* of the Faṭimīd caliph al-Muʿizz, Jawhar, imposed the regulations of the *ghiyār* upon the *dhimmīs*.[39] Most famous of all is al-Ḥākim, who went to much greater lengths, not only inflicting the restrictions upon the *dhimmīs* ruthlessly and mercilessly but also demolishing all synagogues and churches and confiscating property.[40] The question remains, of course, whether the regulations attributed to these rulers were enforced or whether they were merely a dead letter.

Enforcement of *Dhimmī* Restrictions

The decrees regarding the *dhimmīs* issued by al-Mutawakkil are well-known and undoubtedly authentic. Yet information concerning the enforcement of the decree is partial and insufficient. As emphasized in the opening paragraph of this essay, scholars have claimed, on the basis of this paucity of evidence, that al-Mutawakkil's restrictions were not enforced systematically or consistently within the caliphate and that these restrictions were soon disregarded and ignored. What evidence, then, do we have for their enforcement?

On the Muslim side, al-Ṭabarī reports that in Muḥarram of 239 AH (June 12–July 11, 853) al-Mutawakkil ordered that *dhimmīs* affix two yellow sleeves to their outer cloaks. In Ṣafar (July 12–August 9), he ordered that they restrict their mounts to mules and donkeys and avoid riding and pack horses.[41] Ibn al-Jawzī recounts that in 236 AH, following the general edict issued in Shawwāl 235,[42] Christians were ousted from public office, discharged from the *wilāyāt* (provincial administration), and in general no longer to be employed in anything related to the affairs of the Muslims.[43] In agreement with al-Ṭabarī, he relates that in Muḥarram 239 the order that non-Muslim men should wear honey-colored patches on their gowns and overcoats and that women should wear honey-colored veils was enforced; in Ṣafar that year, the *dhimmīs* were prohibited from riding horses and were restricted to using donkeys and mules.[44] In 240, it was announced in public that the children of the *dhimmīs* were to be taught Syriac or Hebrew and were forbidden to learn Arabic.[45] All of these restrictions demonstrate that Muslim authorities indeed meant to enforce these specific clauses of al-Mutawakkil's edict in the years following its publication. If so, how strictly, how widely, and how efficiently were the instructions implemented?

Non-Muslim sources offer especially important evidence regarding the degree and efficiency of this implementation. Information regarding the enforcement of the edict both in Egypt and around the capital itself is adduced by Severus b. al-Muqaffaʿ, who reports that al-Mutawakkil ordered all churches to be demolished, a claim that is not corroborated elsewhere; forbade *dhimmīs* to wear white and ordered that they should wear only dyed garments so that they might be distinguished from Muslims; and commanded that frightful pictures should be made on wooden boards and be nailed over the doors of the Christians.[46] The Jacobite chronicler Gregory Barhebraeus mentions the new requirements concerning appearance, the prohibition on exhibiting crosses in processions on Palm Sunday, the destruction of new churches, and the appropriation of partial areas of large churches. He also notes that similar restrictions were enforced upon the Jews.[47] These sources mention only some of the restrictions found in al-Mutawakkil's edict.

A chronicle written in Samaria at the time of the events by members of the local Samaritan community provides substantial new evidence on this issue.[48] This is a continuation of the Samaritan chronicle of Abū ʾl-Fatḥ. It appears in a unique manuscript found in the Bibliothéque Nationale and was known to Vilmar, the first editor of Abū ʾl-Fatḥ's chronicle. Due mainly to linguistic considerations, Vilmar chose not to publish this unique manuscript, which continued up to the time of the caliph al-Rāḍī (r. 934–40 CE). As a result, this part of the chronicle has until now been disregarded despite its importance as a well-informed source based on an eyewitness account. The *Continuatio* clarifies the picture regarding both issues under discussion: the degree to which al-Mutawakkil's restrictions were enforced and their long-term influence.[49]

He was succeeded by his brother Jaʿfar [al-Mutawakkil], who afflicted the world with every kind [of affliction]. He ordered at first that that people should wear distinguishing clothes, except for the black and the blue, which he reserved for his faith. He ordered that there should be no scribe or public official (*ʿāmil*) except from his faith, and that there should be no one in charge of a fort or holding any kind of position except from his faith. There were Christians whom he cast out, and he appointed all the officials from his faith. He ordered that no one should wear a garment with an embroidered edge (*ṭirāz*)[50] except the members of his faith, and no one should ride a horse [except the members of his faith]. He commanded that every *dhimmī* should wear a distinguishing sign in front and back,[51] and that he should not sit in front on a velvet-like sofa, that no one except the members of his own faith should have iron stirrups[52]—the rest [would have] wooden ones. He ordered that every grave resembling the graves of the members of his faith be destroyed,[53] and the grave of the *raʾīs* Nethanʾel was destroyed. Before that occurred, he ordered that every *dhimmī* should affix to his door a wooden idol bearing the label of "idol" (*wathan*).[54]

The Samaritans who resided in Nablus, may God remember them favorably, having presented the governor (*wālī*) of Nablus with something [i.e., a gift], asked him to grant them a delay so they could go down to Ramla, and he agreed to that. [Now] in Dājūn there was a man possessed of dignity and power, whose word was accepted by the ruler (*sulṭān*), by the name of Abū Yūsuf ibn Dhāsī, may his memory be forever blessed. He called on the governor and petitioned him, and he [the governor] told him that it was not possible to annul the order of the king but [said]: "Choose for yourself an image which is not offensive." He chose the image of a candelabrum that we make; it was put in an envelope, and he stamped it and sent it to the governor of Nablus. [The governor] commanded that a Samaritan should only make [an image] like that which Yūsuf ibn Dhāsī made—[that is,] a candelabrum. They rejoiced greatly in this and profusely thanked God, may He be praised and exalted. As for those [Samaritans] who were in [the province of] Jordan, this [concession] was not granted to them, and an image was made [by them] like the other peoples according to the law.

> In his days it was decreed that a man shall not raise his voice in prayer, and shall not raise his voice in…, a funeral shall not be seen, and a *dhimmī* shall not lift his face to a Muslim's[55] face in order to speak or respond to him.

Unlike the other non-Muslim sources cited, the *Continuatio* gives us a nearly complete list of al-Mutawakkil's restrictions, many of which overlap. Thus, the *Continuatio* mentions the requirements of the *ghiyār*, specifically the patches in front and rear; the prohibition on the use of iron stirrups; the prohibition on riding horses (which is mentioned by al-Ṭabarī[56] but not in the actual edict he cites); the prohibition on holding public office; the prohibition on holding public funeral processions; the order to level all *dhimmī* graves so that they do not resemble Muslim ones; and the order to affix idols to the doorposts.

On the other hand, the *Continuatio* includes many additions not found elsewhere. These include the prohibition on raising the voice in prayer and the order that a *dhimmī* not speak to a Muslim face to face but rather, presumably, with eyes cast down. These decrees appear in *shurūṭ ʿUmar* as "we will not raise our voices in church services or in the presence of Muslims" and as the requirement to show respect toward Muslims.[57]

Three regulations mentioned by al-Ṭabarī are, however, missing. The first is the decree that renovated places of worship be destroyed. The most likely explanation for this is that this decree was not relevant at the time for the Samaritans and that no Samaritan prayer-house had been destroyed. The second is that one-tenth of the houses owned by *dhimmīs* should be confiscated. This decree was most likely not carried out, since it is hard to believe that if this decree were executed in Palestine, or at least among its Samaritan population, it would have gone unmentioned. It may well be due to the fact that there was no shortage of land or housing in the area of Samaria in particular or Palestine in general. The other decree not mentioned in our text concerns the prohibition against *dhimmī* children being educated in Muslim schools. In this case, too, it may be conjectured that the Samaritan population was not bothered by this decree since they had no interest in giving their children a Muslim education.

The report given here concerning the restrictions imposed upon the *dhimmīs* during the days of the caliph al-Mutawakkil is very detailed and of considerable significance. The Samaritan text confirms unequivocally that not only were *dhimmīs* in Palestine and Jordan familiar with the details of these decrees but the restrictions were indeed enforced quite strictly. This is well in line with al-Mutawakkil's letter cited by al-Ṭabarī and in *shurūṭ al-naṣārā*,[58] which demands that "what they do shall be inspected to ensure that the orders of the Commander of the Faithful are carried out by their clear compliance. The inspector should be able to spot compliance readily, it being immediately apparent. . . . You shall instruct the officers concerning the orders of the Commander of the Faithful, and do so in such a way that they are motivated to carry out their examinations as commissioned."[59] This, incidentally, is well in line with the edict of ʿUmar b. ʿAbd al-ʿAzīz to his governor, which ends with the directive that "he shall watch out for anything that I have prohibited and stop those who commit it."[60]

This enforcement of the orders is well demonstrated by the practical consequences related in the Samaritan chronicle, such as the story of the image that the *dhimmīs* were ordered to attach to their doorposts. The Samaritans of Palestine went to great trouble to evade this order, which in their eyes was equivalent to idol worship; nonetheless, they had to settle for a compromise: the use of an image of a candelabrum. The Samaritans of Jund al-Urdunn were not granted even this concession from their governor and had to abide by the original decree. Another example of the strict execution of the decrees is the leveling of the grave of the Samaritan head Nethanʾel because it resembled a Muslim grave. It may be presumed that these decrees were imposed in equal severity upon all the other *dhimmīs* in the *junds* of Filāsṭīn and Urdunn as well. It can, moreover, be deduced safely that this would have been the situation all over the caliphate. It seems it can no longer be claimed that al-Mutawakkil's regulations were not fully enforced.

The Long-Lasting Enforcement of al-Mutawakkil's Restrictions

It nevertheless remains to be asked whether this policy had any long-lasting influence after al-Mutawakkil's days. It has been noted above that there are succinct references to similar restrictions imposed by al-Muqtadir, by al-Ikhshīd, and by al-Muʿizz, even prior to al-Ḥākim's notorious decrees. Yet these were not regarded seriously by scholars, as already noted. Fattal, for example, adopted ʿArīb b. Saʿd al-Qurṭubī's[61] evaluation that al-Muqtadir's restrictions concerning the prohibition on employing *dhimmīs* in government did not last and applied this evaluation to the whole set of prohibitions. This conclusion is problematic, given that al-Qurṭubī refers specifically to this one decree that was not adhered to in Cordoba, while Ibn Taghrī Birdī, who refers not only to this prohibition but also to the elements of *ghiyār*, does not state that these restrictions were left unenforced.[62] It is well-known that the prohibition concerning the service of *dhimmīs* in public office was the most difficult to carry out. This was not only because Christians and Jews had so much experience and knowledge in the field of administration and management that they became almost irreplaceable but also because rulers were reluctant to replace these loyal and efficient officials who, in contrast to their Muslim counterparts, posed no threat to their rule. This is well documented by Ibn Qayyim al-Jawziyya, Ibn al-Naqqāsh, and al-Qalqashandī, who focus almost obsessively on this issue.[63]

Here, too, the Samaritan chronicle supplies us with material evidence that discredits the accepted opinion that al-Mutawakkil's decrees were but a short-lived episode characteristic of their initiator, and that attempts made by other rulers to impose such regulations were not put into effect. The Samaritan chronicle adduces new information that shows that al-Mutawakkil's decrees were in fact a turning point. Although his restrictions had not automatically stayed in force, they were renewed in a surprisingly short time.

The information concerns Aḥmad b. Ṭūlūn, the founder of the Ṭūlūnid dynasty, who ruled Palestine between 878 and 884.[64]

> He [i.e., Ibn Ṭūlūn] oppressed the people in every way. In the second year a governor (*wālī*) came to [rule over] the people on his behalf and oppressed [them] in every way; he ordered that the *dhimmīs* should wear distinguishing signs, engraved [lit., made] idols (*awthān*) on their doors, [ordered that] a *dhimmī* should not raise his head in the presence of a Muslim [lit., *goy*] and that he should not raise his voice in prayer and that he should not blow the horn; he also destroyed a synagogue of the Jews. All the religious communities were in fear of him, lest he extend [his] hand to their houses of worship so as to put them to his own use. He prohibited the drinking of wine[65] and oppressed [them] in every possible manner.

Although more succinct than its predecessor, this set of regulations is almost identical to that of al-Mutawakkil, the distinctions in appearance of the *dhimmīs* being encapsulated under the title *ghiyār*. There are two regulations missing: the lack of reference to funerals likely results from the carelessness of the author, who refers to parallels such as blowing the horn and raising the voice in prayer. The order concerning the leveling of graves is likely absent because after al-Mutawakkil's actions, Samaritan graves no longer resembled Muslim graves but were built without tall tombstones in the first place. An additional Ṭūlūnid decree not listed among al-Mutawakkil's restrictions is what seems to be a generalized prohibition on drinking fermented beverages. This prohibition is rooted in the edict of ʿUmar b. ʿAbd al-ʿAzīz, which prohibited non-Muslims from drinking wine,[66] and it may have resulted in a prohibition on the possession of wine in Muslim cities, as is claimed by Theophanes.[67] Al-Shāfiʿī's *Kitāb al-umm* includes a prohibition on selling fermented drinks to Muslims,[68] while in *shurūṭ ʿUmar* the prohibition seems to be on its sale altogether.[69] Thus, it may well be that by Aḥmad b. Ṭūlūn's time, the ban on wine was already being imposed not only upon Muslims and non-Muslims in the *amṣār* but even upon non-Muslims living in the more neglected agricultural periphery of the caliphate.

There seems to be no other evidence regarding Ibn Ṭūlūn's restrictions. The text, written by members of the local Samaritan community, clearly shows that these measures were imposed upon the population and strictly enforced. It can be safely assumed that these restrictions were enforced in the same manner in all provinces under Ibn Ṭūlūn's jurisdiction. Ibn Ṭūlūn's restrictions are therefore a case in point demonstrating that one cannot deduce from the silence of the sources that the restrictions were not applied. In fact, although it is not part of the current discussion, one should note that the chronicle gives a detailed description of Ibn Ṭūlūn's rule, especially in Palestine; the author complains not only about the restrictions but about the oppressive behavior of Ibn Ṭūlūn's emissaries in general.[70]

The new evidence of the *Continuatio* of the Samaritan chronicle, provided by *dhimmīs* living in a peripheral area of the caliphate, demonstrates that not only were al-Mutawakkil's decrees not forgotten but they were in reality strictly enforced by another Muslim ruler only a few years after al-Mutawakkil's death. This leads us in a rather different direction than the one taken until now. The additional references we have to al-Muqtadir, al-Muʿizz, al-Ḥākim, and al-Muqtadī (1075–94),[71] who also enforced similar decrees, should thus be regarded carefully rather than being nonchalantly discarded. It seems that from al-Mutawakkil's days onward, the regulations published by him were to become the rule that various Muslim rulers strived to impose and enforce.

However, although enforcement of the *ghiyār* thus seems to have been more significant than has been traditionally assumed, this does not mean that from al-Mutawakkil's days onward these regulations were an integral and non-negotiable part of *dhimmī* life. It is quite understandable that *dhimmīs* felt more restricted and humiliated now than they had been before and that they in consequence fought against these new realities, testing and trying the determination of each ruler to enforce the restrictions now and again. It may also be presumed that some rulers were indeed more lenient than others, especially when it suited their internal or external political ends. There are numerous examples of allowances and concessions concerning the building of prayer-houses, the employment of *dhimmīs* in government bureaus,[72] and the like after al-Mutawakkil's reign.[73]

Nevertheless, though the rules were often bent in favor of more lenient policies toward *dhimmīs* and these regulations were often disregarded and evaded, they were never annulled, and they could be imposed or strictly enforced at any given moment. Their enforcement could also be retracted at the ruler's will. This is well exemplified by the behavior of both al-Ḥākim and Ṣalaḥ al-Dīn, who first imposed these regulations and then retracted them.[74] The set of regulations that began with the ideology promoted and applied by ʿUmar b. ʿAbd al-ʿAzīz and struck deep roots from the second half of the ninth century onward continued to expand. It became increasingly elaborate and more strictly enforced with time, as is apparent later in the Mamlūk period when Ibn Qayyim al-Jawziyya wrote his magnum opus *Aḥkām ahl al-dhimma*.

CHAPTER 3

Thinkers of "This Peninsula"

Toward an Integrative Approach to the Study of Philosophy in al-Andalus

SARAH STROUMSA

Andalusian Communities

The development of philosophical thought among Muslims in al-Andalus is often described in contradictory terms. On the one hand, scholars agree that, in many ways, the Iberian peninsula witnessed the acme of Islamic philosophy. On the other hand, medieval and modern scholars alike often regard the development of philosophy in this region as something of an anomaly.[1] Medieval Muslim writers such as Ibn Ḥazm (d. 1065) and Ibn Ṭumlūs (d. 1223) speak apologetically regarding the scarcity of philosophical interest and of philosophical and theological compositions in al-Andalus, while al-Maqqarī (d. 1631) reports animosity toward the study of philosophy in this region.[2] The discrepancy between these apparently unfavorable conditions and the seemingly sudden burst of philosophy requires explanation, one that can bridge the gap between these contradictory descriptions. Such an explanation, however, is not to be found in most studies on the topic, and the few scholars who address this problem tend to refine the presentation of the question rather than offer a satisfactory explanation for it.

Jewish philosophy in al-Andalus, on the other hand, is depicted in a much simpler and more homogeneous way. The effervescence of Jewish philosophy is seen as part and parcel of the so-called Golden Age of Jewish culture in Islamic Spain. Like Jewish culture in al-Andalus in general, philosophy is painted in rosy—or should we say golden—colors. The appearance of luminaries like Judah Halevi (d. 1148) and Moses Maimonides (d. 1204) is regarded as the natural outcome of a flourishing Jewish community whose cultural activity reflected its interest in philosophy as well as the influence of the surrounding Muslim society.

The circumstances in which thought in general, and philosophy in particular, developed in Muslim and Jewish communities are usually studied as separate questions, although dutiful nods acknowledge the existence of the other community. This last statement, which may seem unfair at first sight and may trigger a protesting denial by students of these literatures, deserves elaboration.

Students of Judeo-Arabic philosophy are, of course, well aware of the strong connections between it and its Muslim counterpart. Halevi has been shown to depend on al-Ghazzālī[3] as well as on Ṣūfī and Ismāʿīlī Shīʿī texts,[4] while the eleventh-century Baḥyā ibn Paqūda depends on al-Muḥāsibī.[5] Maimonides' philosophy, continuously and thoroughly examined, has been shown to draw upon works by al-Fārābī, Avicenna, and Andalusian authors like Ibn Ṭufayl and Ibn Bājja.[6] For students of Muslim philosophy, the connection with Jewish philosophy imposes itself less forcefully. Nevertheless, contemporary scholars (such as Miguel Cruz Hernández and Dominique Urvoy) have attempted to present a coherent synthesis that includes the Jewish philosophical output in their mapping of Andalusian philosophy.[7] And yet, all these studies present the connection either as background to the discussion of their main focus of interest (in the case of Jewish philosophy) or as mere chapters in it (in the case of Muslim philosophy).

A comparison with the modern study of the Christians of al-Andalus can highlight the oddity of the compartmentalized approach to the study of Andalusian intellectual history. The history of al-Andalus, from the eighth to the fifteenth centuries, can be described as a chronology of its continuous war with Christian Spain. An uninterrupted Christian presence within the borders of al-Andalus, combined with the Christian pressure from outside, made the Christians a determining factor of Andalusian culture. In the realm of philosophical thought, however, the Christian presence seems to have played only a minor role in the period that concerns us. In the East, the Christians' heritage fostered interest in philosophy, and Christians played an active role as translators and as facilitators of the transmission of philosophical and scientific traditions.[8] Nothing like this decisive Christian intellectual presence is witnessed in this period in al-Andalus.[9] Dominique Urvoy has argued for the existence of some evidence of a transmission of pre-Islamic Spanish philosophical works to Arabic, but the limited evidence for this phenomenon justifies its treatment as rather minor, and Urvoy also notes the "faiblesse relative de la vie intellectuelle mozarabe" as compared to that of the Jews.[10] Ann Christys likewise notes that the Christians were only a footnote in the history of al-Andalus and explains this marginality as resulting from the fact that the Christians did not write (which is to say, they wrote little).[11] One could therefore argue that the explanation for the separate treatment of the Christian community in the historiography of al-Andalus and the marginal place it is accorded in the history of Andalusian thought can be found in the objective sociological characteristics of that community. This explanation, however, does not hold in the case of the Jewish community in al-Andalus: the Jews had a flourishing philosophy, which they did write, and yet they, too, remain little more than a footnote in modern historiography of Islamic philosophy in al-Andalus.[12] This last fact obliges us to look for another explanation for the disjointed historiography of Andalusian philosophy, one that would focus on the preconceptions of the historians who write it as much as it does on the historical developments themselves.

An integrative approach to the history of philosophy in al-Andalus should seek to view the various products of philosophy in the Iberian Peninsula—Jewish, Muslim, and Christian—as parts of a common intellectual history and as stages in a continuous trajectory. This task obviously requires a comprehensive study, which I hope to present elsewhere. This essay has the limited purpose of introducing the methodology of such a study. It will focus on the dynamics of interaction between intellectuals of the different religious communities in al-Andalus and on the method of extrapolating this dynamic from sometimes recalcitrant texts.

"This Peninsula"

The self-perception of the inhabitants of al-Andalus supports the adoption of an integrative approach to their intellectual history. Within the Islamic world, al-Andalus represents a distinct cultural unit with unique characteristics. The territorial borders of this unit are dependent on the fluctuating territorial borders of Islamic Spain (though they are not necessarily identical to them at all periods). At times, these borders encroach upon Maghreban territory; Andalusian intellectual history is thus closely linked to the Maghreb and to its culture. The philosophy engendered within this cultural unit developed as a continuation of the philosophy in the Islamic East and in dialogue with it. Books and theories were imported from the East, and their content was studied and assimilated. The philosophical and theological compositions of Andalusian authors, however, are not servile replicas of Maghreban or Oriental sources.[13] They have a distinct character which, while reflecting the influences of their sources, displays their originality and the fact that they belong to the world of al-Andalus. Muslim writers themselves were quite conscious of the distinct character of their region. The Cordoban Ibn Ḥazm, for example, attempted to spell out "the merits of al-Andalus," while Ibn Rushd (d. 1198) included in his *Commentary on Plato's "Republic"* several observations concerning the peculiarities of political regimes in what he calls "our precinct," and in his Commentary on Aristotle's *Meteorology* he discusses the specific characteristics of the inhabitants of "this peninsula."[14]

Like their Muslim counterparts, Andalusian Jewish philosophical writings also display close connections with currents of thought in the Maghreb. And they, too, notwithstanding their close dependency on the literary output of the Jewish centers in the East, developed their own local characteristics. Jewish thinkers saw themselves as "the diaspora of *Sefarad*," and they cultivated their own local patriotism. Thus, Moses ibn Ezra extolled the literary and linguistic purity of the "Jerusalemites who were exiled to *Sefarad*" above all other Jewish communities;[15] Maimonides, exiled from al-Andalus as a young adolescent, continued to call himself "*ha-sefaradi*."[16]

The distinctiveness of Andalusian intellectual life is taken into account, as a matter of course, in the study of Muslim theology, where regional differences often offer the main framework for historical studies.[17] Students of Jewish philosophy, however, usually prefer a classification that aligns Jewish medieval thinkers with the schools of Islamic thought (*kalām*, *falsafa*, Sufism, and so on).[18] Paradoxically, the underlying assumption for this approach (initiated by Julius Guttmann and in itself quite legitimate) is that the development of Jewish philosophy was, by and large, an integral part of a common Islamic culture.[19] But the logical result of this approach favors the connection of a Judah Halevi with his Eastern sources (both Jewish and Muslim) while ignoring his immediate, neighboring intellectual environment. Such an approach would be justifiable only if one could claim that Jews in al-Andalus lived a segregated intellectual life, an indefensible claim.

The strongly felt Andalusian identity of both Jewish and Muslim intellectuals, along with their close proximity, requires an integrative approach to the study of philosophy in al-Andalus. Such an integrative history should focus on intellectual developments in al-Andalus, attempting to evaluate the local, Andalusian character of this philosophy and to see how it is connected to the development of Islamic philosophy in the Orient.

In what follows, I will discuss the intellectual context in which this philosophy grew and attempt to illustrate what can be learned through an integrative approach.

Ibn Masarra

Very little is known about the early infiltration of speculative thought into al-Andalus. The tenth-century Muslim thinker Muḥammad b. ʿAbd Allah Ibn Masarra (d. 930) provides an apt illustration of the thick fog that covers these beginnings. Much speculation has been published concerning his philosophical tendency. Ibn Masarra has been described as a Muʿtazilī theologian, a mystic, a Neoplatonist follower of the *Bāṭiniyya*, a follower of the so-called Pseudo-Empedocles, and a combination of all of these. Most of these suggestions, however, are not based on an examination of his extant writings and even less on an appraisal of his probable intellectual environment. A cursory examination of his writings discloses some striking, hitherto unnoticed, unmistakably Jewish elements. When these elements are followed and closely checked, they can add significant information to our meager knowledge of the beginnings of Islamic and Jewish philosophy in al-Andalus.[20]

The idea that the paucity of information in Arab sources needs to be supplemented by the examination of other available material has been emphasized by Pierre Guichard, who used Christian and archaeological sources to study the social, administrative, military, and demographic history of al-Andalus.[21] In the case of Ibn Masarra, the discovery of a Jewish element in his thought can help us trace, for example, the transmission lines of theological (*kalām*) material in al-Andalus. It can help us rethink questions concerning the character of this material—for instance, the real or imagined character of Muʿtazilite presence in al-Andalus or the role played by Jews, and in particular by the Karaite Spanish community, in the transmission of Muʿtazilite material. It would also serve as a starting point for a reexamination of the emergence of Jewish and Muslim pietistic movements in al-Andalus, related to figures like Ibn Masarra, Baḥyā ibn Paqūda, or Ibn al-ʿArīf (d. 1141).

Libraries, Scholars, and Pirates

Ibn Masarra's mystical philosophy, with its intriguing echoes of Jewish thought, is our sole witness for this aspect of the development of philosophy and science in al-Andalus in the first half of the tenth century. The second half of the tenth century was, in many ways, a turning point in Andalusian intellectual history. The story of this turning point has two parts. Although the first part, relating to the introduction of sciences to al-Andalus, has been told many times, it deserves to be retold and to be complemented by some "less direct and immediately exploitable sources," as suggested by Guichard. The main source for the story is Ṣāʿid al-Andalusī (d. 1068), who says:

> After the beginning of the fourth century, the emir al-Ḥakam [r. 961–76] . . . son of ʿAbd al-Raḥmān al-Nāṣir li-dīn Allāh [r. 912–61]—and this was still in the days of his father's reign—was moved to attend to the sciences and to favor scientists. He brought (*istajlaba*) from Baghdād, Egypt and other places in the Orient the main outstanding compositions and wonderful tracts, in the old sciences as well as in the modern ones. He gathered, in what remained of his father's reign and then in his own, books in quantity that equaled what the ʿAbbasid kings gathered over a long time.[22]

According to Ṣāʿid, it was mainly al-Ḥakam II who introduced philosophical, theological, exegetical, and scientific lore into the Iberian peninsula on a large scale and established a huge library.[23] Ṣāʿid also tells us of a parallel move, where al-Ḥakam's Jewish vizier, Ḥasdāy ibn Shaprūt, imported religious books for the use of the Jewish community.[24]

> Ḥasdāy ibn Isḥāq, the minister of ʿAbd al-Raḥmān al-Nāṣir li-dīn Allāh... was the first to open for the Andalusian Jews the gates of religious law, computation and the like. Prior to his days, they were obliged to turn to the Jews of Baghdād in matters concerning their religious law, their computation and fixing the dates of their holy days. . . . But when Ḥasdāy attached himself to al-Ḥakam, . . . he used his good offices to bring (*li-istijlāb*) whatever he wanted of the compositions of the Jews in the Orient. The Jews of al-Andalus thus came to know that regarding which they were ignorant before.[25]

Sāʿid clearly sees Ḥasdāy's initiative to import books (*istijlāb*) as connected to that of his master's, a fact that has already been noted by several scholars.[26] The connection is not limited to the purpose of the two initiatives but also has implications regarding the lot of the books at the receiving end. It requires little dramatic imagination to realize that the same ships must have carried the books ordered by the caliph and his vizier and that when the ships arrived at the docks in Seville, for example, their literary cargo was not divided strictly according to religious affiliation. Although Ḥasdāy had ordered Jewish religious books, the books ordered by al-Ḥakam could just as well reach the hands (and the libraries) of Ḥasdāy and his co-religionists (as well as those of Christians). Ḥasdāy ibn Shaprūt was no stranger to the sciences. When the caliph received, as a gift from Byzantium, a manuscript of Dioscorides' *Materia Medica*, Ḥasdāy was a member of the team that was called upon to translate it into Arabic. He probably perused or purchased more books than he ordered, and he must not have been the sole Jew to have done so.

Ṣāʿid's information is corroborated by a Jewish source, the twelfth-century Abraham Ibn Daud (d. ca. 1180). In his *Book of Tradition,* Ibn Daud recounts the story of four Oriental Talmudic scholars who were captured by pirates in the service of ʿAbd al-Raḥmān III. Ransomed by four different Jewish communities, so the story goes, these captives lay the basis for an independent Jewish scholarship in the West. In the case of al-Andalus, the ransomed captive was Rabbi Hannoch. Ibn Daud recounts the speedy spread of the rumors regarding Rabbi Hannoch's erudition, and adds: "[At this point] the commander [of the pirates] wished to retract his sale. However, the king [i.e., the caliph, presumably ʿAbd al-Raḥmān III] would not permit him to do so, for he was delighted by the fact that the Jews of his domain no longer had need of the people of Babylonia."[27]

Ibn Daud's account tells us that the importation of books was often accompanied by traveling scholars, and he testifies to the dramatic effect the migration, whether voluntary or forced, had on the life of the Jewish communities. Ibn Daud does not connect this account to Ḥasdāy ibn Shaprūt, but Ḥasdāy's involvement with pirates may be attested in yet another source, this time by a Christian writer. Liudprand of Cremona recounts that Otto I had sent John of Gorze to carry letters to ʿAbd al-Raḥmān III. The background for this mission was a dispute between the two rulers over the attacks on Otto's land by the pirates of Fraxinentum (LaGarde Freinet in the Gulf of St. Tropez). The letters that John of Gorze was charged to bring were offensive to Islam, and the mission went sour and dragged on for years. Several local mediators were involved in this affair, among them a Jew named Hasdeu, who may well have been Ḥasdāy ibn Shaprūt.[28]

The snippets of information culled from Christian, Jewish, and Muslim sources allow us to flesh out the image of Ḥasdāy: his role in sensitive missions in the service of both ʿAbd al-Raḥmān III and his son al-Ḥakam II; the diplomatic ease with which he crossed the boundaries of religious communities; and his interest in scholarly entrepreneurship. The various stories in which Ḥasdāy appears depict him as a facilitator of intellectual transport from Byzantium and from Christian Europe via Christians, from the Orient via Jewish books and captives.

As mentioned above, this part of Ṣāʿid's story is well known. Reading the Jewish, Muslim, and Christian texts together, however, allows us to flesh out the story and to appreciate the intricacy of the picture. The dissemination of philosophy and science in al-Andalus owes much to the determination of people like al-Ḥakam, Ḥasdāy or John of Gorze, who turned adverse situations like pirate attacks or diplomatic crises into a channel for purchasing books and acquiring new knowledge.

The Porous Iron Curtain

The oft-told story, however, has a second part, which, although as famous as the first, is usually reported in a curtailed fashion. This is the part regarding al-Manṣūr's censorship, a key source for which is the continuation of the account of Ṣāʿid, who says:

> [Al-Ḥakam] died in 366 [976]. His son Hishām became king after him, and he was then a boy . . . and his chamberlain Abū ʿĀmir [r. 976–1002] took control of managing his kingdom. As soon as [Abū ʿĀmir] took control, he turned to the treasuries of [Hishām's] father al-Ḥakam, in which the above-mentioned books were kept, and he took out, in the presence of his close entourage of religious scholars, the various kinds of compositions that were found in them. He commanded [his servants] to put aside the books of the Sciences of the Ancient, which were composed in logic, astronomy etc. . . . and he ordered that these books be burnt and destroyed. Some were burnt, others were thrown into the palace's wells and covered with rocks and dirt, or were disfigured in all kinds of manners. . . . The people who have been moved to [search for] science were thus silenced, their souls were suppressed and they took to conceal whatever they had of these sciences.[29]

Ṣāʿid's depiction of "the iron curtain" that descended on libraries and their users is much exaggerated; al-Ḥakam's library was not wholly destroyed, and other libraries continued to function.[30] Nevertheless, this story is commonly accepted as faithfully reflecting the difficulty encountered by scholars of philosophy.[31] One should notice, however, that, unlike the first part of the story, Ṣāʿid's story of censorship does not have a Jewish part, nor is it attested in any Jewish text. Indeed, there is no indication that the censorship of al-Manṣūr targeted the intellectual activity of Jews.[32] In fact, the eleventh century saw a steady growth in the quantity and quality of Jewish philosophical writings. Jews could thus serve as the custodians of philosophy when its study was deemed heretical by Muslims. They (and their private libraries) played a crucial role in the preservation, transmission, and cultivation of philosophy and sciences in al-Andalus.[33] Among Muslims, philosophical activity was kept alive on a minor scale during the following century, in the courts of the so-called party kings (*mulūk al-ṭāʾifa*).[34] As argued by Martínez Lorca, the continuation of this activity, recorded by Ṣāʿid, prepared the ground for the seemingly sudden appearance of philosophy in the twelfth century. At the same time, as Ṣāʿid's report also shows, Jewish scholars seem often to have served as an important link in the line of transmission of philosophy and science to their Muslim neighbors.

One example of this continuous line of transmission may suffice. The first in the line of great Muslim philosophers of the twelfth century, the Saragossan Ibn Bājja (d. 1139), corresponded with Abū Jaʿfar Yūsuf ibn Ḥasdāy, an Andalusian physician who emigrated to Egypt. Ibn Bājja reported to him about the order in which he had learnt the various sciences, and this order closely resembles the one followed, according to Ṣāʿid, by another outstanding scholar of Saragossa, Abū al-Faḍl Ḥasdāy Yūsuf ibn Ḥasdāy.[35] Whether or not Ibn Bājja's correspondent is identical to Ṣāʿid's Saragossan scholar, or just related to him, it is clear that the two belonged to the Jewish community and that both of them were accomplished in the sciences and philosophy.[36] Like Ibn Bājja, Abū Jaʿfar Yūsuf ibn Ḥasdāy and Abū al-Faḍl Ḥasdāy belonged to a minority group, "the minority (quite a large minority in Saragossa) of the followers of the sciences of the ancients."[37] In terms of their intellectual position, the fact that these two Jewish scholars also belonged to a religious minority seems to have been almost insignificant.

Influences, Currents, and Whirlpools

The history of philosophical thought in al-Andalus can be discussed on two parallel levels: one concerning the way in which this thought was formed and fashioned, the other concerning the way it is studied by modern scholars. The examples cited above attempt to show that, on both levels, examining the history of the various religious communities together provides a comprehensible and more accurate picture.

An examination that focuses on the output of only one religious community is similar to examining an object with a single eye and is likely to produce a flat, two-dimensional picture. Reading Jewish, Christian, and Muslim intellectual history together is a sine qua non for a well-rounded picture of this history. One should emphasize that, for a correct application of the multifocal approach, a parallel but separate study of the different communities will not suffice. If one were to close successively one eye then the other, one would still obtain only a flat, two-dimensional picture.

In this complex intellectual world, the ideas flow into each other, brazenly oblivious to communal barriers. In the domains of theology and of polemics, the dynamic character of the interaction has been depicted by the metaphor of a marketplace, where the same coins change hands. This metaphor, however, is misleading, since in the fiscal transaction the coins remain intact and unchanging (except for the usual wear from continuous use). In the medieval intellectual marketplace, on the other hand, ideas and motifs moved from one religious or theological system to another, slightly modifying the system into which they were adopted and, in the process, undergoing some transformation themselves. The flow of ideas was never unilateral or linear but went in all directions, creating a "whirlpool effect." Like a drop of colored liquid which, when falling into the turbulent water of the whirlpool eventually colors the whole body of water, an idea introduced into this intellectually receptive world had an impact on all its components.

The whirlpool metaphor may also convey some of the difficulties involved in our approach. It is much easier to trace the course of neatly divided currents and trends than to reconstruct the ways in which they contributed to the whirlpool. This understanding, however, does not free us from the need to try to detect direct contacts, proximate channels, and possible influences.

PART II

Adopting and Accommodating the Foreign

CHAPTER 4

Translations in Contact

Early Judeo-Arabic and Syriac Biblical Translations

SAGIT BUTBUL

The histories of biblical translations into Greek, Latin, Syriac and Judeo-Arabic reveal remarkable similarities, particularly in matters of strict literalism. Although literalism can vary, it seems that, by and large, the principle underlying these literal biblical translations was very much opposed to that of Horace in his *Art of Poetry*: "And care not thou with over anxious thought / To render word for word."[1]

Syriac and Judeo-Arabic biblical translations seem to reveal a particular affinity to each other in many respects, including their tendency toward literalism. While the Syriac tradition of translating the Bible is well attested and documented, the emergence of early Judeo-Arabic biblical translations is yet in need of elucidation. The Syriac tradition may help us shed some light on this obscure episode in the history of biblical translation into Arabic. I will attempt to establish this hypothesis in the following pages.

Literal and Free in Ancient and Medieval Biblical Translations

In bird's eye sketches of the history of biblical translation, ancient and medieval biblical translations are usually considered to be very different from modern versions. It is customary to draw an imaginary line, a spectrum, one pole of which, with reference to the ancient and medieval translations, is labeled "literal," whereas the opposite pole, that of modern translations, is defined as "free." This seemingly neat pair of opposed categories, "literal" and "free," is far from being simple or clear-cut. In an attempt to elucidate the two, there is a need for yet another spectrum, the two poles of which this time are the point of departure, "the original text," and the destination, "the reader." According to this view, a literal translation would be described as "text-oriented," whereas a free translation would take the opposite position and be "reader-oriented." In other words, "text-oriented" translation is directed toward the original text; it is a translation that, in an attempt to be faithful to the language of the source text, will strive to represent every detail in it and is therefore described as *verbum e verbo*, "word for word." In contrast, the "free" translation, which is oriented toward the reader, does not linger too much on the details of the original text but rather wishes to give the reader the general meaning by way of a free paraphrase of the source text to the reader and thus is described as *sensus de sensu*, "sense for sense." The mediator between these two poles—the source text and the reader—is none other than the translator. It is thus clear that the character of a translation will always depend to a great extent on the attitude of the translator toward the source text.[2]

This division is, clearly, a rather simplified portrayal of biblical translation technique. Without a doubt, as any closer examination of the long tradition of biblical translation will prove, there are different ways for a translation to be literal or free, as James Barr has shown in his *Typology of Literalism*.[3] Yet, at the same time, it is convenient for the sake of argument to use this terminology, and for this reason these two terms will be used throughout the following discussion.

Another distinction should be made: I use the two traditional poles "literal" and "free" to describe the difference between the ancient and medieval translations on the one hand, and the modern translations on the other. "Free" translations, however, were not a complete novelty, restricted to modern times alone. The same division is to be found within the boundaries of ancient biblical translations themselves. While certain sections of the Septuagint, such as Ecclesiastes, are viewed as extremely literal, others, such as Job and Proverbs, are usually considered to be free.[4] Over the course of time, the practice of literalism was modified by later biblical translators. Following these modifications, biblical translations became more reader-oriented.[5]

Before turning to Bible translations in Judeo-Arabic, it is useful to first consider the history of Greek and Syriac biblical translations.

Greek and Syriac Bible Translations

The histories of both the Greek and the Syriac Bibles reveal a very similar course of development. The earliest translations do not show a consistent tendency to be either literal or free. According to Brock, this was because "the translators lacked experience and precedent."[6] Whatever the reason, the fact remains that in their early stages, Greek and Syriac Bible translations are of inconsistent character, and it is only during their advanced stages that the more meticulous literal tendency appears. The culmination of this tendency in the Greek Old Testament is Aquila[7] and in the Syriac New Testament, the Harklean.[8] Once it was adopted, literalism gained dominance, at least for some centuries. It was initially a corrective technique, for compared with the original text, the earliest inconsistent translations came to be regarded as inaccurate. Translators aimed at perfecting these early and inexact translations in such a way that every single element of the original text (be it in Hebrew or Greek) would be reflected in the translation. Literalism was merely the natural means to achieve this end.[9]

Sebastian Brock has pointed out that "the history of Syriac translation technique up to the early eighth century falls into three periods, each with its own ideal of translation." Translations belonging to the first period—the fourth and fifth centuries—are essentially reader-oriented; the second period—the sixth century—is a period of transition between that early tendency and the one to follow in the third period—the seventh century—which is strictly literal.[10]

How might this history of translation technique in Syriac shed light on Judeo-Arabic biblical translations? Or, to be more precise: since there are missing pieces in the picture of early Judeo-Arabic biblical translations, how might our knowledge of parallel phenomena in the Syriac Bible enrich our understanding of the Bible as rendered in Judeo-Arabic?

Early Judeo-Arabic Bible Translations

Until the 1980s, the monumental enterprise of Saadya Gaon (882–942), the *tafsīr*, had opened all discussions of Judeo-Arabic Bible translations. No reliable data existed concerning earlier translations into Arabic, and Saadya's *tafsīr* in the Judeo-Arabic environment took a position parallel to that of the Septuagint in the Judeo-Hellenistic period.[11] While the dominant position of Saadya's *tafsīr* still stands, we now have concrete, written evidence in support of earlier activity in the field of biblical translation within Arabic-speaking Jewish communities, including glossaries and word-lists.[12]

These early manuscripts, though fragmentary and scanty, present positive evidence for the existence of *written* Judeo-Arabic translations prior to that of Saadya.[13] They also display several distinctive characteristics. Two of these are revealed in their external traits: (a) most of these translations are written on parchment or vellum; and (b) the transcription that they use is phonetic (dependent largely on Hebrew orthographic habits) rather than the standard transliteration of Judeo-Arabic (modeled upon Arabic spelling). These two features alone suffice to indicate their antiquity, and it is likely that these pre-Saadian translations were composed during the eighth and ninth centuries.[14]

The scope of the present article does not permit comprehensive discussion of these early translations and other such distinct features, some of which further demonstrate their antiquity. I would note just one other such striking trait—one that lies at the core of the present discussion—namely, an extremely literalist tendency. Two such distinctive linguistic peculiarities serving to illustrate this literalist tendency are the automatic use of *iyyā* to translate the Hebrew accusative particle *eṯ* and the use of the artificial *aysa* to translate the Hebrew *yeš*.[15]

To sum up thus far, the oldest Judeo-Arabic biblical translations that we possess are from the eighth and ninth centuries, and they reveal a distinct literal tendency. However, the plot is further thickened since, as has been shown by Simon Hopkins,[16] these early Judeo-Arabic translations—the earliest we have—show signs of having been preceded by an even earlier *Vorlage*. Furthermore, certain of these old translations reveal clear traces of having previously circulated in Arabic script, viz., errors and blunders that can be understood only if we ascribe them to faulty deciphering of a manuscript written in unpointed Arabic letters. A well-known such blunder was due to the confusion caused by the writing of the proper name Yeḥezqʾel ("Ezekiel") in Arabic letters; unpointed, it was misunderstood and considered to comprise two words: *yajuz qāla* > *yajūz qāla* (in later copies this was shortened into *yajūz*).[17] The most instructive example, however, is the rendering of Proverbs 6:15, *ʿal ken pitʾom yavo edo*, "therefore shall his calamity come suddenly,"[18] as found in MS Adler 2779.27: *ʿalā ḏāka ʿaqluhu yajī taʿsuhu*. Since the translation is so literal, it is easy to see how every word of this rendering stands as an equivalent of its corresponding Hebrew word, except the word *pitʾom* ("suddenly"), which is rendered by *ʿaqluhu* ("his intelligence"). This puzzle can only be understood if we think of the Arabic writing of the word *ʿaqluhu*, without the diacritical points, which can also be read as *ġaflatan*, the expected rendering, that is, "suddenly."[19]

Early Judeo-Arabic translations in Arabic script are as yet unattested, and thus there is a missing link in the history of Judeo-Arabic biblical translations. But this is not the only missing link. If it is assumed that the written translations were preceded by oral translations, it follows that there are at least two stages of development currently unattested: oral translations and written translations in Arabic script. Only the latter are subject to discovery, but until such concrete texts are discovered, educated hypotheses are the only way to remedy the lack. I would like to suggest the following scenarios and to connect them to the history of the Syriac Bible.

Judeo-Arabic and Syriac Bible Translations in Contact

Possible Scenarios

Two possibilities come to mind: one, the missing link in the history of Judeo-Arabic translations contains translations that are inconsistent in character, being neither literal nor free in any rigorous way. These were followed at the next step by the translations we do have: the literal translations. According to this scenario, Bible translations in Judeo-Arabic went through a course of development very similar to that of Greek and Syriac translations.

While this possibility cannot be excluded, there is another, more satisfying, scenario, which suggests that the missing link consists of Judeo-Arabic translations that were literal from the very beginning. Timing makes this scenario more likely, for the time frame during which Judeo-Arabic translations are likely to have been put into writing, some time after the Arab conquests, is the same period in which Syriac translations took a turn toward very strict literalism.

Now, this could have been nothing more than a mere coincidence, a natural process of a similar fashion of translation developing in two separate channels, one alongside the other. However, to accept that would be to suggest that translators worked in a vacuum, having no interaction with their surroundings, and we know this is unlikely to have been the case. Studies by Rina Drory and Sarah Stroumsa[20] have emphasized the necessity of examining the connection between Jewish and Christian biblical literature. Although it is an intricate matter to establish a direct relationship between Jewish and Christian development of translation technique, Jewish and Syriac sources nonetheless present similar motifs and ideas, which point to some degree of interdependence. Thus, it would be reasonable to assume that at the outset, Judeo-Arabic Bible translations were exposed to some influence by the contemporary Syriac translations. If so, it would not be too wild a speculation to suggest that it was the literary model of the Syriac Bible that served the early Judeo-Arabic translators.[21]

Evidence

Jews and Syrian Christians were neighbors in Palestine and Mesopotamia. They also shared the Aramaic language before the Arab conquests and thereafter. In a recent article, Joshua Blau and Simon Hopkins deal with the Aramaic vocabulary found in early Judeo-Arabic Bible translations written in phonetic spelling.[22] They point out that the Aramaic words that appear in these texts were borrowed not only from the eastern layer of Targumic Aramaic or Eastern Judeo-Aramaic (Babylonian Talmud and gaonic literature), but also from spoken Aramaic of the early Islamic period. Some of these Aramaic words are not attested in Jewish Aramaic literary sources at all. They do, however, appear in non-Jewish eastern dialects, namely Syriac and Mandaic.[23]

To the many examples given by Blau and Hopkins,[24] I would like to add the following. An early Judeo-Arabic glossary to Genesis, found in MS T-S Ar.31.245,[25] offers no fewer than four renderings of the word *kenim*, which appears repeatedly in the story of Joseph and his brothers (Gen. 42:11, 19, 31, 33, 34): (i) *tujjār* ("merchants"); (ii) *murattabīn* ("established, ordered"); (iii) *dahāqīn* (pl. of *dihqān*, of Persian origin: "headman, chief of a village or town" or "a merchant");[26] and (iv) *bunkiyīn*. The first three appear side by side as renderings of the first occurrence of the word in Genesis 42:11. The fourth translation appears a few lines below, seemingly as a separate rendering of the later occurrences of the word but most probably simply because the writer recollected or was reminded of another plausible rendering of *kenim*.[27]

The word *kenim* is usually understood as "honest men"[28] or "true men,"[29] and yet none of the four renderings offered corresponds to this accepted meaning of the word. Moreover, none of them is self-evident. While only the fourth rendering has a close connection to the present argument, the first three are essential to understanding the fourth. All three derive the word *kenim* from the biradical root *kn*. The word *ken* appears in the Bible (Gen. 40:13, 41:13) with the meaning of "position" or "rank."[30] This explains the first three renderings: all point to men of position or rank, whether merchants or headmen. *Murattabīn* is not attested thus in Arabic, but it seems reasonable that it was derived from *martaba*, "position" (cf. "the upper part of a place or mountain").[31]

As for the fourth rendering, the very few Arabic dictionaries that mention the word *bunk* point to its foreign origin.[32] In these dictionaries it is accepted as a Persian word with the meaning of *aṣl* ("source, origin").[33] The word *bunk*, however, is also found in Syriac dictionaries, both as *bunkā* and *bukhnā*, with the meaning expected here in light of the three former renderings, viz. "native, noble inhabitants."[34] Therefore, all four renderings point to the same idea: well-born noblemen of high and established position, who could not possibly be *meraglim* ("spies")—the apparent antonym of *kenim* in the verse.

Nevertheless, the mere appearance of this word in Syriac is not enough. Another point should be made that is crucial to the present argument: the word *bunkā/bukhnā* with the meaning of "native, noble inhabitants" is found in Syriac and is not attested in Jewish Aramaic literature.[35]

A translation like this, attested in Christian varieties of Aramaic but not in Jewish ones, helps establish the contacts Jews and Syrian Christians had in Palestine and Mesopotamia. Other distinct renderings found in early Judeo-Arabic translations provide further proof that at least some kind of contact—whether literary or spoken—existed between Judeo-Arabic translations and the Syriac tradition.

Early Judeo-Arabic Bible Translators

Despite the fact that the period discussed here is one of the most obscure periods of Jewish history, I would like to venture a hypothesis and take the suggested scenario one step further. The reason given for the development of literal translation is that when the early Greek and Syriac "free" translations were compared with the original text, translators regarded them as inaccurate or defective and therefore aimed to bring the translation as close to the Hebrew source text as possible. If we accept the scenario that Judeo-Arabic translations emerged at the very beginning as literal translations, as well as accept the relevance of the Greek-Syriac model for the Judeo-Arabic translations, what was the inconsistent or inaccurate model of translation that prompted the early Judeo-Arabic translators to compose deliberately literal translations? It stands to reason that the Aramaic Targums and Midrash were that rejected model. The Targums and the Midrash are abundant with additions and expansions of the original text, replete with creative etymologies and so on. These are most certainly inaccurate translation, often of the freest kind.

If these were indeed the rejected model of translation, who could be the translators who dismissed this model as inaccurate and aimed at perfecting the translation by adopting literal methods? The one group in Judeo-Arabic biblical literature that we know to have rejected the rabbinic tradition, its free translation technique, and indeed any addition to scripture, is the Karaites.

There are a number of features that link Karaite and early Judeo-Arabic translations. Karaite biblical translations as a whole are extremely literal.[36] The Arabic in the translations of Yefet ben ʿElī, for example, unlike the Arabic of his commentaries, has been described many times in a similar way to Aquila's Greek, that is to say, as unnatural and somewhat barbarous.[37] Karaite, Christian, and early Judeo-Arabic translations are all characterized by their extreme literalism and use of alternative renderings. The affinity between Karaite and early Judeo-Arabic translations is also indicated by the discovery that the latter were transferred from Arabic to Hebrew script; use of Arabic script for the biblical text, whether for the transcription of the Hebrew original or for its translation into Arabic, is a phenomenon thus far known only among Karaites.[38] Furthermore, at times, the renderings found in early Judeo-Arabic Bible translations and glossaries are found in later Karaite biblical translations. To name one example, the word *kenim* discussed above is rendered by Yefet ben ʿElī in the same way as that of the early glossary: *bunkiyīn*.[39]

That said, this extension of the scenario remains a suggestion and a hypothesis. Despite the fact that the Karaites would make the perfect initiators of the Judeo-Arabic translations, one problem is that the question of the origins of the Karaites remains open. We do not have evidence for the existence or crystallization of the Karaite movement before the ninth century.[40] And thus, while it is not impossible that the early Judeo-Arabic translators were forerunners of the Karaites, and while such a group would fit very well as the missing link we have in the history of Judeo-Arabic biblical translations, we do not have any direct evidence for the existence of such a group.

While we are left with the question of the identity of the early Judeo-Arabic biblical translators, the role of the Syriac tradition in illuminating the emergence of the Judeo-Arabic Bible is becoming progressively more and more evident.

CHAPTER 5

Claims About the Mishna in the *Epistle* of Sherira Gaon

Islamic Theology and Jewish History

TALYA FISHMAN

In an Aramaic *Epistle* of 987, Sherira Gaon, head of the rabbinic academy at Pumbeditha, responded to questions posed by Jews of Kairouan about the genesis of the ancient corpora of rabbinic tradition.[1] Reconstructing the circumstances under which Mishna, Tosefta, Talmud, and Midrash were formed, Sherira described the pedagogic practices of earlier rabbis, traced intellectual lineages linking many generations of sages, and identified political and geographic developments that precipitated internal cultural changes. Sherira pointedly disabused his questioners of their assumption that the rabbinic corpora had begun as written works. Tradition, he emphasized, was transmitted orally through face-to-face encounters between masters and disciples, precisely the practice maintained in the geonic academies.[2]

Though not the first chronology of the rabbinic generations,[3] the *Epistle* almost single-handedly shaped rabbinic culture's subsequent understanding of its own literary foundations. Sherira's late tenth-century document informed the vision of the rabbinic past purveyed in Rashi's eleventh-century Talmud commentary[4] and the historical survey of rabbinic literature set forth by Maimonides in the introduction to his twelfth-century legal code, the *Mishneh Torah*.[5] Medieval Jewish writers eager to establish their bona fides prefaced their own works with updates of Sherira's narrative. Whether they started their intellectual genealogies with Adam, Moses, or a later tradent, each inscribed his own teachers into the chain of tradition before describing the circumstances that had motivated him to undertake his own composition.[6] In short, rabbis of many generations have found in Sherira's *Epistle* an expandable template for filiating with the authoritative past.

Yet some aspects of the *Epistle* had, at best, an inconsistent afterlife in subsequent rabbinic culture. Two of them, specific claims made by Sherira about the Mishna's formation, are examined in the present study. One, advanced through a series of pointed remarks, is the assertion that the Mishna is something other than a conventional composition. According to Sherira, Rabbi Judah the Patriarch, the Mishna's compiler, was the human agent of a divinely guided project. Among subsequent Jewish writings, this claim was perpetuated only by the twelfth-century thinker Judah Halevi[7] and by kabbalistic writers down through the sixteenth century.[8] Halakhic writers, on the other hand, ignored Sherira's claim and, instead, valorized Gemara (in which the Mishna was absorbed). Though there was little overt disparagement of Mishna,[9] its virtual absence from the rabbinic curriculum until the early seventeenth century is noteworthy.[10]

A second claim made by Sherira that left little or no cultural echo concerns a distinct shift that occurred in the process of the Mishna's transmission. Up until the end of the tannaitic period, writes Sherira, masters imparted received teachings using whatever language they needed in order to convey the pertinent meaning; over the course of these generations, tradition was transmitted "free-style." It was not until the early third century that Rabbi Judah the Patriarch established a linguistically fixed formulation of Mishna, *ipsissima verba*.

This chapter situates these two claims within a broader cross-cultural context in order to illuminate their pertinence, both conceptually and terminologically, to discussions that actively engaged Muslim theologians of Sherira's time and place. Given the rich evidence of geonic immersion in the pan-religious discourse of tenth-century Baghdad,[11] Sherira's awareness of contemporaneous ideational debates is not surprising, but the proximity of these two claims to contemporaneous threads of discourse raises questions about whether Sherira had received them as traditions from rabbinic predecessors or was articulating them, for the first time, in response to intellectual provocations in his own environment.

The Origins of Mishna and the Muslim Doctrine of *Iʿjāz al-Qurʾān*

According to the *Epistle*, the production of Mishna was abetted by a number of rare circumstances—and above all, by the contribution of divine assistance. For one thing, Rabbi Judah the Patriarch (known simply as "Rabbi"), the agent of the Mishna's standardization, was uniquely endowed: "Heaven bestowed upon Rabbi, at one and the same time, Torah and grandeur. For all those years, all those generations were subject to him. As they say, 'From the days of Moses until Rabbi, we never found Torah and grandeur in one place.'"[12] Beyond this, the time and place in which Rabbi Judah undertook this project was unusually fortuitous: "In those days, the sages rested from all destruction, because of [the Roman Emperor] Antoninus' affection for him [i.e., Rabbi Judah]."[13]

Moreover, in the days of Rabbi Judah, unanimity once again came to reign in the rabbinic academies, following generations of discord that had been set in motion when the students of Hillel and Shammai failed to fulfill their discipleship obligations. The restoration of intellectual clarity, with divine assistance, enabled R. Judah the Patriarch to recover insights that had been taught by the earliest tannaitic scholars who flourished before the era of divided opinions.[14] In his day, the entire rabbinic cohort regained the sense of legal certainty that had been the hallmark of sages who lived prior to the Destruction in 70 CE: "And [because] heaven helped them, the meanings of Torah were as clear to them as *halakha le-Moshe mi-Sinai*. And there was no division[15] nor dispute."[16] Indeed, writes Sherira, the teachings of the Mishna approximated divine thought: "And in the days of Rabbi, matters were aided such that the words of our Mishna were as if they had been said from the mouth of the Almighty. And they seemed like *a sign and a wonder*.[17] And Rabbi did not compose these from his heart."[18] According to the *Epistle*, supernatural aid also affected the Mishna's semantically muscular literary form. The compactness of the Mishna's formulations could never have been attained without such intervention: "Had Rabbi wished to say everything that was taught, the matters would have been lengthy and [thus, ultimately forgotten and] uprooted.[19] But Rabbi only arranged the principles of matters, so that even from a single matter one might learn several principles and terse formulations and great and wondrous meanings and numerous details. For our Mishna was said with the aid of heaven."[20] Concluding his words of praise, Sherira again alludes to the element of divine assistance evident in the Mishna's elegant style and linguistic perfection: "Not every wise person knows how to compose in this manner, as it is written '*A man may arrange his thoughts, but what one says depends on God*' (Prov. 16:11)."[21]

The *Epistle*'s repeated allusions to the Mishna's superhuman origins bring to mind Islamic discussions of *iʿjāz al-Qurʾān*, a theological doctrine whose definition was intensely debated and refined by Sherira's intellectual contemporaries.[22] The notion that the Qurʾan was a matchless literary creation had already been adumbrated in that work's "challenge" verses, daring skeptics to compose anything of comparable literary excellence;[23] that none ever did was seen as confirmation of the Qur'an's inimitability. According to the *ṣarfa*, or "turning away" strain of the inimitability argument, God had intentionally intervened to prevent other Arabs from composing anything that would match the Qur'an in linguistic eloquence.[24] Yet another argument for its inimitability focuses on the Qur'an's inclusion of information that no living person could possibly know, such as knowledge of the remote past, the eschatological future, God and spirits. Since the presence of this information was deemed evidence of the Qur'an's miraculous nature, the work itself was identified by theologians as the miracle that served to authenticate Muhammad's prophecy.[25]

Claims that the Qur'an's inimitability was a function of its stylistic perfection date back to al-Jāḥiẓ in the ninth century, but this theme was most richly elaborated in the tenth century by an array of theologians and literary scholars that included al-Khaṭṭābī (d. 996 or 998), al-Ruwarmmānī (d. 994 or 996), ʿAbd al-Jabbār (d. 1025), and al-Bāqillānī (d. 1013).[26] In the words of a twentieth-century scholar of medieval Arabic poetics, "[i]t was the contribution of the tenth century to insist on the formal or rhetorical uniqueness of the Koran to such an extent that it became part and parcel of the theological argument for the Book's supernatural character."[27] When tenth-century Islamic thinkers composed lists enumerating the characteristics of *balagha*, that is, rhetorical eloquence or aesthetic effectiveness, they took the Qur'an as the reference point against which all other compositions were to be measured. In this way, perspectives that had first been articulated in a theological context came to shape literary ideals. Of all the stylistic features on which a work might be judged,[28] it was the ideal of conciseness that came to be identified with the term *iʿjāz* itself.[29]

Jewish intellectuals living in the environment were hardly oblivious to this doctrine, particularly because Muslim theologians often linked it with the polemical charge that the Jews had abrogated the original divinely revealed Torah.[30] Muslim writings exhibit awareness of Jewish reactions to the doctrine of *iʿjāz al-Qurʾān*,[31] and, before the *Epistle*'s composition, it was the subject of a debate between Sherira's in-law, R. Samuel ben Ḥofni, and the Muslim theologian, Abū ʿAbd Allāh al-Baṣrī, who died in 980.[32] Samuel ben Ḥofni also refuted this doctrine in writing,[33] as did David al-Mukammaṣ[34] and the Karaites Yaʿqūb al-Qirqisānī[35] and Yūsuf al-Baṣīr.[36]

Jewish intellectuals in the Islamic environment did not only parry the anti-Jewish elements of the *iʿjāz al-Qurʾān* doctrine. From Saʿadya Gaon's early tenth-century *Sefer ha-egron* through Moses Ibn Ezra's twelfth-century *Kitāb al-muḥāḍara wa-ʾl-mudhākara*, they appropriated and transformed some of its constituent features, arguing for the perfection of Scripture and of scriptural Hebrew.[37] This development was also noticed by Muslim theologians.[38]

When viewed against the backdrop of Muslim—and Jewish—ruminations on *iʿjāz al-Qurʾān*, the *Epistle*'s description of the stylistic qualities that made the Mishna and its underlying source, R. Meir's formulation of tradition, superlative creations assume greater resonance. Indeed, Sherira's claims about the Mishna may be seen as analogues of certain arguments articulated by Muslim theologians in promoting the doctrine of the Qur'an's inimitability. According to Sherira's narrative, Rabbi Judah the Patriarch could have chosen the formulation of any of the earlier sages as the basis for his standardized Mishna, but he selected Rabbi Meir's formulation of tannaitic teachings because the latter was concise and it lent itself to easy recall. This, writes Sherira, was because of its intelligent and elegant concatenation.[39] Since the preservation and oral transmission of tradition depends not only on the storage of data but also on retrieval of the appropriate material when needed, the creation of compelling mnemonic links is crucial. The chain of associations constructed by Rabbi Meir was memorable, writes Sherira, because it made sense; R. Meir had succeeded in connecting tradition's many subjects in ways that drew upon their natural affinities (*kol davar ve-davar ʿim mah she-domeh lo*). When Rabbi Judah created an elegant, properly arranged, and tersely worded composition, he used R. Meir's notebook as a scaffold.[40] As a *ḥibbur*, literally a work of links (i.e., *catenae*), the Mishna was bound together in patterns that were easy to memorize and retrieve.

> In the matter of *halakhot* [i.e., legal traditions], Rabbi Judah took the way of Rabbi Meir (which was the way of [R. Meir's teacher] Rabbi Akiva)—since he saw that it was succinct and easy to learn.[41] And its matters were linked in an elegant concatenation, each and every matter with that which was similar to it [and] far more precise than [the ways of] all the [other] *tannaim*. And there was no excess verbiage in them; each and every word achieves its meaning without saying unnecessary synonyms, and without anything lacking in their information, except in a few places. Great and wondrous things are in each and every word.[42]

Additional evidence of the Mishna's wondrousness is that it was accepted by all Jews. According to Sherira, Rabbi Judah's standardization of tannaitic teachings spread immediately[43] and was received with unanimous acclaim.

Though other formulations had been in circulation, these could not compete with a work of such elegance and power. The Mishna's most effective marketing agent was its own perfection: linguistic, organizational, and stylistic.

> And when everyone saw the beauty of the Mishna's arrangement and the truth of its meanings and the precision of the words, they abandoned all those [other] *mishnayyot* that they had been reciting. And these *halakhot* [legal traditions] spread throughout Israel and became our *halakhot*. And all the others were abandoned, and became, for example, *beraita*,[44] which one hears and analyzes as an interpretation or an auxiliary remark. But Israel relies on these *halakhot* [of the Mishna] and all Israel accepted them with faith, once they saw them. And none differ with this.[45]

The Notoriety of Mishna in Sherira's Environment

Why did Sherira apply the constituent arguments of *iʿjāz al-Qurʾān* to Mishna, a work of Oral Torah? In the absence of any definitive answer, I will identify several developments that might have provoked Sherira's claim.

The rejection of Oral Torah by Karaites, Jewish scripturalists living in Muslim lands, dated back to the eighth century, but by the early tenth century, the written Mishna had become the target for a singularly pointed barb. A passage in *Book of the Wars of the Lord* by the Karaite Salmon ben Yerūḥīm explicitly ridicules the inscription of putative Oral Torah: "You say the Rock has given Israel two Laws, one which is written, and one which was preserved in your mouths. If this is as you say, then indeed your deeds are but falsehood and rebellion against God. The Holy One has given you an oral law, so that you would recite it orally. For, you say, He had deemed it in His wisdom a laudable command. Why then did you write it down in ornate script?"[46] Earlier Karaites had attacked rabbinic tradition for deigning to arrogate authority to non-scriptural traditions and for issuing legislation that critics reviled, borrowing from Isaiah 29:13, as "a commandment of man learned by rote."[47] By the time of Salmon ben Yerūḥīm, this allegation was compounded by the charge of Rabbanite hypocrisy. How could a corpus of ostensibly Oral Torah now be consulted in writing?

Whether or not Karaites posed an active challenge in Kairouan and informed the concerns of the questioners,[48] Sherira's distinctive claims about the Mishna's superlative style and its creation with divine assistance might be construed as a strategic response to the above-mentioned Karaite challenge.

Just as Ashkenazim and Sephardim of later centuries would articulate regulations and make pronouncements that "sacralized" the inscribed corpora of Oral Torah by setting them apart from other human compositions,[49] Sherira's assertion that Mishna was more than a conventional human composition removed this work from the category of "laws learned from men" and moved it into the domain of prophetic, or inspired, writings.

* * *

Sherira's claims about the Mishna's exceptionalism might also be explored in relation to Muslim expressions of scripturalism. Some individuals and groups in the early Muslim community took issue with the ascription of legal authority to *ḥadīth*; they argued that these reports about the sayings and deeds of the Prophet Muhammad and his companions ought never be construed as comparable to the Qur'an, the Book of God.[50] The authority accorded *ḥadīth* was greatly advanced by demonstration that the Qur'an itself demanded obedience to the Prophet[51] and by al-Shāfiʿī's (d. 820) formulation of the doctrine of dual revelation,[52] but the scripturalist perspective continued to be viable and compelling for some Muslims over the course of several centuries. Not only did *ḥadīth* specialists feel the need to justify specific *aḥādīth* that were criticized for their offensive or irrational content,[53] they needed to defend the very status of *ḥadīth* as a source of authority. Opposition to the authority of *ḥadīth* can be reconstructed from a range of works by Islamic theologians,[54] heresiographers,[55] and jurists that were composed through the eleventh century.[56] Indeed, the polymath, al-Khaṭīb al-Baghdādī (d. 1071) referred to contemporaries who feared that *ḥadīth* would lure Muslims away from the Book of God.[57]

In a recent work, Aisha Musa suggests that the persistence of this fear in the post-Shāfiʿī era might have been linked to the growing authority of *ḥadīth* in Islamic society. She posits that widespread circulation in the mid-ninth century of *ḥadīth* collections composed by al-Bukhārī and Muslim led to a revival of the debates that had been addressed by al-Shāfiʿī and to their redirection.[58] The new prominence of *ḥadīth* intensified concern that traditions about the Prophet's sayings and behaviors would compete with, or be seen as more authoritative than, the Word of God.

Opposition to the authority of *ḥadīth* was particularly strong within the various subsects of the Khārijite movement,[59] especially among the Ibāḍīs of

North Africa. A late eighth-century Ibāḍī critique of the shameful anthropomorphisms that permeate *ḥadīth* cautioned believers to rely only on the Qur'an,[60] and a document identified by Michael Cook as an Ibāḍī letter of the eighth century censured the Muslims of Kufa for privileging the counsel of humans over that of God: "They abandoned the judgments of their Lord and took *ḥadīths* for their religion; and they claim that they have obtained knowledge other than from the Koran. . . . They believed in a book which was not from God, written by the hands of men; they then attributed it to the Messenger of God."[61] By the time that Sherira Gaon composed his *Epistle*, Ibāḍism had passed its peak in North Africa, but a revolt against the Fāṭimids in 980 once again gave the Ibāḍīs control of a swath of the Maghrib that included major sites of Jewish settlement, like Gabes and Kairouan.[62] If Sherira knew that the *Epistle*'s addressees, the Jews of Kairouan, lived within a region where some Muslims were inclined toward scripturalism, his incentive to bring Mishna into the realm of "extended Scripture" may have been even greater.

* * *

Even among non-scripturalist Muslims, there were many who acknowledged the authority of *ḥadīth* but actively opposed its commitment to writing.[63] Within certain regions, this attitude persisted well into the ninth century, a time when resistance to inscription had otherwise died down and *aḥadīth* were circulating in written collections.[64] Several expressions of this opposition refer, with derision, to the Mishna of the Jews. *Kitāb al-ṭabaqāt al-kubrā*, a biographical encyclopedia of great Muslims from the time of Creation through the 870s ascribed (nonetheless) to the Baghdadi polymath Ibn Sa'd (d. 845),[65] invokes the experiences of earlier Peoples of the Book as a cautionary tale. One passage cites a story about 'Umar's appointment as caliph that had been told by Sufyān al-Thawrī (d. 778) on the authority of Ibn Shihāb al-Zuhrī (d. 741–42):[66] "'Umar wanted to write the Traditions (*al-sunan*), so he spent a month praying for guidance; and afterward, he became determined to write them. But then he said: I recalled a people who wrote a book, then they dedicated themselves to it and neglected the book of God."[67] The identity of this people is spelled out quite explicitly in another of Ibn Sa'd's accounts, reported by 'Abd Allāh ibn al-'Alā' of Damascus (d. 786). The narrator, a student of al-Qāsim ibn Muḥammad (d. 728), grandson of the first caliph,

Abū Bakr, recounts that when he asked his teacher to dictate *ḥadīth*, al-Qāsim refused to do so. It was essential, from al-Qāsim's perspective, that the ontological distinction between Scripture, that is, Qur'an, and oral traditions, that is, *ḥadīth*, be preserved. Explaining this position to his student, al-Qāsim recalled something that had occurred in the time of the second caliph, ʿUmar: "The *aḥādīth* proliferated during the time of ʿUmar, so he called on the people to bring them to him. When they brought them to him, he ordered them to be burned. Afterward he said, '*Mathnaʾa ka mathnaʾat ahl al-Kitāb*.' From that day on, al-Qāsim forbade me to write the *ḥadīth*."[68]

Writing about this passage more than a century ago, Ignaz Goldziher noted that the Arabic phrase left untranslated above can be rendered in one of two ways: "Do you really want a mishna like the Mishna of the People of the Book?!" or "This is indeed a mishna like the Mishna of the People of the Book!"[69] Either way, it is hard to miss the import of the caliph's comment. The case of the Jews and their Mishna presented those who invoked this story with an important admonitory lesson about the dangers of accepting any source of authority other than Revelation itself.

Inasmuch as Ibn Saʿd's *Kitāb al-ṭabaqāt al-kubrā* circulated in several recensions during Sherira's lifetime[70] and was widely cited by subsequent Muslims,[71] the gaon could easily have been familiar with its contents. Though Sherira's sacralizing claims about the Mishna hardly refuted these disparaging remarks by Muslim critics, they might conceivably have given succor to vulnerable Rabbanite Jews by assuring them that their Mishna was something other than a mere human composition.

Why Mishna and Not Another Corpus of Oral Torah?

Why did Sherira wax effusive about the special qualities of Mishna, while saying nothing comparable about Midrash and Talmud, the other corpora of Oral Torah whose formations the *Epistle* discusses? The preceding remarks suggest one answer: Mishna was the only rabbinic work that Muslim critics attacked by name. Within the context of Karaite criticisms, Sherira's singling out of the Mishna might have been strategic as well, for unlike the corpora of Midrash and Talmud, Mishna does not contain *aggadot*, the non-legal narratives that were targets of Karaite derision. Like Muslim scripturalists who ridiculed particular *ḥadīth* for their irrationality and anthropomorphic content, Karaites disparaged rabbinic *aggadot* for their irrationality, their depiction of God in anthropomorphic terms, and their unflattering portraits of the Patriarchs.[72] Rather than reject these charges, geonim from the time of Saʿadya (882–942) onward, Sherira among them, declared that the *aggadot* were not authoritative.[73] Whether or not this was a factor in Sherira's calculations, the *Epistle*'s lionization of Mishna avoided some of the *aggadah*-related pitfalls that might have attended celebratory remarks about the corpora of Midrash or Talmud.

Finally, the *Epistle*'s special arguments about the Mishna might conceivably offer testimony to the fixed language of this corpus (and to Sherira's consciousness of its fixity) at a time when the language of Talmud was still fluid.[74] Sherira presents the Mishna as the premeditated composition of one individual and the Talmud as a corpus whose formulation was far less orchestrated.[75] In this sense, the discrepancy between Sherira's portraits of the two works offers a valuable snapshot of a particular historical moment in the formation of rabbinic literary culture, one whose accuracy has been corroborated in recent scholarship.[76]

From Freestyle Transmission of Tannaitic Tradition to Formulation of *Ipsissima Verba*

Sherira carefully describes Rabbi Judah the Patriarch's transformation of Mishna from a body of tradition transmitted by teachers who related its content using any words that accomplished this goal to a work that was tightly scripted, in which only verbatim recitation would do. Setting the historical stage for Rabbi Judah the Patriarch's undertaking, Sherira explains that students of the earlier tannaitic sages were exposed to divergent oral formulations of the mishnaic traditions. Where meaning was concerned, however, these variants all "amounted to the same thing." Lexical latitude posed no problems in those times, for the essence and purpose of oral teaching was to relay content rather than precise words: "Our sages did not recite it in one voice and one formulation, but rather, the meanings [*teʿamim*] that were known to them—and this knowledge was widespread among them. . . . There was no known Mishna with an established formulation, such that all recited it in one voice, but only those meanings [*teʿamim*]. Even though each of the sages [relayed these] in equivalent manners, each would recite to his students in whichever manner and in whichever concatenation he wished."[77] In making this claim, Sherira may have drawn on information he had derived from earlier geonim. Saʿadya Gaon posited a similar shift—from freestyle oral transmission to fixed oral transmission—in a passage that compares the Mishna's early history with that of the esoteric *Sefer Yetsira*, a work ascribed to the patriarch Abraham.

> They [i.e., the Early Ones] do not say that he [Abraham] fixed the words of this book [*Sefer Yetsira*] in this particular order. Rather, they say that he derived these matters from his intellect. . . . He taught them to himself and he taught them to the Unifiers [of God] who were with him. These [matters] did not cease being transmitted, unwritten, within our nation—like the Mishna, which was transmitted in unwritten form. . . . And in that time when the sages of the nation gathered and pulled together [*rikkezu*] the matters of Mishna and dressed them in their respective words and fixed them, they did the same, or something like it, to the matters of this book.[78]

Sherira's remarks on the shift in Mishna's transmission offer details that are missing from Saʿadya's earlier account or are only vaguely adumbrated. The *Epistle* precisely dates the imposition of transmission *ipsissima verba* to the time of Rabbi Judah the Patriarch and to his specific agency, and it forcefully asserts that the "fixing" of Mishna in specific words had nothing to do with inscription.[79] According to Sherira's account, Rabbi Judah's scripted mishnaic formulation displaced the freestyle transmission that had prevailed earlier, but even this was relayed through oral recitation.[80]

The two modes of oral transmission, freestyle and scripted, distinguished by Saʿadya and Sherira correspond to the Arabic terms *riwāya bi-ʾl-maʿnā*, that is, transmission focusing on the sense of the text, and *riwāya bi-ʾl-lafẓ*, that is, transmission in which lexical accuracy is paramount. These categories were of concern to Muslim grammarians and philosophers,[81] and they featured prominently in a debate between Muʿtazilite and Ashʿarite theologians in ninth- and tenth-century Baghdad that diverted the *iʿjāz* conversation away from its earlier focus on the unique circumstances of the Qurʾan's revelation.[82]

Both groups of thinkers accepted the doctrine of *iʿjāz al-Qurʾān*, but they differed in identifying what it was about Qurʾan that made it inimitable.[83] From the Ashʿarite perspective, the Qurʾan was without peer because it was God's speech. This meant, in effect, that while the Qurʾan, as an aspect of the divine essence, was neither God nor something other than God, it *was* eternal and uncreated.[84] Muʿtazilites found this definition—an analogue of the Christian doctrine of the Logos—offensive, heretical, and theologically untenable; in their radical defense of God's unity, they could not countenance the suggestion that anything other than God Himself was eternal. Attacking the Ashʿarite notion of "inner speech," *kalām nafsī,* the Muʿtazilite theologian ʿAbd al-Jabbār (937–1024/25) insisted that ideas and verbal expression, or meaning and speech, were two totally distinct matters. As a literary production, the Qurʾan must, necessarily, have been created in time, he asserted, for its commandments and prohibitions are temporally contingent and its messages are relayed through words and letters that are rooted in particular historical coordinates.

The reorientation of *iʿjāz al-Qurʾān* discussions in the tenth century toward a focus on the Qurʾan's literary qualities may be seen as a function of the Muʿtazilite impulse to parry the Ashʿarite understanding of Qurʾan as God's speech. Rejecting the assertion that the Qurʾan's matchlessness was a function of its divine origin, ʿAbd al-Jabbār and other Muʿtazilites went on to locate the text's inimitability in the clarity of its words, the beauty of its meaning, and the arrangement of its speech.[85] Under these circumstances, it is not surprising that a range of Muslim compositions produced in Sherira Gaon's milieu emphasized the difference between transmission for meaning and verbatim transmission. ʿAbd al-Jabbār's twenty-book compendium, *Al-mughnī fī abwāb al-tawḥīd waʾl-ʿadl* (Book 16 of which was devoted to *iʿjāz al-Qurʾān*), *Al-nukat fī iʿjāz al-Qurʾān* by al-Rummānī, *Bayān iʿjāz al-Qurʾān* by Ḥamd b. Muḥammad al-Khaṭṭābī (d. 996 or 998), and *Iʿjāz al-Qurʾān* by al-Bāqillānī all weighed in on the theological question of whether the Qurʾan's inimitability resided in its ideas (*maʿnā*) or in its specific formulation (*lafẓ*).

When considered in light of this debate, the *Epistle*'s description of a shift in the transmission of mishnaic traditions—from freestyle to fixed formulation—might be seen as relevant to a contemporary theological conversation. If Sherira was influenced by Muʿtazilite thought, as were many Rabbanites and Karaites of his era,[86] his claim about the shift to *ipsissima verba* in the time of Rabbi Judah the Patriarch may have signaled his alignment with the Muʿtazilite notion of a created text's inimitability and his rejection of the Ashʿarite view.[87]

Sherira's efforts to evaluate the Mishna's perfection using standards of literary excellence to which all might assent also bears some affinity to the perspectives of Muʿtazilite theologians. According to the *Epistle,* the circumstances of the Mishna's composition were decidedly unusual and abetted by divine assistance, but the strongest evidence of the Mishna's peerless status is its stylistic perfection and the fact that it attained acceptance by all of Israel.

* * *

Awareness that certain claims in the *Epistle* engage issues that were of importance to Muslim theologians of the tenth century must inevitably raise questions about the extent to which Sherira's account reflects longstanding Jewish traditions about the formation of rabbinic corpora and the extent to which its emphases were responses to contemporary stimuli.[88] (These claims had little reverberation in subsequent rabbinic writings, though this observation, in and of itself, need not tip the balance in favor of the latter possibility.) What cannot be doubted is that the *Epistle*'s snapshots of attitudes, concerns, and practices that prevailed at the time of its composition make it a valuable witness to its own moment in Jewish cultural history.

CHAPTER 6

Maimonides and the Arabic Aristotelian Tradition of Epistemology

CHARLES H. MANEKIN

Recent years have witnessed increased scholarly interest in Maimonides' epistemology, especially his understanding of the nature, scope, and justification of human knowledge.[1] These studies have often viewed Maimonides within the context of Aristotle's epistemology and the Arabic philosophical tradition but less often within the Arabic Aristotelian epistemological tradition that we have strong reason to believe was known to him.[2] I say "strong reason to believe was known to him" because of the scholarly propensity in recent Maimonidean studies to look far and wide for possible influences, as the writings of his era become better known.[3] That Maimonides crossed religious and ethnic borders in his quest for knowledge is well-known; as he famously put it, one should accept the truth from whomever says it.[4] In trying to chart this crossing, it is important to continue to pay attention to the immediate intellectual context that emerges from the sources he mentions, sources that generally belong to the Aristotelian commentarial tradition in Arabic.

I wish to focus here on two issues: first, Maimonides' goal of attaining certainty through demonstration (and of attaining near-certainty through proofs approximating demonstration); and second, his advocacy of Alexander of Aphrodisias's method of theory acceptance, that is, that an undemonstrated theory should be accepted when it arouses less serious doubts than rival theories. Shlomo Pines pointed out over a half century ago that Alexander of Aphrodisias's *On the Principles of the All*, to which Maimonides makes two explicit references, is extant in two Arabic versions,[5] yet I am not aware that scholars have examined the work further for its relevance to Maimonides' epistemology. As for Maimonides' view on demonstrative certainty, although he does not mention a source explicitly, it is well-known that he praises Alfarabi as a logician and uses some of his commentaries on books of the Organon.[6] His characterization of certainty in *Guide* 1.50 has already been related by Michael Schwarz to Alfarabi's definition of certainty in the short treatise on the *Posterior Analytics*.[7] The reinterpretation by Arab Aristotelians of Aristotle's "science" (*epistēmē*) as objective, demonstrative "certainty" (*yaqīn*), or simply "certain knowledge" (*ʿilm yaqīnī*) is a key to understanding Maimonides' project in the *Guide*, which is to provide the reader with such certainty, dispel doubts, and reduce perplexity as much as possible. This is not to say that the Arabic Aristotelian epistemological tradition devalues *epistēmē*; as we shall see, for Alfarabi and Maimonides it remains the highest species of certain knowledge. But it is not the *only* species, and that consideration has important ramifications for understanding Maimonides' epistemology, especially his view that humans can have certain knowledge of metaphysical and theological truths.

Certain Knowledge (*ʿIlm yaqīnī*)

Maimonides does not provide a formal definition of certain knowledge, but one can infer the conditions of certainty from his brief characterization in his discussion of divine attributes in *Guide* 1.50: "Belief is the affirmation that what has been represented is outside the mind just as it has been represented in the mind. If, together with this belief, it is realized (*ḥaṣala*) that a belief different from it is in no way possible, and that no starting point can be found in the mind for a rejection of this belief, there is certainty (*yaqīn*)."[8] These conditions can be formulated as follows: *S* is certain of *p* (or "*S* believes *p* certainly") if and only if

(1) *S* represents *p*.
(2) *S* assents (*ṣadaqa*)[9] that *p* conforms to extra-mental existence.
(3) *S* realizes that not-*p* is in no way possible.
(4) *S* realizes that any *q* leading to rejecting *p* is impossible.
(5) *S* realizes that any *q* leading to supposing not-*p* is impossible.

The certainty described here is objective rather than subjective, a point that is brought out more clearly by Alfarabi, as we shall see. Moreover, conditions

(3), (4), and (5) require that the subject realize not only the impossibility of not-*p*, but the impossibility of anything implying the rejection of *p* or the supposition of not-*p*. These are strong conditions that require the subject to see the connection between that which is believed with certainty and that which implies its negation.

Maimonides continues, "When you shall have cast off desires and habits, shall have been endowed with understanding, and shall reflect on what I shall say in the following chapters, which shall treat of the negation of attributes, you shall necessarily have certainty in this matter."[10] Given that "the following chapters" contain philosophical speculation, one can infer that certainty in at least *some* theological matters can be achieved through philosophical speculation. At this point in Maimonides' exposition, however, it would be rash to conclude that *only* philosophical speculation can provide certainty.[11]

Certainty is associated by Maimonides in some passages with knowledge achieved through demonstration (*burhān*). Thus, certainty of the existence of God, His Unity, and His incorporeality is achieved through the demonstrations of the philosophers.[12] A person labors to possess true knowledge of the premises of a science in order to achieve certainty with respect to that science.[13] Among those who have delved into speculation concerning the fundamentals of religion there is one "who has achieved demonstration, to the extent that it is possible, of everything that may be demonstrated, and who has ascertained in divine matters, to the extent that it is possible, everything that may be ascertained, and who has come close to certainty in those matters in which one can only come close to it."[14] The distinction between achieving demonstration and achieving near-certainty seems to rest on the distinction between demonstrations and near-demonstrations, that is, proofs approximating demonstrations, as in the proof for the world being produced as a result of Divine purpose.[15] Such proofs cannot dispel all doubts, hence unlike demonstrations they cannot provide certainty. But, as we shall see below, they dispel the gravest of the doubts and provide near-certainty.

There are passages in the *Guide* that indicate that certainty can be achieved by ways other than philosophical demonstration. Thus, those who actually see miracles achieve certainty regarding them, but those who merely receive miracle reports do not.[16] That the celestial orbs are living and possess intellect is a certain truth, not only according to the philosophers but also from the standpoint of the Torah.[17] The prophetic vision is known by the prophet with certainty, even though it is perceived in a dream or through the imaginative faculty, just as existing things that are apprehended through the senses and the intellect are known with certainty.[18] In the *Treatise on Logic* attributed to Maimonides, we learn that the three sources of certainty are intelligibles acquired by the mind, either primary or secondary (e.g., geometric theorems and astronomical calculations), sensibles apprehended by one possessing a healthy sense, and knowledge obtained from critical experience (*tajriba*).[19]

The conditions implicit in the characterization of certainty in *Guide* 1.50, especially (4) and (5), appear to exclude sense-certainty. When I see a book before me, I may then realize that the nonexistence of the book is impossible, but it is hard to attribute to sense-knowledge the further realization that anything implying the nonexistence of the book is impossible. I am certain that the book exists when I see it, but I cannot be certain that it will always exist or that nothing will render its existence impossible. That is not the case when we grasp a geometrical theorem. So taken jointly, the conditions of certainty that emerge from Maimonides' characterization of certainty, at least with regard to theoretical matters, relate mainly to certainty of primary and secondary intelligibles, the latter being obtained through scientific investigation.

Do any of the implied conditions of certainty in *Guide* 1.50 include or exclude prophetic certainty? The question is important for our consideration of the epistemic value of certainty because the knowledge that prophets consider to be certain is achieved through the imagination rather than the intellect, and it is possible to read Maimonides' characterization of prophetic certainty as subjective rather than objective.[20] While there is no clear-cut implication one way or the other in the passage, I suggest that both the context and the language exclude prophetic and other forms of non-rational certainty. The context is that of certain *knowledge* (*ʿilm*) rationally achieved, that is, the certain knowledge of the negation of attributes. Moreover, the fifth condition requires that the knower realize the impossibility of any premise that "leads to" the opposite of the thing known with certainty. If "leads to" means "implies" or "entails," then this involves inferential reasoning, and we are in the realm of rational knowledge.

It is not surprising that the quest for certainty and near-certainty is fundamental to Maimonides' project in the *Guide*. The book is, after all, a guide that promises to reduce perplexity by dispelling doubts.[21] Some doubts can be dispelled through solving the problems that led to them, either via speculation or revelation, others by showing that they arise inevitably because their solution lies beyond human comprehension. While Maimonides' quest for certainty is not without precedent in the Jewish philosophical tradition,[22] it is colored here by a certain metaphysical picture: The final end of man is to possess and to contemplate true convictions and accurate representations of eternal matters, thereby bonding with the Divine intellect, and through this bond to love and worship God. Hence it is crucial for the knower to achieve certainty and near-certainty so that the true convictions and accurate representations cannot be dislodged, thereby breaking the bond between the knower and God.[23] One might say that Maimonides transforms the quest for *epistēmē* (i.e., scientific knowledge), known to us from Aristotle, into the quest for *ʿilm yaqīnī* (i.e., certain knowledge), so as not to break the bond between the human and the divine.

Actually, this transformation precedes Maimonides; the Arabic Aristotelian logical tradition had already understood *epistēmē* in terms of *yaqīn*. According to Deborah Black, the Arabic term *yaqīn* "functions as a technical term in Arabic accounts of demonstration, to a large extent displacing the traditional identification of the end of demonstration as the production of 'knowledge' or 'science' (*ʿilm*, equivalent to the Greek *epistēmē*)."[24] Already in Abu Bishr Matta's Arabic translation of the *Posterior Analytics*, the terms "certain knowledge" and "certain syllogism" are used to render the Greek terms for "knowledge" and "scientific syllogism." But the replacement of *epistēmē* by *ʿilm yaqīnī* is found most prominently in Alfarabi's two extant writings on scientific demonstration, *Conditions of Certainty* (*Sharāʾiṭ al-yaqīn*) and *Short Treatise on the Posterior Analytics* (*Kitāb al-burhān*). In the former, Alfarabi defines *yaqīn* as follows: "Certainty, without qualification, is to believe (*yaʿtaqid*) of a thing that it is such, or not such; to assent (*yuwāfiq*) that it conforms, and is not opposed, to the existence of an external thing; to know (*yaʿlam*) that it conforms to it, and that it is impossible for it not to conform to it, or for it to oppose it; nor can it at any time not conform to it, or be opposed to it, and that all this is realized (*haṣala*) not accidentally, but essentially."[25] We can unpack this as follows. *S* believes *p* with certainty if and only if:

(1) *S* believes *p*.
(2) *S* affirms that *p* conforms (and is not opposed) to extra-mental existence.
(3) *S* knows that *p* so conforms (and is not opposed).
(4) It is not possible for *p* not to so conform, or for its contradictory to so conform.
(5) It is not possible for *p*'s contradictory at any time to so conform.
(6) This [epistemic/psychological state] is arrived at not accidentally but essentially.

Conditions (1) through (4) are requisite for all kinds of certainty, including sense-knowledge and knowledge obtained through critical experience (*tajriba*). The reason that condition (4) does not exclude the certainty of sense-knowledge is the same as we saw above for Maimonides' condition (3): the impossibility is related to the epistemic state of the knower and not the metaphysical state of the object known. Conditions (5) and (6) are needed for the certain knowledge of intelligibles, both of primary intelligibles through intuition and of secondary intelligibles through demonstration.

In his *Short Treatise on the Posterior Analytics*, Alfarabi characterizes certainty as "our believing that the state of affairs to which we have assented as true cannot contain any entity contrary to our belief—and, together with this, we believe concerning this believing that it cannot be otherwise, to the extent that any [further] belief that is held concerning this believing will be considered to be not possible otherwise, and that *ad infinitum*."[26] This characterization seems to capture the first four conditions above and can hold of sense-certainty, as well as of critical experience. Alfarabi goes on to divide certainty into the necessary, which pertains to primary and secondary intelligibles, which are certain at all times, and the non-necessary, which pertain to objects that are certain only at some time and whose contradictory can be conceived in one's mind. As Black points out, "necessary certainty" in the *Short Treatise on the Posterior Analytics* seems to be synonymous with "absolute certainty" in the *Conditions of Certainty*.[27] I may add that it seems to be equivalent with the sort of certainty referred to in *Guide* 1.50.

Alfarabi writes that Aristotle required that this state be arrived at essentially (the sixth condition) because it is possible for the first five conditions to obtain in the subject through chance, through factors that do not come about naturally (i.e., in knowledge obtained through induction), or through the unanimous testimony of others. Various passions may be responsible for an opinion appearing certain: personal preference for the opinion or its author, bias, loyalty, habit, the high importance in which the opinion is held, the abhorrence of its opposite, and so forth. Such passions induce the believer to hold that the opinion has been established through reason. Moreover, many people lack the ability to perceive their own errors. Hence it is necessary to examine putatively certain beliefs to see whether they have been attained accidentally or essentially:

> Aristotle explained this in his book *On Demonstration*. This is the sort of certainty that is employed in philosophy and in general the speculative sciences. It is possible that this certainty not be attained through deduction, i.e., if it is the certainty that is prior by nature

> and in time. This sort of certainty is relevant to propositions that are primary intelligibles and that are the principles of speculative sciences. But it is possible that it is obtained through deduction, and that is of two sorts: The first should stipulate, in addition to the aforementioned six conditions, the condition that the subject know the existent together with its cause. And the second should stipulate its opposite, namely that it be said without the subject knowing the cause of the existent. Each of these two kinds should be arranged between the fifth and sixth conditions.[28]

The distinction between knowing the existent without knowing its cause and knowing both it and its cause is Alfarabi's formulation of Aristotle's distinction between knowing the fact (*to hoti*) and knowing the reason why (*to dioti*) (*Posterior Analytics* 89b23–25). Aristotle distinguishes between two types of demonstrations, explanatory demonstrations (*to dioti*, known in the Latin tradition as *quare sit* or *propter quid* demonstrations) and factual demonstration (*to hoti*, known in the Latin tradition as *an sit* or *quia* demonstrations). For Aristotle, only explanatory demonstrations are said to yield scientific knowledge ("*epistēmē*"), and it is one of the conditions of the demonstrative syllogism that the premises be explanatory of the conclusions. But for Alfarabi, *both sorts of demonstration, factual and explanatory, yield demonstrative certainty.* This is a crucial move for our purposes, for we have seen that according to Black, the Arabic Aristotelian tradition largely replaces *epistēmē* (*ʿilm*) with certainty (*yaqīn*). And since for Alfarabi absolute certainty is obtained not only through explanatory demonstrations but also through factual demonstrations, this means that the Aristotelian ideal of *epistēmē*, when transformed by the Arabic Aristotelians into certainty, is attainable where (only) factual demonstrations are obtainable. And where there is certainty, there is no possibility of doubt. As Black puts it, "Farabi claims that if all the conditions for absolute certitude are met, one's belief in a proposition is in all respects unassailable: the only way that the belief itself can cease to exist is through 'death or insanity and the like, or through oblivion.'"[29] This is not to say that Alfarabi erases the distinction between explanatory demonstrations and factual demonstrations or places explanatory knowledge on the same footing as factual knowledge, or abandons the Aristotelian ideal of explanatory knowledge. But from the standpoint of absolute certainty arrived at through demonstration, demonstrations of the fact are not inferior to explanatory demonstrations, especially when the latter are beyond human capacities.

This last point is also significant because the proofs for the existence of God in the Arabic Aristotelian tradition are factual and not explanatory demonstrations, since the First Principle has no prior causes explaining it. Indeed, the lack of explanatory demonstrations led Themistius to claim that *no* demonstration for the existence of the First Principle was possible.[30] He appears to have limited demonstrations in this context to explanatory demonstrations. But against his view we have the view of Avicenna, who writes in his section on Demonstration in the *Shifā* that a factual demonstration (*burhān anna*) provides certainty as much as an explanatory demonstration (*burhān limā*) and that in order to attain certainty, one does not need to know the cause of something's existence.

> Our investigation in this book is not entirely devoted to explanatory proofs, to such an extent that if the demonstration is not explanatory, it will not be considered here, and it will be considered dialectical or sophistical, etc.... Rather, this book includes the explanation of the absolute demonstrative proof, which applies to what provides certainty solely through a factual proof, and what provides certainty through a factual proof together with an explanatory proof. It is sufficient to consider the error of the one who says that there is no certainty in something whose cause is unknown. For that implies that there will be no certainty with respect to the Creator, may His name be Exalted, because there is no cause of His existence! We must inform him that he has lost his way in the pursuit of science, for he lacks the thing for the sake of which wisdom is sought, namely, certainty with respect to the Creator, may His highness be Exalted.[31]

Avicenna does not, in this passage, go so far as to claim explicitly that the existence of God is proven through factual demonstration, only that factual demonstrations provide certainty and that one may have certain knowledge of the existence of God despite the fact that He has no causes. Yet his own proof for the existence of the Necessary Existent is a factual demonstration.[32] Later in the section on Metaphysics, he writes, "[Metaphysics] is also the wisdom that is the best knowledge of the best thing known. For it is the best knowledge, i.e., certainty (*ʿilm ay al-yaqīn*) of the best thing known, i.e., God, exalted be He, and the causes that are after Him." It should be noted that Avicenna glosses *ʿilm* with *yaqīn* and speaks of certain knowledge. There is no indication in this passage that certain knowledge arrived at through factual demonstrations is *significantly inferior* to certain knowledge arrived at through explanatory demonstrations, much less that it is not, strictly speaking, "knowledge." In fact, it would be odd to argue that for Avicenna, one can have certain demonstrative knowledge about God's existence but that, strictly speaking, such knowledge does not count as "knowledge" because it is not achieved through a knowledge of (nonexistent) causes. True, but who says that it has to?

At first glance these passages appear to conflict with Avicenna's twice-repeated claim in the *Shifā* that God's existence cannot be demonstrated "since there is no cause of Him."[33] But as Michael Marmura argues, Avicenna is referring here to explanatory rather than factual demonstrations.[34] Neither the present passage nor a similar statement in the *ʿUyūn al-masāʾil* provides any support for the claim that God's existence cannot be known with certainty through demonstration.[35]

In short, both Alfarabi and Avicenna agree that factual demonstrations are true demonstrations; that they provide certain knowledge; and that humans can know God's existence and unity with certainty. Like them, Maimonides provides factual and not explanatory demonstrations of God's existence in *Guide* 2.1, both those of the philosophers and his own, "for He, may He be exalted, has no causes anterior to Him that are the cause of His existence."[36] Through the "correct demonstration" of the philosophers, "perfect certainty is obtained with regard to those three things, I mean the existence of the deity, His oneness, and His not being a body." In this part of his project in the *Guide*, at least, the part where he lays claim to certain knowledge, Maimonides is a faithful disciple of Alfarabi and Avicenna.

Aside from its importance in the Arabic Aristotelian epistemological tradition, why is certainty emphasized by Maimonides? Part of the answer may be found in Alfarabi's explanation of his third condition for certainty, that is, that the knower know that his belief is true. Alfarabi states that for one who knows with certainty, "the state of the intellect with respect to the intelligibles . . . comes to be like the state of vision with respect to the visible at the time of perception."[37] In certainty, not only has the mind acquired an intelligible, it has a reflexive awareness of this acquisition and the necessity of the intelligible obtaining, which prevents it from doubting or disbelieving it. Certain knowledge of an intelligible provides, as it were, a psychological/epistemological lock on the intelligible, which as a result cannot be budged or dislodged, not only while the person is contemplating it (as in the case with the sense-certainty) but *ever.* This may explain the importance of certain knowledge, that is, knowledge acquired through demonstration, for Maimonides, who requires the acquisition and retention of the intelligibles for the well-being and immortality of the soul.

Opposed to the condition of certainty is the condition of doubt. To doubt one's beliefs is to break the psychological/epistemological bond between the knower and the intelligible. Maimonides' evaluation of doubt is quite negative. Thus, in his *Code of Law*, the *Laws Concerning Idolatry* 2:3, he warns against philosophical speculation by the inept, who are easily led astray by doubts and false beliefs. In *Guide* 1.32, he extends this warning to those who wish to know things beyond the limitations of human knowledge. For Maimonides, then, certainty provides the firm and rooted experience of the intelligibles, and that is why the quest for certainty is an important part of Maimonides' epistemological project. It is not the *only* part of his project, since he allows for varying degrees of belief and epistemic appraisal, ranging from the possible to the near-certain and certain. Still, we have seen that Alfarabi and Avicenna consider certain knowledge to be the highest sort of knowledge (*ʿilm*) and demonstration as the way to attain it. We have also seen that Maimonides presents certainty as his epistemic ideal, that certain knowledge can be reached through demonstration, and that God's existence, unity, and incorporeality are demonstrable. Given all this, it seems that this aspect of Maimonides' epistemological position strongly excludes skepticism as an ideal. To concede that Maimonides allows for certainty but to claim that this is not good enough since the further ideal of explanatory knowledge is still beyond our reach assumes, without justification, that nothing less than *explanatory* knowledge works for him. And while something like this thesis seems to appear in the commentarial tradition, we just saw that Avicenna rejects it, and there is no indication that Maimonides accepts it.

The claim has been made that since the philosophical demonstrations for the existence of God do not meet that ideal, they do not provide true knowledge, and while Maimonides may occasionally say that they are demonstrations, he doesn't consider them to be true demonstrations.[38] Let us examine some passages that have been put forth as evidence for the claim that Maimonides limits substantive knowledge[39] to explanatory knowledge, that is, knowledge of something through its causes, the original notion of Aristotelian *epistēmē*.

In *Guide* 1.73, Maimonides lists as one of the functions of the activities of the intellect its apprehension of intelligibles "in their true reality and with their causes (*bi-ḥaqīqatiha wa-bi-asbābiha*)." This has been taken to imply that the apprehension of something in its true reality *requires* apprehension through its causes, as if the conjunction *waw* should be as *yaʿnī* or *reṣoni lomar* ("meaning" or "i.e."). Yet it is implausible to think that intellection per se requires knowledge of causes. That would exclude from the activity of intellection the intuitive apprehension of primary intelligibles, which are self-evident, as well as God's intellectual apprehension of his own true reality, since God has no causes. Be that as it may, the context makes it clear that the distinction Maimonides draws is between the activity of the intellect and that of the imagination. The imagination apprehends the particular through its accidents and without apprehending its causes; the intellect apprehends the particular in its true reality and through its causes. There is no indication whatever that Maimonides is stipulating necessary conditions for what constitutes substantive knowledge.

In several places in the *Guide* Maimonides uses the terms *burhān qāṭiʿ* and *burhān*, which are often translated by Pines as "cogent demonstration" and "demonstration," respectively.[40] If *burhān qāṭiʿ* refers exclusively to explanatory demonstration, then where there is no possibility of a *burhān qāṭiʿ*, there is no substantive knowledge. The difficulty with this argument is that there is no evidence that *burhān qāṭiʿ* means an explanatory demonstration, and in some uses of the phrase by Maimonides it cannot mean that,[41] a point that bewildered some of Maimonides' commentators.[42] Nor do any of Maimonides' commentators suggest that the phrase always means "explanatory demonstration." It could simply mean the sort of proof that provides certainty and rules out doubt. Thus in *Guide* 2.11, Maimonides claims that astronomers lack a cogent demonstration of the number and form of the celestial orbs. He goes on to say that the astronomers have demonstrated that the path of the sun is inclined against the equator, "about this there is no doubt." Now this latter demonstration about the path of the sun is at best a factual demonstration, since the purpose of the astronomer "is not to tell us in which way the spheres truly are." So when Maimonides says that the astronomers lack a cogent demonstration of the number and forms of the celestial orbs, his point is that they lack *any* demonstration, even a factual one, of the form and the number of the spheres. This can be seen from his immediate contrast with what demonstrations the astronomers do possess, namely that the path of the sun is inclined against the equator, "about which there is no doubt." In all these cases demonstrations leave no room for doubt; where there are doubts, no demonstrations, factual or explanatory, are possible.

Finally, the distinction Maimonides draws in *Guide* 1.32 and 1.46 between "guidance leading to the existence of the thing" and "an investigation of the true reality" is not to be identified with the distinction between factual and explanatory demonstrations. Rather, it has do with the difference between the methods of educating the multitude and the philosophers. Just as factual demonstrations of the sort described by Alfarabi and Avicenna are not used in the education of the multitude, there is no indication that philosophers investigate the true essence of things only by explanatory proofs. As for the philosophers, in *Guide* 1.33, Maimonides writes that the perfect man "attains a rank at which he pronounces the above-mentioned correct opinions to be true, and in order to arrive at this conclusion, he uses the veritable methods, namely demonstration in cases where demonstration is possible or strong arguments where this is possible. In this way he represents to himself these matters, which had appeared to him as imaginings and parables, in their truth and understands their essence."[43] This passage implies that the perfect man can understand the essence of things *even through strong arguments* and not only through demonstrations, explanatory or factual.

But perhaps the strongest argument against Maimonides' adopting the strict requirement of *epistēmē* in his quest for substantive knowledge is simply one *ex silentio*: nowhere in the *Guide*, nor in the Arabic epistemological tradition to which he appeals, is that requirement found. While Maimonides mentions certainty and certain knowledge often, where does he mention explanatory knowledge? And if the distinction between factual and explanatory demonstrations is crucial for him, so crucial that factual demonstrations should not be considered strictly speaking demonstrations (despite the fact that he explicitly calls his proof for the existence of God a "cogent demonstration"), then why does he leave this fact for the modern reader to uncover?

In short, the *Guide* contains no textual evidence that restricts the sort of knowledge deemed desirable by Maimonides to *epistēmē*, that is, knowledge of a thing through its cause. Maimonides, moreover, explicitly claims that demonstration yields certainty and certain knowledge of metaphysical truths such as the existence of God. We have seen, furthermore, that the Arabic *Posterior Analytics* tradition replaces the Aristotelian concept of *epistēmē* with the concepts of *ʿilm* and *ʿilm yaqīnī*. For these reasons, it seems hard to justify the thesis that demonstratively certain knowledge of the intelligibles does not count as substantive knowledge for Maimonides and that factual demonstrations are not, strictly speaking, demonstrations.[44]

Near-Certainty and Alexander's Method of "Less Grave Doubts"

To show that God created the world after absolute nothingness, Maimonides first argues that the proofs for the eternity of the world are not demonstrations and thus do not prove the eternity thesis conclusively. He then argues, "by means of speculation," that the creation thesis "outweighs the other in the scales." To do this he argues "by means of arguments that come close to a demonstration" that the world exists by virtue of a particularizer and purposer, and that this further requires that the world be created after absolute nothingness. In the final stages of his argument, he opposes his thesis to that of the eternity thesis and argues that the latter is accompanied by graver doubts than the former.

Maimonides advances the following methodological principle, which he claims to find in the treatise *On the Principles of the All* by the late second- and early third-century commentator of Aristotle, Alexander of Aphrodisias.[45] When comparing two opinions, neither of which is demonstrable and both of which are accompanied by doubts, it is reasonable to adopt the opinion whose doubts are less grave.

Maimonides admits that the aforementioned argument for creation is not demonstrative, but he never informs the reader what he thinks it is. He apologizes for employing a "rhetorical mode of speech,"[46] but it is difficult to view the formal structure of the argument as rhetorical. Since, as scholars have noted, his argument for creation possesses certain similarities to the structure of dialectical arguments—the appeal to universally agreed-upon propositions, the engagement with the opponent's thesis, the attempt to prove that difficulties or contradictions follow from the opponent's thesis—one may be tempted to conclude that Maimonides considered both this and the Aristotelian arguments for the eternity of the world to be dialectical in nature. This has led some scholars to examine what Aristotle and the Arabic Aristotelians have to say about the positive value of dialectic in order to see what light can be shed on Maimonides' argument.[47]

The difficulty is that while the Arabic philosophical tradition does find some benefit in dialectic, it prohibits its use in serious scientific discussion.[48] The only time Maimonides mentions the term "dialectic" is he when accuses certain Kalam theologians of "shouting defamatory polemics and various complicated kinds of dialectic arguments and sophistries."[49] At best, Maimonides' attitude toward dialectic (if he indeed employs it in his proofs for creation) is ambivalent; he may draw on some of the resources of the method without openly admitting to it. So committed is he to the demonstrative method that he is willing to concede, at least hypothetically, that if the philosophers would succeed in demonstrating eternity, as Aristotle understands it, "the Law as a whole would become void, and a shift to other opinions would take place."[50] While he does not believe that such a demonstration can be found, he provides no conclusive argument against one, leaving the question, in principle, open. There is a difference between the negative claim that some theoretical issues cannot be determined by demonstration and the affirmative claim that those issues are best approached by dialectic. I see evidence for the former but not the latter.[51]

Instead of adopting Aristotelian dialectic, Maimonides appeals to a method that he finds in Alexander: "For Alexander has explained that in every case in which no demonstration is possible, the two contrary opinions with regard to the matter should be regarded as hypotheses, and it should be seen what doubts attach to each of them: the one to which fewer doubts attach should be believed. Alexander says that things are thus with respect to all the opinions regarding the divine that Aristotle sets forth and regarding which no demonstration is possible."[52] Shlomo Pines considered the source of these remarks to be two passages from Alexander's *On the Principles of the All*, a work that Maimonides cites by name in *Guide* 1.31 and 2.3. The first states that one determines the principles of the All not through demonstration, since demonstration proceeds from prior things and from the causes, and First Principles have no causes or anything prior to them. Rather one shows "that the principles that lead up (*tuṭaʾu*) to them are in necessary agreement with things that are evident, manifest, and well-known."[53] Among the things sought by this method are to know what is the First Cause, what is its action, what sort of motion belongs to the body moved by it, why do the motions of this spherical body become many and diverse, and are the things generated below the sphere of the moon by these motions generated by choice and by knowledge. It should be noted that Alexander does not list here the *existence* of God as undemonstrable.

The second passage is at the end of the treatise. After giving an Aristotelian account of Divine governance, he writes:

> This opinion, besides the fact that it is the only one, to the exclusion of others, suitable for the divine governance, is that to which we must look and assent to the exclusion of other opinions, because it corresponds to the things observed in the world and is appropriate to them. Whoever lays claim to being a philosopher must work according to this opinion and prefer it to others, whatever the conditions, since it is the most correct of the opinions put forward concerning God Most High and the divine [celestial] body. This alone among the opinions accounts for the continuity and order (*intiẓām*) of things which issue from the two of them and because of the two of them. . . . We should not, on account of a slight difficulty that

> might appear in it, give up the care and effort we have expended in examining all this doctrine . . . but we must hold firm in this opinion and uphold it, since it is, of all opinions held about God Most High, the best and fittest to be regarded as sound. . . . [We must] refute all opinions opposed to it and correct the errors previously encountered in them as far as we can; for we believe that it is difficult to find a theoretical opinion devoid of doubts.[54]

Then Alexander lists the three causes of divergence of opinions to which Maimonides refers in *Guide* 1.31: love of domination, the difficulty of the subject matter, and the "weakness of our nature and our incapacity to apprehend true realities." And he concludes,

> But we should not for all that reject what we have come to believe and think by way of reflection and philosophizing. Generally speaking, we must believe what we have investigated, scrutinized and clarified, and before examining the doubts that have been raised about it and solving them, [we must] examine the matter itself and try to discern its truth . . . and we should not, on account of some slight doubts, aim at expanding out discourse . . . rather we should obtain by means of the sciences which are not doubtful, confirmation of what we previously fancied to be doubtful in these sciences, and not reject it.[55]

The upshot of these passages is that when demonstration is not possible, the proper method is to accept the opinion that (a) accords with the phenomena; (b) follows from principles that agree with evident, manifest, and well-known things; (c) accounts for the continuity and order of things; (d) employs the sciences that are not doubtful to accept what previously was imagined to be doubtful; and (e) is the best and most appropriate concerning God.

As mentioned above, Maimonides attributes to Alexander the further methodological principle that when faced with two opinions, the one with the smallest number of doubts is to be accepted, or more precisely, the one whose doubts agree less with what exists is to be rejected.[56] This is not found explicitly in the text before us, but it perhaps may be inferred from Alexander's point that there is no theoretical opinion devoid of doubts, and yet Aristotle's opinion should not be rejected because of its "slight doubts."

This last methodological principle, that of weighing doubts of various theories and accepting the one with the least grave doubts, plays a well-known role in Maimonides' argument for accepting the opinion of creation over that of eternity. But it is also important to view this principle within the context of Maimonides' larger epistemological project in the *Guide* of relieving perplexity through eliminating or reducing doubt (*shakk*) and difficulty (*ishkāl*):[57] "I do not say that this Treatise will remove all difficulties for those who understand it. I do, however, say that it will remove most of the difficulties, and those of the greatest moment."[58] The constant study of the *Guide* will "elucidate most of the obscurities (*mashākil*) of the Law that appear as difficult to every intelligent man (*ʿāqil*)."[59] Most, but not all—one should not abandon an opinion because it is accompanied by some doubts or because it has not been demonstrated,[60] as for example in the case of the celestial and separate intellects, regarding which the proofs are "well-hidden though correct; many doubts arise with regard to them."[61]

Where proofs and arguments are possible but demonstration not, Maimonides adopts, implicitly or explicitly, Alexander's methodological principle, setting up the positions so that the graver doubts are on the side to be rejected. Thus, in rejecting the Kalam methods of arguing for the creation of the world, he writes, "For every argument deemed to be a demonstration . . . is accompanied by doubts and is not a cogent demonstration."[62] That the arguments are not cogent or conclusive demonstrations is not enough to rule them out—after all, Maimonides himself does not claim to have a cogent demonstration for creation, though his arguments are close to a demonstration. But that Kalam arguments are accompanied by doubts which turn out to be quite serious is enough to forego them. All their arguments are based on two premises, that of the impossibility of the infinite by succession and that of admissibility. The former premise was refuted by Alfarabi; the latter, in its Kalam form, implies the abolition of the stable nature of existence. Maimonides writes that the *mutakallimūn* abolished the stable nature of existence, and hence, no arguments could be adduced from it; also they did not "leave the intellect with a sound, inborn disposition by means of which correct conclusions could be drawn." This sounds like he is accusing the *mutakallimūn* of skepticism, which is not surprising since his project is one of guaranteeing knowledge against doubt, perplexity, and skepticism.

Yet this project does not shy away from employing an Alexandrian method of doubt against the claims of worthy opponents like the Aristotelians. Given the impossibility of refuting their position on eternity, the next best thing is to point out the doubts accompanying that position, first to show that their arguments do not serve as demonstrations and next to show that their position should be rejected using Alexander's criteria above. The clearest example of this methodological doubt is in Maimonides' argument against the Aristotelian "physical" demonstrations for the eternity of the world. That argument goes something like this: Assume that the world was created by God after it did not exist. Isn't it possible that when the world was being created, its nature differed from the nature it was to have after it was completely created, just as the nature of a fetus differs in certain important respects from that of an adult? But if that is so, then how are we to know for certain that the principles of nature we derive from our experience of the world after its creation apply to the world during its generative period? This is one of the few instances of a skeptical argument in the *Guide*: for Aristotle to argue from the present stable nature of what exists to the past assumes that the past is conformable to the present, but this is precisely the point under debate. The structure of this argument is reminiscent of Hume, who argues that we cannot know for certain that the future is conformable to the past.[63] While it is directed specifically against the Aristotelians, it could be used as a broader skeptical argument against Aristotelian science were Maimonides inclined to do so. That he is not so inclined shows that his goal is limited: first, to undermine confidence in the demonstrative character of Aristotelian physical demonstrations for eternity, and second, to suggest the weakness of physical arguments: "Whenever you err in this and draw an inference from the nature of a thing that has achieved actuality to its nature when it was only in potentia, grave doubts are aroused in you."[64]

The fact that Maimonides appeals to a general principle to justify his claim shows how restricted his skepticism is here. In fact, his skeptical consideration is designed to undermine the confidence in the Aristotelian demonstration for eternity, but it does not concern the science of the world as we know it today, and so it is not relevant to our question of the limitations of human knowledge of the heavens. After all, Maimonides believes that the sublunar realm has already achieved scientific closure and that both celestial and sublunar realms operate according to a stable nature after they have been generated.

The principle of "less grave doubts" is the only criterion of theory acceptance that Maimonides explicitly attributes to Alexander, but other criteria, such as that a good theory accords with observed phenomena, that its principles agree with evident, manifest, and well-known things, and that it accounts for the continuity and order of things, are implicit in some of his criticisms against the Aristotelians. As for the order criterion, Maimonides devotes *Guide* 2.24 to expounding "the grave doubts that would affect whoever thinks man has acquired knowledge as to the order (*intiẓām*) of the motions of the spheres, and as to their being natural things going on according to the law of necessity, things whose order (*al-niẓām*) and arrangement are clear."[65] Aristotle indeed "wished to bring order for our benefit into the being of the spheres," but "this task has not been accomplished by him, nor will it be accomplished." Rather, all that he has said concerning the cause of the motion of the spheres "does not follow an order for which necessity can be claimed."[66] As for Aristotle's celestial science lacking accord with the observed phenomenon, the inability to square that science with the observed motions of the spheres and stars is the message of *Guide* 2.24. This is not to say that Maimonides rejects Aristotelian celestial science entirely; on the contrary, what he rejects is the principle of necessity on which it is based, that is, that the world proceeds from God as the effect proceeds necessarily from the cause, and not from Divine purpose. It is the principle of necessity that conflicts with the observed phenomena, and that is an "Alexandrian" reason for rejecting the Aristotelian theory. Finally, Alexander's condition that the theory be the best and most appropriate concerning God is reflected in Maimonides' attempts to show the disgraceful consequences of the eternity theory for divine action and omnipotence. This condition is mentioned independently of the "less grave doubts" condition[67] but should not be understood as unphilosophical or somehow connected merely to the question of religious belief and morality, much less to the necessary beliefs of the multitude. On the contrary, it was the Aristotelians themselves who argued for the eternity of the world by appealing to the disgraceful implications for Divine action that would follow had the world originated at a certain time.[68]

In short, what Maimonides appears to do throughout his argument for creation is to turn the tables against the Aristotelians by appropriating the Alexandrian method of theory acceptance in the absence of demonstration for his own purposes. Of course he is aware, and indeed anticipates, that the Aristotelians will not concede that the eternity thesis carries with it disgraceful consequences for the deity or that they will consider the doubts he has raised concerning Aristotle's celestial science especially grave.[69] But his appropriation of Alexander's method and his adherence to Alfarabi's shift from *epistēmē* to *yaqīn* show that he wishes, as much as possible, to stay within the tradition of the Arabic Aristotelian epistemology familiar to him.

CHAPTER 7

Ibrāhīm Ibn al-Fakhkhār al-Yahūdī

An Arabic Poet and Diplomat in Castile and the Maghrib

JONATHAN P. DECTER

In his monumental anthology *Nafḥ al-ṭīb min ghusn al-andalus al-raṭīb* (The Fragrant Breeze from the Succulent Branch of al-Andalus), Shihāb al-Dīn al-Maqqarī (ca. 1577–1632) includes a section of several pages dedicated to six Arabic Jewish poets including one Ibrāhīm Ibn al-Fakhkhār al-Yahūdī (d. ca. 1239).[1] Among al-Fakhkhār's several poems is a couplet composed in honor of Alfonso VIII of Castile, under whom al-Fakhkhār served as a diplomat during key negotiations with the Almohads of the Maghrib. The verses, along with the introductory superscription by al-Maqqarī, read as follows:

> He said praising Alfonso, may God exalted curse them both:
> The court of Alfonso is a wife still in her succulent days,
> Take off your shoes in honor of its soil for it is holy.[2]

The verses are striking on several levels, three of which will be discussed in this article. First is the mere phenomenon of a Jew composing Arabic poetry in honor of a Christian king, a possibility owed to the particular cultural circumstances of thirteenth-century Toledo, where al-Fakhkhār was active. Second is the literary quality of the verses, which make intertextual reference to a passage from the Moses story in the Qur'ān and bear an affinity to the parallel passage in the Hebrew Bible. Third is the ambivalent place of the verses in al-Maqqarī's anthology, specifically the tension between cursing the poet on one hand while deeming his poem worthy of preservation on the other. For al-Maqqarī, al-Fakhkhār embodied the ideal qualities of the Andalusian intellectual even as he served a Christian king who contributed significantly to the decline of al-Andalus.

Although al-Fakhkhār has been mentioned sporadically in modern scholarship as a public figure, Arabic poet, and patron of Hebrew writing, he has not been the subject of an independent study; although some of his poetry has been translated (into Hebrew), it has not been discussed on a literary or cultural level.[3] The present article is divided into three sections, treating al-Fakhkhār's life and career, his literary output, and his place in Arabic anthologies.

Al-Fakhkhār's Life and Career

Abū Isḥāq Ibrāhīm Ibn al-Fakhkhār was active as a diplomat largely during the long reign of Alfonso VIII of Castile (r. 1158–1214). The early years of Alfonso's rule were characterized by weakness and disorder and the expansion of neighboring Christian and Muslim kingdoms into the territory of Castile. Alfonso remained king through the reigns of the most potent Almohad caliphs—Abū Yaʿqūb Yūsuf (1163–84), Abū Yūsuf Yaʿqūb al-Manṣūr (1184–99), and Muḥammad al-Nāṣir (known to Christian writers as Miramamolín, a distortion of *amīr al-muʾminīn*) (1199–1213). Alfonso was thus at the helm during a great period of Muslim expansion and Christian humiliation. In particular, the Battle of Alarcos (known as al-Arak in Arabic sources) in 1195 is recalled as a crushing defeat for Alfonso.

The great turnaround in the balance of Muslim-Christian power occurred toward the end of Alfonso's reign in 1212 at the Battle of Las Navas de Tolosa (known in Arabic as al-ʿIqāb). This battle saw the defeat of al-Nāṣir, last of the great Almohad caliphs, who died in 1213. Al-Nāṣir was succeeded by several other caliphs, the first of whom was Abū Yaʿqūb Yūsuf al-Mustanṣir (1213–24), who ascended at a young age and was compelled to sign truces with Castile and Aragon. Alfonso died in 1214, leaving the crown to his young son Enrique I.

According to Ibn Idhārī (d. ca. 1295) in his *Al-bayān al-mughrib fī ikhtiṣār akhbār muluk al-andalus wa-ʾl-maghrib* (The Remarkable Exposition Summarizing the History of the Kings of al-Andalus and the Maghrib), al-Fakhkhār first came to Marrakech as a diplomat in 1203, eight years after Alfonso's defeat at Alarcos, when Alfonso sent him to negotiate a new truce and the deferment of tribute payments. This was followed by several years of peace between Muslims and Christians. We next hear of al-Fakhkhār in 1214, two years after Alfonso's victory at Las Navas de Tolosa and after the death of al-Nāṣir, when al-Mustanṣir became caliph. Sent by Alfonso, al-Fakhkhār traveled to Marrakech to begin negotiations for the definitive peace between Castile and the Almohads. Alfonso died on October 6, 1214, without seeing the truce completed, though al-Fakhkhār continued the negotiation after his death under the direction of Doña Berenguela, guardian of the minor Enrique I.

Al-Fakhkhār was thus a key diplomat at the moments of greatest Christian weakness and greatest Christian strength; he was a witness to and agent in a transformative moment during the Reconquista, when the Almohads fell into decline and power tipped in favor of Castile. As a figure who moved easily among the settings of the Jewish community and Christian and Muslim courts, he was able to speak several languages and assume various modes of cultural discourse. He spoke Arabic in Marrakech (and probably in Toledo as well), undoubtedly spoke Castilian to Alfonso VIII, and had a command of Hebrew that allowed at least for the appreciation of Hebrew literary works.

Al-Fakhkhār appears in numerous Arabic literary compilations, among them *Al-mughrib fī ḥula al-maghrib* (Novel Tidings About the Ornaments of the West), a biographical anthology of Arabic poets by al-Fakhkhār's younger contemporary Ibn Sa'īd al-Maghribī (1213–86), and al-Maqqarī's *Nafḥ al-ṭīb*.[4] Ibn Sa'īd, who relates that he met al-Fakhkhār personally, identifies the Jew as a "doctor" (*ṭabīb*) who "was widely known in Toledo and became an emissary (*rasūl*) from its Christian King Alfonso (Adhfunsh) to the nation of the Banū 'Abd al-Ma'amūn at the court of Marrakech. My father described him as a master of poetry, learning in ancient sciences (*ma'arifat al-'ulūm al-qadīma*) and logic (*al-manṭiq*)."

Al-Fakhkhār is mentioned in several Jewish sources, where he appears as a diplomat, a learned leader of the Jewish community, and a tax collector. He served as a patron for Hebrew writers, including Judah Ibn Shabbetai, who dedicated his *Minḥat Yehudah sone' ha-nashim* (Gift of Judah the Misogynist) to al-Fakhkhār and featured the patron as a character within the text. Ibn Shabbetai writes in al-Fakhkhār's praise (in 1208), noting his eminent position among Muslims and Christians:

> The Lord established him to determine justice for his people. He bears sovereignty upon his shoulder. Whose greatness can compare

> with his? Tongues fail to declare his praise. Because of him lands are elevated even above the skies! Of him the prophets spoke. For his sake all creation was made. The kings of Arabia purify themselves in the waters of his wisdom, and the chiefs of Edom wage war at his command: "They set out at his word and at his word they return" (Numbers 27:21). Before him they are dumbfounded[5] and upon them falls his dread for they behold things never told before. He is the "father of many nations" (Genesis 17:4) and the master of Torah.[6]

The quotation from Genesis evokes the sobriquet of al-Fakhkhār's namesake, the biblical Abraham, yet here the moniker refers to the diplomat's status among contemporary religious communities. The passage from Numbers is apposite in that it makes reference to Joshua, precisely at the moment of his being invested with Moses' authority. Hence al-Fakhkhār too is being represented as a legitimate heir to Moses' rule (though the troops referred to here are obviously Christian rather than Israelite).

It is striking that the praise found in Judah al-Ḥarizi's (b. Toledo, 1166?; d. Aleppo, 1225) *Taḥkemoni*, a later work by another of al-Fakhkhār's contemporaries, is far more brief and restrained: "He possesses precious moral qualities (*middot yeqarot*) and upright actions (*peʿulot meyusharot*)."[7] Joshua Blau and Joseph Yahalom comment that al-Ḥarizi's encounter with al-Fakhkhār likely took place prior to 1208 (when *Minḥat Yehudah* was published), which might explain al-Ḥarizi's reticence, both about al-Fakhkhār's patronage of Hebrew writing and his diplomatic career.[8] It is also possible that al-Ḥarizi did not think al-Fakhkhār remarkable among the Jews of Toledo, many of whom merited praise. Most important, the discrepancy in the type and magnitude of praise between Ibn Shabbetai and al-Ḥarizi may simply derive from the fact that al-Fakhkhār served as patron to the former but not the latter.

Meir Abulafia, a renowned legal scholar and Hebrew poet of significant skill, addressed two poems to al-Fakhkhār during the latter's lifetime and composed an elegy upon his death.[9] The earliest poem is dated (Nisan) 1194 and is written on the occasion of al-Fakhkhār's marriage to the daughter of the vizier Abū ʿUmar, that is, Joseph Ibn Shoshan, Abulafia's sister-in-law. The second poem is written as an appeal for deferment on behalf of Abraham ha-Yarḥi, from whom al-Fakhkhār had requested payment of a tax (called *jizya* in the Judeo-Arabic superscription to the poem). The elegy, which was inscribed on al-Fakhkhār's tombstone, reads as follows (introduced by a scribe with a Judeo-Arabic superscription):

He said when his brother-in-law, the most illustrious vizier Abū Isḥāq bin al-Fakhkhār, may God be satisfied with him, passed away in the year 1229. He said what was engraved on his tomb:

1. You, drunk with the wine of reeling,[10] turn to the cave of Makhpelah!
2. It has given you to drink another goblet of reeling that will make you forget all [previous] reeling.
3. For there is buried Abraham, the glory among every community's leaders.
4. A Nagid and Prince (*sar*) but only of refined culture (*musar*). All other dominion he despised!
5. How a tower of strength, who was a refuge for the poor, has become a heap of ruins!
6. A vine whose shade covered mountains, whose branches [covered] all,[11]
7. Passed like chaff before a storm,[12] taken down to Sheol.
8. When his pen spat myrrh,[13] a flame rushed like lightning, a blaze of devouring fire.
9. His pen glided on the wings of the wind and answered all who petitioned.
10. Doom has brought an end to Dominion so that she is stripped of her adornments.
11. [Doom] speaks, "You may come this far but no farther."[14] The stumbling block has come.
12. The night is desolate; also the day is darkness and gloom.
13. Pant and gasp for the Earth plots even against the mighty!
14. Weep and lament and say, "No man endures any longer than a breath!"[15]

Associating the deceased with the cave of Makhpelah ensconces al-Fakhkhār hyperbolically within the pantheon of Israel's patriarchs, associating him, again, with his namesake Abraham. In lines 4 and 5, Abulafia alludes to al-Fakhkhār's political power even as he insists that such power was of no importance to him. The poem also dwells on the might of Abraham's pen, not an unusual theme for medieval Hebrew (and Arabic) panegyric but particularly apposite for a diplomat who authored epistles and signed treaties. Whether Abulafia intends al-Fakhkhār's skill in writing Arabic and Hebrew or Arabic only is open to interpretation, though no Hebrew writing by al-Fakhkhār has come down to us.

Al-Fakhkhār's Literary Output

Like many individuals whose verses have been preserved, al-Fakhkhār was not a "professional poet" in the sense that he did not earn his living by writing poetry. Rather, he possessed a range of learning and an ability to compose verse, almost prerequisites for a political career within Islamic courts. Striking, of course, is that he served a Christian king rather than a Muslim king. Alfonso VIII undoubtedly knew that such skills were essential attributes of a successful diplomat to the Islamic world and may have appreciated these abilities himself.

Al-Fakhkhār was by no means the only Jew known for composing Arabic poetry in the Islamic West. In various collections, verses have been attributed to Ismāʿīl Ibn Naghrīla (Shemuel ha-Nagid), Abū Ayyūb Ibn al-Muʿallim, Nisīm al-Israʾīlī, Ibrāhīm Ibn Sahl al-Israʾīlī, Elias Ibn al-Madūr al-Yahūdī, the poetess Qasmūna bint Ismāʿīl, and others.[16] What separates al-Fakhkhār is his origin in Christian Castile, from the city of Toledo, which was obviously still highly Arabized over a century after the Christian conquest, and the ease with which he moved between Islamic and Christian domains and modes of cultural discourse.

The selection of verses that are preserved in al-Maqqarī's anthology likely represent a fraction of the poems the diplomat composed; al-Maqqarī's selection is based on several earlier anthologies, notably that of al-Fakhkhār's contemporary Ibn Saʿīd. Al-Maqqarī includes an anecdote on the authority of Ibn Saʿīd in which al-Fakhkhār addresses a "Muslim littérateur (*adīb*) who knew him before his station was elevated and [before he] worked as an emissary among kings. [The Muslim] did not interact with him in a manner any better than when [al-Fakhkhār] had been in ignominy (*idhlāl*); Ibn al-Fakhkhār lost his patience and wrote to him":

> O one who makes two matters alike, having no sense of intelligence
> with which to investigate!
> You have made wealth and poverty, lowliness and loftiness
> equivalent. You do not cease being miserable and troubled.
> Are the high land and the valley equivalent on the earth? Will you
> seek a level path when your course is ascending?

You were not distinguished by the one whom you sought because
you had become accustomed to idleness.
What has occurred between us has become an occupying matter, so
do not make demands of me in the manner you are accustomed!
If you insist upon foolish audaciousness, you will continue to be
reviled and driven out.
Why is it that when you come to his door on every journey you
shift about uncomfortably?[17]

It is interesting to consider the extent to which religious difference was a factor in the exchange. Conceivably something similar could have occurred between two Muslims, though Ibn Saʿīd's reference to al-Fakhkhār's previous state of "lowliness" or "ignominy" (*idhlāl*) and al-Fakhkhār's reference to "lowliness" (*dhull*) in the poem evoke the assumed status of People of the Book, ironically employed in Judah Halevi's reference to Judaism as the "lowly faith" (*al-dīn al-dhalīl*). The anecdote indicates the power of political ascendance to overcome the status inherent in religious identity, even when the source of the ascendance lay with a Christian rather than a Muslim sovereign.

Another poem preserved by al-Maqqarī is a couplet on the common homoerotic theme of hairs sprouting on the face of the youthful beloved:

When the night of his beard darkened his cheek, I was certain that
night was most concealing, veiling.
My reprovers reached the point of saying to me, "[Be his]
companion!" So I met with him publicly and did not conceal
myself.

The poem adheres to standard elements of the genre, such as the likening of sprouting hairs to night (concealing the day, the whiteness of the cheek) and the presence of reprovers (though here even they feel compelled to urge the poetic speaker not to restrain himself). The homoerotic topos also remains current among Hebrew authors from Castile in the twelfth and thirteenth centuries.[18]

Perhaps the most interesting poem is the couplet in honor of Alfonso VIII cited at the beginning of this article; it is included in Ibn Saʿīd's anthology and later by al-Maqqarī. Ibn Saʿīd writes, "I saw him in Seville when he had become quite famous. He recited to me himself what he said concerning Alfonso":

The court of Alfonso is a wife still in her succulent days,
Take off your shoes in honor of its soil for it is holy.

First, we might ask whether the verses were recited before Alfonso VIII or were disseminated among Arabic speakers only. Ibn Saʿīd only reports that he heard the verses from the poet in Seville, not that they were recited before the king. Still, the verses must have been composed long before the encounter between Ibn Saʿīd and al-Fakhkhār since Alfonso died just after Ibn Saʿīd was born and the content of the poem suggests that the court was fully functional.[19] It is even possible that the verses originally stood as part of a longer panegyric of the type delivered to Muslim patrons, though nothing conclusive can be said on this point.

If the poem was recited to Alfonso VIII in Toledo directly, it would attest to the value Arabic held within the court culture of Castile. This would not have required that the king or others at court possess knowledge of Arabic sufficient to understand the poem: even the non-Arabic speaker would recognize the political performance of a panegyric being delivered before a king. In the second half of the thirteenth century, Todros Halevi Abulafia delivered at least two Hebrew poems to Alfonso X (the Wise) of Castile, one of which was inscribed on a chalice given to the king when the Jewish courtier first entered royal service.[20] Although the Hebrew poems may not have been understood by Alfonso X without translation, they were likely of value to him as objects, as gifts offered by a Jewish subject, signifying the fealty of the Jew (or maybe even the Jews). In comparison with Hebrew, Arabic had a more complex valence to which we will return after a brief point about the literary character of al-Fakhkhār's poem.

The second line of al-Fakhkhār's couplet—*fa-akhlaʿ al-naʿalaini takrimatan fī tharāha innaha qudusu,* "Take off your shoes in honor of its soil for it is holy"—is a clear play on Moses' appearance before the burning bush recounted both in the Qurʾān (20:11–12) and in the Hebrew Bible (Exod. 3:5). The Arabic phrasing closely mimics the verse in the Qurʾān, *fa-akhlaʿ naʿalaika innaka bi-ʾl-wādī al-muqaddasi tuwan,* "remove your shoes for you are in the holy valley of Tuwa." The verse therefore evokes a point of overlap between two (really three) scriptural traditions and resonates within multiple literary/cultural worlds. It utilizes the well-known intertextual technique known as *al-iqtibās,* literally the "lighting of one candle with another," describing the practice of lacing a poetic verse with a verse from the Qurʾān. Here it has the effect not only of beautifying the verse but of likening appearing in Alfonso's court with holding audience before God himself in a moment charged with religious significance. The effect is not lost for a Christian or Jewish audience in translation since the verse still evokes the scene of Moses at the burning bush, where he is also told to remove his shoes.

The dynamics of a Jewish poet evoking the Qurʾān in an Arabic poem in honor of a Christian king are intriguing and seem open to multiple interpretations. One might see in the verses testimony to the remarkable and complex multiculturalism for which medieval Iberia is famed. In this case, this would mean that the Crown of Castile tolerated and respected the culture of the Muslim-Arabic tradition, the bearer of which could even be an Arabized Jew. Such a reading would contribute to the longstanding image of medieval Iberia as a *convivencia,* a state of "living together" wherein Muslims, Christians, and Jews lived side by side according to a general spirit of cooperation.[21] Although the notion of *convivencia* holds true in certain respects, the shortcoming of this reading lies in its failure to account for the role of power in the production of cultural forms, not to mention the difficulty inherent in portraying the medieval past as an illustrative model for contemporary issues of multiculturalism and interreligious relations.

More productively, al-Fakhkhār's poem could be seen as an early example of the mudejarism phenomenon, referring to Christian patrons' cultivation of literary or artistic forms presenting an admixture of Muslim and Christian elements. More famous examples include the twelfth-century church of San Roman in Toledo, whose niche is adorned with a quasi-Arabic script; the sarcophagus of Ferdinand III (d. 1252) in Seville, inscribed in Latin, Arabic, and Hebrew; Alfonso X's (1221–84) patronage of Muslims within the intellectual entourage of his court; and Pedro I's (1350–69) Alcazar, an Islamic-style royal palace replete with Arabic inscriptions. (The fourteenth-century synagogue of Samuel Halevi Abulafia in Toledo should also be considered within the rubric of mudejarism.)

Mudejarism studies have been reformulated in recent years in light of postcolonial theory, notably the concept of "hybridity" as delineated by Homi Bhabha.[22] Bhabha studies the complex dynamics between colonizing powers and their colonized subjects, which, contrary to the view of previous theorists, are also not devoid of agency. Bhabha argues that unique "hybrid" cultural forms emerge as a colonized subject invariably assumes, sometimes in subversive ways, the cultural forms of its colonizing power while the colonizing power also appropriates the cultural forms of its colonized subject, often with the aim of furthering colonial power and influence. Of course, we must use caution when applying theories derived from modern situations to the Middle Ages, for the dynamics between Castile and Muslim territories were not identical to those between modern colonial states and their colonies. Still, the notion of hybridity is helpful because it accounts for the new cultural forms that inhere in and emerge through the relationship between political bodies of disparate power, be they the colonizer and the colonized or the conqueror and the conquered. Bhabha's theory imagines this relationship as highly dynamic, where neither political body is considered stable or inert and both are rendered changed by the encounter.

As noted in a recent journal volume dedicated to the mudejarism phenomenon, "hybridity must be considered . . . the product of a protracted Iberian imperial process."[23] Mudejarism reflects not only a certain taste among Christian patrons but also, at least at times, a type of appropriation and co-option obtaining calculating, often political, effects. While we need not be so cynical as to suspect Christian patrons of having no genuine interest in Arabic literature or architecture, we must consider individual artifacts within their full and specific sociopolitical contexts. Languages, whether written or performed, had value as vehicles of power and prestige in the court of Castile and in the territories of its influence. Being praised in Arabic presented Alfonso VIII as a king with all the pomp characteristic of his Almohad foes, thus promoting an essential image of royalty within the culture of Christian expansionism. If al-Fakhkhār's verses, either alone or as part of a longer panegyric, were recited before Alfonso VIII himself, they would speak further to an Arabized court culture in Christian Toledo, though it remains possible that the sole purpose of the verses was to spread the monarchal image among Castile's Arabic-speaking subjects and abroad.

Was it of any significance that the author and speaker of the verses was a Jew? Would it have made a difference to the Christian king or to Muslims in al-Andalus and the Maghrib? One imagines that Alfonso VIII, to the extent that he was aware of the verses, would have been equally or more pleased had the author been a Muslim. What could confer greater legitimacy upon a Christian king than to have Muslim subjects aggrandize him within their particular mode of political discourse? It may have been feasible to receive such a poem from an Arabized Jew only. For the Muslim listener in Almohad territory, Jewish performance would not be as poignant as Muslim performance, though it was also likely significant that the author was not a Christian. The Jewish courtier loyal to a Muslim ruler was certainly a familiar type to Muslims in al-Andalus and the Maghrib, and the redirection of Jewish fidelity toward a Christian sovereign may have been a subject of concern. The

Muslim listener may have marveled that a Jew as thoroughly Arabized as al-Fakhkhār paid homage to a king who was Christian and not Muslim.

Another issue that is raised by al-Fakhkhār's verse for Alfonso VIII is the extent of Jewish knowledge of the Qurʾān in Christian Iberia. Al-Fakhkhār references the Qurʾān not only in this verse but also in an anecdote related about him by al-Maqqarī. According to the story, al-Fakhkhār went to Marrakech, to the court of al-Mustanṣir, on a diplomatic mission during the period of Almohad decline, when al-Mustanṣir was greatly compromised. Al-Fakhkhār comes to the gate of the palatine garden and there beholds a hideous gatekeeper. A vizier asks how he is enjoying his surroundings and al-Fakhkhār responds, "I saw Paradise, though I heard that Paradise would have Riḍwān by its gate, but by this gate is Mālik." (According to Qurʾān 43:77, Mālik is the gatekeeper of Gehenna, while Islamic tradition associates Riḍwān with Paradise.) The vizier laughs and relates the story to the caliph, who also laughs and says to the vizier, "Tell [al-Fakhkhār] that we did this by design. Were Riḍwān the guard by the gate, we would fear that he would turn [the visitor] away [from the garden] and say to him, 'You are not in the right place.' But because he is Mālik, he ushers [the visitor] into [the garden] since he does not realize what is behind him and imagines that it is Gehenna." Upon hearing the caliph's words, al-Fakhkhār responded, quoting Qurʾān 6:124 (*Surat al-anʿām*), "'allahu aʿalamu haithu yajʿalu risālatahu,' 'God knows best how to carry out his mission.'"

The anecdote reveals that al-Fakhkhār held two pieces of Islamic knowledge: the fact that Mālik and Riḍwān are associated with Gehenna and Paradise, and the quotation from *Surat al-anʿām*, which makes a nice cadence to the story.[24] As the story illustrates, knowledge of such matters constituted a useful, perhaps even requisite, tool for the Jewish diplomat in gaining the caliph's favor.

But how much did al-Fakhkhār and Jews in general know about the Qurʾān and Islam in Christian Iberia? In Islamic al-Andalus, Qurʾānic verses are quoted explicitly by Jewish authors. Ismāʿīl Ibn Naghrīla is said to have mastered all the formularies of Arabic epistle writing, which undoubtedly included knowledge of Qurʾānic quotations. He is also accused by Ibn Saʿīd al-Maghribī of trying to versify the Qurʾān, which, if true, would presume thorough knowledge of the text (at the very least, it seemed conceivable to his Muslim critic that he possessed such knowledge).[25] The great Hebrew poet and literary theorist Moses Ibn Ezra illustrated literary and aphoristic points with direct quotations from the Qurʾān.[26]

Hava Lazarus-Yafeh[27] maintains that certain Qurʾānic phrases had entered Arabic parlance in general and may not have been recognized as Qurʾānic per se. This might have been the case with the quotation that concludes the anecdote of al-Fakhkhār in Marrakech, though the cadence of the story seems more forceful if the phrase is considered Qurʾānic. Familiarity with Mālik and Riḍwān is not indicative of deep Islamic learning but perhaps only of Muslim popular beliefs. However, such an explanation is not sufficient for al-Fakhkhār's close mimicry of Qurʾānic language in the panegyric for Alfonso VIII, whose meaning is contingent upon mediation through the Qurʾānic verse as the words evoke an entire scenario.

We cannot assume a priori that Jewish knowledge of the Qurʾān remained as strong in Christian Iberia as it had been in al-Andalus, even in a highly Arabized city such as Toledo. Still, evidence suggests that Jewish knowledge of the Qurʾān remained considerable. In Abraham Ibn Ḥasdai's (Barcelona, first half of the thirteenth century) Hebrew translation of al-Ghazzālī's *Mizān al-ʾaml*, the translator transforms a passing reference to *al-Fātiḥa* into a translation of the entire *sura*.[28] Judah al-Ḥarizi, a renowned translator from Arabic to Hebrew and an original author of Hebrew as well as Arabic literature, in all likelihood recognized many instances of Qurʾānic usage when he translated the *maqāmāt* of al-Ḥarīrī of Baṣra into Hebrew. It thus seems that Jews in Christian Iberia had *some* knowledge of the Qurʾān, at least of pervasive passages such as *al-Fātiḥa* and the verse from *Surat al-anʿām*, as well as of verses of special interest to a Jewish audience, such as that describing Moses at the burning bush. From the few examples before us, it is impossible to conclude that Jewish knowledge of the Qurʾān remained as rich as it had been in al-Andalus, though this is not certain. It is likely that Jewish knowledge of the Qurʾān varied according to individual proclivities and needs. As in other subjects, al-Fakhkhār at least possessed the knowledge appropriate for an able diplomat, but this is not necessarily indicative of deep or systematic study of the Qurʾān.

Al-Fakhkhār in Arabic Anthologies

Finally, I wish to comment on the placement of al-Fakhkhār in Arabic literary anthologies. As Ross Brann has demonstrated in the case of Ismāʿīl Ibn Naghrīla, representations of Jews in Arabic literature shift in accordance with the political and social climate in which the representations are produced.[29] In comparison with works produced during the Taʾifa period, during which Ibn Naghrīla was active, twelfth- and thirteenth-century sources amplify the villainy and sedition of the Jewish courtier. The Ta'ifa period came to be viewed as a failed experiment wherein the Party Kings' permissive attitude toward minority power opened the door to being trounced by the Christian Reconquista. Authors pointed to Ismāʿīl (whose impudence and arrogance were now conflated with that of his less diplomatic son Yūsuf) as a cautionary example of the ill fate that awaits rulers who empower Jews set upon humiliating Islam and denigrating Muslims.

In comparison with Ibn Naghrīla, al-Fakhkhār is seldom mentioned, with only a few lines dedicated to him at best. As mentioned, al-Fakhkhār is included in Ibn Saʿīd's *Al-mughrib fī ḥula al-maghrib*, where the description of the powerful Jew is quite positive, noting his political fame and citing his accomplishments in literature, ancient knowledge, and logic. This is striking given that Ibn Saʿīd's literary and biographical anthology is among the works that vilify Ibn Naghrīla. Would not the thirteenth-century Muslim author have recoiled upon encountering a Jew appointed to a position of influence, especially given his role in reducing Almohad power? Did it not seem paradoxical to Ibn Saʿīd that Muslims who employed Jewish courtiers seemed destined to peril whereas Christians who did so seemed destined to triumph? Perhaps he was not as concerned with Jews serving Christian rulers as he was with them serving Muslim rulers, or perhaps he felt that al-Fakhkhār represented an acceptable model of Jewish power while the impudent Ibn Naghrīla did not. Perhaps it was not yet apparent to Ibn Saʿīd that the victories of the Reconquista would amount to the irreversible reduction of Muslim territory on the Iberian Peninsula. Perhaps Ibn Saʿīd's appreciation for al-Fakhkhār as a man of letters and learning outweighed any urge he may have had to denounce him as an ally of the enemy.

In any case, al-Fakhkhār's power did capture the imagination of other contemporary Muslims who found it more problematic. Preserved in a section on *muḥāwarāt* ("dialogues" or "disputes") in the literary anthology *Lamḥ al-siḥr min rūḥ al-shiʿr wa-rawḥ al-shiḥr* (The Gleaming of Sorcery from the Wind of Poetry and Refreshment from the Narrow River Bank) is the following anecdote:[30]

> It was said to ʿIsā Ibn ʿAbāhil al-Bayyāsī,[31] "If you were charged with coming between Alfonso (Idhfunsh) and his Jewish vizier, what would you say?" He recited,
>
> > O you who conquers for the religion of the Messiah with his sword

And whose fathers and forefathers protected it,
Verily, the one for whose faith your ancestors conquered,
The Jews claim that they crucified him!

This poem was not actually recited before Alfonso or al-Fakhkhār; rather, the prestige of the Jewish courtier provided a hypothetical situation wherein a Muslim could confront a Christian king about the overextension of Jewish power. The fantasy is one of revealing the ironic hypocrisy of a Christian investing a Jew with power, given that the king's ancestors were soldiers for Christ whereas the courtier's ancestors were ostensibly his crucifiers.[32] Importantly, the suspicion of the Jew is essentially the same as it is in the case of Ibn Naghrīla; he is the religious Other charged with sedition, undermining the religion of the monarch he ostensibly serves. The preoccupation was probably inspired more by concern over Jewish power within the Muslim sphere than within the Christian sphere. By the time that Ibn Luyūn recorded the anecdote, Islamic Iberia had been reduced to the small kingdom of Granada for a century and the reign of Alfonso VIII, especially the Battle of Las Navas de Tolosa, was viewed as a watershed event that led inevitably to Almohad collapse. Anxiety over the extent of Jewish power is at the heart of the anecdote; this is confirmed by the fact that the anecdote is preceded immediately in the anthology by a related anecdote in which the ʿAbbāsid poet Yaḥyā Ibn Aktham recites a couplet to Harūn al-Rashīd that causes the caliph to banish a Jew with whom he had developed close relations.

Al-Maqqarī was born in Algeria ca. 1577 and spent most of his life in Morocco and significant time in Syria where he taught widely on the Andalusian tradition. He ultimately settled in Egypt, where he died ca. 1632. The representation of al-Fakhkhār in al-Maqqarī's monumental anthology is double-edged. On one hand, al-Maqqarī generally follows Ibn Saʿīd in creating a positive portrayal of a learned Jew endowed with power. This is not surprising given that al-Maqqarī compiled his great anthology from a perspective that combined nostalgic recollection with pure imagining. The segment on Jewish poets is included within a very long section given the heading, "[concerning] the commemoration of the brilliance[33] of the Andalusi minds, the Andalusis' love for knowledge, and their capacity for refutations (*ajwiba*) and other things that indicate their superiority."[34] Here, the Jewish poets are included among hundreds whose memory evokes a lost culture now in need of commemoration. It is striking that al-Fakhkhār is still included within the "Andalusi" rubric despite his origin in and loyalty to Castile. Al-Fakhkhār's status was not a cause for alarm in al-Maqqarī's view. The anthologist relates the anecdote in which the Muslim fails to treat al-Fakhkhār with due respect and includes al-Fakhkhār's acerbic attack on the Muslim, all without a hint of opprobrium or concern over Jewish power.

However, from al-Maqqarī's vantage point in history, approximately a century after the last Muslim kingdom in Granada had been conquered, the anthologist also laments the causes that led to Andalusian failure. Whereas Ibn Saʿīd probably did not recognize the reign of Alfonso VIII as a great turning point in the history of the Reconquista, al-Maqqarī believed that Almohad decline led centuries later to the conquest of Granada. It is therefore not surprising that al-Maqqarī introduces the couplet in honor of Alfonso, "He said praising Alfonso, may God exalted curse them both." In al-Maqqarī's *Nafḥ al-ṭīb*, it is the tension between two interrelated tendencies that accounts for the ambivalent representation of Ibrahīm Ibn al-Fakhkhār al-Yahūdī: the nostalgic evocation of the multifaith culture of al-Andalus on one hand and the lamentation of Muslim decline on the other.

Appendix

Shihāb al-Dīn al-Maqqarī, *Nafḥ al-ṭīb min ghusn al-andalus al-raṭīb wa-dhikr wazīriha Lisān al-Dīn Ibn al-Khaṭīb*, ed. Iḥsān ʿAbbās (Beirut: Dār Ṣādir, 1968), 3:527–28.

As for Ibrāhīm Ibn al-Fakhkhār the Jew: He ascended to power under Alfonso the Christian king of Toledo. [Alfonso] appointed him a delegate between himself and the kings of the Maghrib. He was knowledgeable in logic and in poetry. Ibn Saʿīd said, "He recited to me himself: he was addressing a Muslim littérateur who knew him before his station was elevated and [before he] worked as an emissary among kings. [The Muslim] did not interact with him in a manner any better than when [al-Fakhkhār] had been in ignominy; Ibn al-Fakhkhār lost his patience and wrote to him:

> 'O one who makes two matters alike, having no sense of
>   intelligence with which to investigate!
> You have made wealth and poverty, lowliness and loftiness
>   equivalent. You do not cease being miserable and troubled.
> Are the high land and the valley equivalent on the earth? Will you
>   seek a level path when your course is ascending?

You were not distinguished by the one whom you sought because
you had become accustomed to idleness.
What has occurred between us has become an occupying matter, so
do not make demands of me in the manner you are accustomed!
If you insist upon foolish audaciousness, you will continue to be
reviled and driven out.
Why is it that when you come to his door on every journey you
shift about uncomfortably?'"[35]

Ibn Saʿīd said: "He recited to me himself:

'When the night of his beard darkened his cheek, I was certain that
night was most concealing, veiling.
My reprovers reached the point of saying to me, "[Be his]
companion!" So I met with him publicly and did not conceal myself.'"

He said praising Alfonso, may God exalted curse them both:

The court of Alfonso is a wife still in her succulent days,
Take off your shoes in honor of its soil for it is holy.

[Ibn al-Fakhkhār] said: "They brought me into the garden of the Caliph al-Mustanṣir, which I found to be of the utmost beauty as though it were Paradise. By its gate I saw a guard of the utmost hideousness. When the vizier asked me about my state of delight, I said, 'I saw Paradise, though I heard that Paradise would have Riḍwān by its gate, but by this gate is Mālik.' He laughed and informed the caliph of what occurred. [The caliph] said to [the vizier], 'Tell him that we did this by design. Were Riḍwān the guard by the gate, we would fear that he would turn away [the visitor] from [the garden] and say to him, "You are not in the right place." But since it is Mālik, he ushers [the visitor] into [the garden] since he does not realize what is behind him and imagines that it is Gehenna.'" [Ibn al-Fakhkhār] said, "When the vizier informed me of this I said to him, 'God knows best how to carry out his mission.'"

PART III

Crossing Borders

Agents of Interaction and Exchange

CHAPTER 8

The Impact of Interreligious Polemic on Medieval Philosophy

DANIEL J. LASKER

One of the outstanding characteristics of the academic study of Jewish philosophy from its very inception in the nineteenth century has been the search for the non-Jewish sources employed by medieval Jewish philosophers.[1] Most scholars have assumed that Islamic philosophy was the most significant influence on medieval Jewish philosophy, but in the last few decades students of the field have made increasing efforts to expand the corpus of sources.[2] Thus, some scholars have recently turned to the non-philosophical internal Jewish sources of Jewish philosophers,[3] while still others have investigated external influences on Christian and Islamic philosophy.[4] Diana Lobel's excellent and learned study of Baḥya ibn Paqūda's *Duties of the Heart*, entitled *A Sufi-Jewish Dialogue*,[5] provides a good example of the attempt to marshal the wealth of sources, Jewish and non-Jewish, philosophical and non-philosophical, that underlie a prominent Jewish philosophical/moral treatise.

Let us look, for instance, at the chapter devoted to divine unity. Lobel illustrates what she calls the various crosscurrents that contributed to Baḥya's discussion of God's oneness: Jewish monotheism, Pythagorean and Neoplatonic number mysticism, the philosophical distinctions between the True One and the metaphorical one, and Sufi mystical devotion. She cites authors as diverse as Saadia ben Joseph Gaon, Isaac Israeli, and Solomon ibn Gabirol among the Jews; al-Naẓẓām, al-Ashʿarī, and Shahrastānī among the Islamic *mutakallimūn*; Yaʿqūb al-Kindī and Avicenna among the Islamic Aristotelians; and *Ikhwān al-Ṣafāʾ*, Thābit ibn Qurra, Qushayrī the Sufi, and Baṭalyawsī among other Muslim scholars. Despite Lobel's impressive erudition, however, one complete genre is missing from her discussion: the literature of the Jewish-Christian-Islamic debate, which has, not surprisingly, a great deal to contribute to an understanding of Baḥya's view of divine unity.

In Lobel's discussion of divine unity, al-Kindī's *First Philosophy* is cited at length, but his refutation of the Trinity, known from the counterrefutation by Yaḥyā ibn ʿAdī, is not mentioned; Ibn Gabirol's distinctions in *Keter Malkhut* between various kinds of unity are adduced; and Dāwūd al-Muqammaṣ's much more detailed analysis and the Karaite Yaʿqūb al-Qirqisānī's adaptation of it are missing, even though al-Muqammaṣ is specifically mentioned by Baḥya in his introduction to *Duties of the Heart*, and Lobel does cite him in her discussion of divine attributes. No reference is made to any Christians, such as Nonnus of Nisibis, Ḥabīb ibn Ḥidma abū Rāʾiṭa, or Yaḥyā ibn ʿAdī, despite their relevance to the discussion.[6]

The example of Diana Lobel's book is a particularly good one because of its overall high quality. Her work illustrates the predominant trend in the historical analysis of medieval philosophy: a close exploration of internal and external philosophical sources (and, in this case, mystical sources) without any discussion of the decisive impact of interreligious polemic on philosophical discussions. I will argue here that a close reading of the controversial literature indicates that quite a number of developments in medieval philosophical discourse can actually be traced to polemical motivations. The discussion here will review the impact of polemics on the following philosophical topics as they developed particularly in the Islamic realm: epistemology, the nature of God, and theodicy. The majority of the discussion below treats the impact of polemics on Jewish philosophy. Nonetheless, it is clear that interreligious polemic also made a significant impact on Islamic and Christian thought and that philosophy and polemics are intertwined in all three religious traditions.

* * *

Let us start with epistemology. The philosopher's first problem, whether she believes in God and is a member of a faith community or whether he is an avowed atheist, is: How do we know? This question is sharpened by a conflict of truth claims, especially when the divergent truth claims have their origin neither in perception nor in intellection but in the assumption of divine revelation.

Most philosophers are willing to consider knowledge attained through the use of either sense perception or reason as valid for all human beings. In contrast, however, Jews, Christians, and Muslims claim to have special information that is inaccessible, or at least inaccessible at first blush, to those who are not coreligionists. What is the status of that class of knowledge?

As Sarah Stroumsa has demonstrated, the need to verify the truth of one's religion inspired a genre of discussions regarding signs of prophecy, first by Muslim thinkers who were responding to Christian criticisms of Muḥammad, then by Christians who answered these Muslim ripostes, and then finally by Jews who defended their own religion.[7] Stroumsa demonstrates how thinkers of each religion formulated their discourse on prophecy to answer the challenges of the other religions. As an example, she cites Dāwūd al-Muqammaṣ's response to an unknown theological work, presumably written by a Christian and known to al-Muqammaṣ from the days when he was a Christian before returning to Judaism. That Christian was most likely responding to Islamic claims about Muḥammad.[8]

Sometimes the polemical imperative can come into conflict with epistemological principles. Thus, Saadia Gaon begins his *Beliefs and Opinions* in good kalāmic fashion[9] by outlining the sources of knowledge: sense data, rational truths, and a combination of perception and reason. He adds a fourth source for believers, reliable tradition, which is apparently included for polemical reasons, both internal Jewish and external ones, and which he will justify later in the book. Saadia is aware, however, that some of his co-religionists are uncomfortable with the use of reason to achieve truth, since they argue that revelation alone is sufficient. Although he dismisses the holders of this opinion as the "uneducated," Saadia realizes that there are traditional Jewish sources that can be marshaled in support of this position. Thus, he argues that one may, or even must, use reason to demonstrate that the truths which were accepted on the basis of prophetic miracles can also be verified by reason; revelation, according to Saadia, is a shortcut for humans whose reason alone is not adequate to attain these truths, at least not in a reasonable amount of time. The role of philosophy is not to invalidate the truths of revelation.[10]

The question arises, of course, as to how to recognize the miracles of a true prophet and distinguish them from sorcery. Saadia gives some guidelines: the miracle must be the subjection of elements in nature or the transformation of substances; the prophet must announce the miracle in advance; and there must be a good motive for producing the miracle. Moses' miracles were much more extensive than the magic performed by Pharaoh's soothsayers. The soothsayers, for instance, were able to change the color of only some of the water in Egypt whereas Moses transformed all the water in the Nile into blood; the soothsayers produced frogs in a limited area, but Moses caused them to come up out of the entire river. A further sign of a prophet is his humanity, including human frailty. It would not be proper to send angels on a prophetic mission since one could not know if the angel performed miracles on its own or spoke in its own name; humans are aware of the human limitations and, therefore, can recognize someone doing superhuman actions at God's behest.[11] If a person produces the signs of prophecy with the appropriate miracles, then one is obligated to accept his bona fides; reason can be used solely to provide further validation to his mission.

This is well and good in the context of intrareligious polemics, when Saadia is answering Jewish critics who object to the use of reason. But when he turns to interreligious polemic against Christians and Muslims, who offer their own criteria for signs of prophecy, Saadia adopts a different approach and maintains that miracles are acceptable as a proof of the truth of a prophet only if the prophet's message is determined to be rationally possible. When a litigant sues someone for 1,000 drachmas, he is called upon to provide witnesses; when he claims that someone owes him the Tigris River, the case is thrown out of court without asking the plaintiff to provide proof. A prophet with an irrational message is not accepted no matter how great his miracles.[12] (As Moses Mendelssohn was to say eight hundred years later, if a prophet revived in front of him all the dead who had been buried for centuries but had an irrational message, he, Mendelssohn, would not accept such a prophet.)[13] So, which is it: does one accept miracles first and investigate later (as in the introduction to *Beliefs and Opinions*) or does one investigate first and then accept the miracles (as in the book's polemical passage)? In a sense, it depends on whether one's interlocutors are of the same or of a different religion.

Judah Halevi, who was skeptical of the utility and reliability of the Kalām, must have seen Saadia's unsuccessful attempt to navigate between the Scylla of the use of reason to justify truths known through prophetic miracles and the Charybdis of the threat of Christianity and Islam as vindication of his own rejection of rational proofs for Judaism. Halevi's epistemology in his *Kuzari* was based not on rationalism, either in its kalāmic or Aristotelian garb, but on empiricism, or at least what he considered empirical facts, those perceived by a large number of witnesses and conveyed from generation to generation by reliable transmitters. Judaism may be rationally superior to Christianity and Islam, but the real difference between the three faiths is the number of people who witnessed the theophany that established the religion.[14] This argument, central to Halevi's philosophical enterprise and extremely popular among Jewish apologists to this day despite the fact that it makes Judaism self-validating, was the Jewish culmination of a long three-sided epistemological debate on the polemical question of the signs of prophecy.[15]

Another interesting epistemological issue related to polemics is the question of the extent of divine power and whether God can perform an act that otherwise appears to be impossible. Although this issue has its greatest development in the Christian world, especially in light of Scholastic distinctions between God's ordinary power and His absolute power, preliminary discussions of the subject can already be found in the Islamic world. For instance, the question arises as to God's power to innovate or change His mind (*bidʿa*), an important interreligious polemical issue when one religion claims to supersede another. Similarly, the possibility of an incorporeal God's communicating with corporeal humans is a major theological topic, and such theories as the "created glory" and the "created voice" were postulated to avoid the logical difficulties of revelation.[16] The issue of God's eternal word, whether asserted to be the Logos of Christianity or the Qurʾān of Islam, also plays a role in such discussions.[17]

Maimonides and some of his Jewish predecessors struggled with the distinction between the possible and the impossible in nature.[18] Although Christianity and Islam are not the direct targets of these discussions of possibility, such discussions may very well reflect contemporaneous interreligious discussions.[19] Thus, whereas Maimonides' treatment of the subject appears in the context of his disagreements with the Kalām, some of the examples he adduces very likely refer to Christian beliefs (e.g., God's making another one like Himself or becoming a body). Furthermore, subsequent Jewish anti-Christian polemicists were influenced by Maimonides in their philosophical attacks on Christianity.[20] In any event, distinctions between possibility and impossibility, which originated in the Islamic world, helped set the stage for later discussions of nature and miracle, which are so central to the philosophical polemics between Jews and Christians in Western Europe.[21]

* * *

The nature of God is another theological issue in which philosophy and polemics were intimately intertwined. Thus, Baḥya ibn Paqūda's discussion of divine unity has a polemical background, even if he himself did not explicitly make the connection between God's absolute unity and the refutation of Christianity.[22] Baḥya draws distinctions between the accidental or metaphorical one; the theoretical, conceptual, or intuited True One; and the actual True One, who is God. This discussion originates in Aristotle's definitions of "one" in his *Metaphysics*, as mediated by the Church Fathers and their Syriac- and Arabic-speaking successors, who were looking for a definition of unity compatible with a triune God. Anti-Christian Muslim and Jewish polemicists (such as al-Kindī and al-Muqammaṣ) further refined these discussions of divine unity, which were eventually developed in non-polemical contexts as well, for example, in Ibn Gabirol's philosophy and poetry. It is clear that if it were not for the need to define divine unity in the polemical context, the Jewish and Muslim philosophical discussions of God's unity would look quite different.[23]

The same is true for the various theories of attributes that developed in the Islamic world. In a series of articles, most of which are now incorporated into *The Philosophy of the Kalam* and *Repercussions of the Kalam in Jewish Philosophy*,[24] Harry A. Wolfson has reconstructed the discussions held between Christian theologians, who had a fairly sophisticated explanation of the Trinity, and Muslim thinkers who were in the process of working out the beliefs of the new religion. In response to Christian identification of the persons of the Trinity with divine attributes (such as wisdom and power), the Muslims were forced to define what exactly the Qurʾān means when it says that God is wise and powerful. Some Muslims (the Ṣifātiyya) admitted the ontological existence of divine attributes, while still denying that these attributes could be understood as distinct persons with internal relationships among them (as in Christianity). Others reduced the attributes to mere terms humans use to understand better the nature of God, explaining that these attributes certainly have no independent existence.

Jewish philosophers in the Islamic world, most notably Dāwūd al-Muqammaṣ and Saadia Gaon, also presented refutations of the Christian Trinity based on discussions of divine attributes. These refutations, however, were neither as extensive nor as developed as those of some Muslims, such as Abū ʿĪsā al-Warrāq, who analyzes at extreme length the relationship between the attributes and the persons of the Trinity. Al-Warrāq's refutation of Christianity has been preserved by Yaḥyā ibn ʿAdī, who adduces it in order to refute it.[25] Nonetheless, even in the absence of such all-embracing discussions of the Trinity, the nexus between philosophical theories of divine attributes and polemical attacks on Christianity was firmly established in Jewish literature, both philosophical and polemical.

This connection was maintained in Western Europe, where Christian polemicists explained the Trinity to their Jewish audiences in terms of divine attributes even though most Christian theologians rejected the relationship between Persons and attributes.[26] Thus, a full understanding of the medieval philosophical problem of divine attributes in the Christian world is impossible without consideration of the polemical motivations that informed the medieval debates in the Islamic milieu.

* * *

Another aspect of the threefold religious debate was theodicy and the justification of God's actions.[27] Although such issues as the suffering of the righteous present problems for all revealed religions, the polemical aspect comes into play when historical circumstances are adduced as proof of specific theological positions. For instance, Christians and Muslims argued that their temporal success was a sign of divine pleasure. A tendentious reading of history, then, often resulted in theological triumphalism. This issue was particularly acute for Jews in both Islamic and Christian countries, since Jews as minorities were subjected to the argument that their lowly status in this world was a sign of divine displeasure. Thus, Saadia Gaon records an objection to the truth of Judaism: "One sees that the nation that clings to this Law is in a state of humiliation and contempt." Saadia answers that if Jews were temporally successful, people would accuse them of observing the commandments for personal advantage; only in light of the persecution of the Jews can their true devotion to God be recognized.[28] Judah Halevi's Khazar king is skeptical of Jewish promises for reward in the hereafter when he says: "Correlate their [Israel's] rank in the hereafter with their rank in this world." Halevi's answer is that when the other religions were weak, their believers understood martyrdom as a sign of the truth of their religions.[29] Although one might legitimately question the effectiveness of historical proofs altogether when the willingness to kill and the willingness to be killed in the name of one's religion can both be adduced as a proof of the truth of that religion, nevertheless, in light of interreligious polemics the question of God's providence was especially acute for religionists who suffered for their beliefs. Religious philosophers were forced to confront issues of theodicy if they wished to separate the fate of believers from the truth value of a particular religion.

* * *

In the Middle Ages, the borders between philosophy, theology, polemics, and apologetics were not clearly demarcated, and thus it is sometimes difficult to determine where one pursuit ends and the next begins. Nevertheless, one can generally distinguish between genres of discourse, and a polemical treatise is not a philosophical treatise. When, however, the same authors are writing both genres, for instance, Dāwūd al-Muqammaṣ in the ninth century or Ḥasdai Crescas in the fourteenth, and they are discussing some of the same issues, such as divine unity and attributes, it behooves the researcher at a minimum to contemplate the relationship between the works.[30]

When comparing philosophy and polemics, however, there are a number of methodological considerations to keep in mind. Thus, one should be wary of taking polemical arguments at face value, since the polemicists are not motivated by a desire to analyze objectively the issues at hand; their goal is to make arguments that are convincing or sound convincing. It is nonetheless instructive to see how discussions that are not ostensibly polemical in content are still influenced by the motives and motifs present in polemical arguments.

It is helpful to distinguish between polemics whose chief motivation was interreligious (to convince members of another religion) and those whose motivation was intrareligious (to convince members of one's own religion). It is often difficult to determine if the actual intended audience of a treatise that takes the form of a debate between members of different religions is the author's own co-religionists and not members of the attacked religion. Recently, more and more scholars have adopted the argument that even events or treatises that look most like active proselytizing vis-à-vis another religion (such as forced, public debates) should be understood in the context of the internal needs of the disputants.[31] Here, too, one should be wary about drawing conclusions concerning the history of ideas and the impact of philosophy on polemics or polemics on philosophy. Yet, even if the polemical literature was meant more for internal consumption than as a tool for conversion, it would appear that this genre does reflect issues that were discussed in the context of the encounter between the religions. Polemical literature was partially fashioned by philosophical concerns; then, in turn, the polemical genre made an impact on philosophical developments.

This chapter has presented only a few examples of how recourse to the polemical literature and awareness of the polemical impulses behind certain philosophical discussions can enrich our understanding of the medieval philosophical enterprise. Given the trend to look for more and more sources for medieval works, it is surprising that the polemical literature often continues to be ignored. Greater attention to the interface between these two fields will lead to an enrichment of both.

CHAPTER 9

Arabic into Hebrew

The Emergence of the Translation Movement in Twelfth-Century Provence and Jewish-Christian Polemic

GAD FREUDENTHAL

The Problems

I would like to invite you to join me in approaching my topic as a follower of the philosopher of science Karl R. Popper. By this I mean that our look at the historical facts should be informed by *questions and problems.* "Facts without theory are blind," Kant famously said, and a *problem* at the back of our minds can similarly function as a searchlight that guides us through the thicket of the historical raw material. Rather than simply describe yet again the facts of the Arabic-into-Hebrew cultural transmission, I will sketch what I identify as *problems* calling for explanation. Following this, I will try to make a first step toward offering answers to the questions raised.

Let me formulate the problem as follows: In the year 1140, the Jewish communities north of the Pyrenees, those whose cultural tongue was Hebrew, were still immersed in exclusively traditional Jewish studies. This holds equally for all the centers of learning: northern Italy, the Midi, Tsarfat, Ashkenaz, and England. In the numerous yeshivoth young men studied the Talmud under respected masters and interpreted midrashim.[1] Less than half a century later, the scene in Provence had changed radically. Although talmudic and midrashic studies continued to flourish, a considerable number of Hebrew books of formerly unknown kinds had found their place on the Jewish bookshelf and were now studied by numerous scholars and laymen. These were Hebrew works drawing on Arabic learning or works translated from Arabic into Hebrew.[2] "Probably the most remarkable fact about the development of Jewish culture in Provence," the late Isadore Twersky wrote, "is the manner in which a Torah-centered community, widely respected throughout Jewish Europe for its wide-ranging rabbinic scholarship and deep-rooted piety, whose sages were constantly beseeched for scholarly advice and learned guidance, turned with remarkable zest and gusto to the cultivation of philosophy and other extra-Talmudic disciplines."[3] The question is: What *produced* the Provençal "zest and gusto" for the cultivation of science and philosophy? This question is the Popperian searchlight that will illuminate our path in what follows.

Like all cultural changes, the cultural transformation that took place in the Midi during the second half of the twelfth century must not be taken for granted as the result of some teleological process leading toward enlightenment. It is a truism that cultural contacts between Sefarad and Provence, and in particular the emigration from Sefarad to Provence, played a decisive role in this historical process. In the early decades of the twelfth century, Abraham bar Ḥiyya composed a series of scientific and philosophical books in Hebrew for the Jews in the Midi. In 1140, Abraham Ibn Ezra began his peregrinations, which brought him to Italy, Provence, northern France, and England. A few years later, in the mid-1150s, the Almohad persecutions brought to Provence families of scholars, notably the Tibbonids, who settled in Lunel, and the Qimḥis, who settled in Narbonne. These scholars were deeply immersed in Arabic letters, particularly in Judeo-Arabic learning, and they quickly became agents of cultural transmission. As so often is the case, immigration played a decisive role in bringing about cultural change.

This is certainly an essential part of the picture, but it falls short of providing a full answer to our question. For while the arrival in Provence of scholars immersed in Judeo-Arabic culture was obviously a *necessary* condition for the inception of the cultural transfer, it was hardly a *sufficient* condition. The fact that émigré scholars from Sefarad had something to *offer* their hosts does not itself account for the willingness with which the latter embraced this initially alien culture. Considered from a sociological perspective, we can even venture to say that the odds were against this acculturation.

The traditional intellectual activity in premodern Jewish cultures gravitated around the study of the Jewish canonical texts, sanctified and legitimized through its own tradition. In Judaism's self-understanding, an unbroken line of transmission and reception (*qabbalah*) was assumed to link the present to the Revelation received at Sinai: it legitimized traditional knowledge and, concomitantly, fended off competing bodies of belief. In this scheme, the appeal to any "alien [or: external] wisdom" means to acknowledge an authority other than that of Revelation and Tradition, while sociologically it means conferring power to new elites: premodern Jewish cultures tended to be self-sufficient. Hence, intellectual quests that originated in other cultures—notably science and philosophy—were perceived and referred to as "alien [sometimes: Greek] wisdom," and Judaism's most prevalent attitude toward them has been one of circumspection and hostility.[4] The Torah and philosophy are "contraries, two rival wives who cannot dwell at one and the same place," the erudite Talmudist R. Asher b. Yehiel (Rosh) wrote early in the fourteenth century,[5] expressing in a nutshell a deep-seated religious feeling shared in many circles. The numerous Jewish cultures that remained exclusively traditional and the recurrent Maimonidean controversies amply testify to this deep-seated inherent "isolationist" tendency in Judaism. Maimonides' norm "Hear the truth from whomever says it" was an innovation that broke with the past and remained under continuous attack. Its remarkably rapid acceptance in Provence after 1140, followed by the appropriation of non-traditional, especially philosophical, writings, is striking and calls for an explanation.

A key figure here is of course Judah Ibn Tibbon, the "Father of the Translators." We owe him the Hebrew versions of such Judeo-Arabic classics as *Ḥovot ha-levavot*, *Tiqqun middot ha-nefesh*, *Kuzari*, *Emunot ve-deʿot*, and the two parts of *Sefer ha-diqduq*. I recently devoted a "microanalysis" to this figure in which I looked as closely as the evidence allows at how his translation program was defined in collaboration with his patrons in Lunel, R. Meshullam b. Jacob and his son R. Asher b. Meshullam.[6] Put in a nutshell, I showed how the list of works to be translated resulted from a series of particular, local negotiations that led to choices made conjointly by the émigré scholar and his patrons. As the translation of a work progressed, Judah Ibn Tibbon even taught it to the masters and students in R. Meshullam's yeshivah, thus obtaining immediate feedback from his future readers; this was indeed indispensable in order to introduce them to the entirely unfamiliar ideas conveyed by his translations. As Judah Ibn Tibbon himself once remarked, science and philosophy cannot easily be transmitted by written documents alone—they have to be taught orally. At least at its beginning, the contents of the cultural transfer were thus shaped through a social process of continued discussion. The intellectual supply and demand were constantly attuned to one another and evolved in harmony. At this first phase of the translation movement, what interested Judah Ibn Tibbon's hosts were distinctively *Jewish* cultural goods: theology, ethics, spirituality, and Hebrew grammar. The universal components of the Sefardic culture, notably philosophy and science, were to come only later.

I believe that this microanalysis of the motivations of Judah Ibn Tibbon and his patrons affords some insight into the considerations that shaped the choices of the works to be translated. After all, even a Long March begins with a first step. Yet I now wish to broaden the perspective and situate the inception of the appropriation process of "alien wisdom" by the medieval Jewish culture in the Midi in a larger historical context.

The acculturation processes in the Islamic settings that began in the eighth and ninth centuries followed the adoption of Arabic both as a vernacular and as a cultural tongue by the Jewish societies concerned. As the intellectuals, along with members of other strata within Jewish society, acquired access to Arabic culture, a drive ensued to appropriate it, at least in part. The case in Provence was very different: the vernacular, which Jews shared with the majority population, was not a cultural language, and Jews (like most gentiles) usually had no access to the cultural language, which was Latin. Access to the majority culture was thus very limited. This circumstance makes the acculturation process in Provence particularly intriguing, indeed exceptional. For acculturation as a rule results from a "pull" the surrounding majority culture exerts on the minority culture via a multitude of channels, all of which pass via a shared language. But Provence is characterized by a process of acculturation that resulted from the "importation" not of the immediately environing majority culture but of a distant culture (notably Andalusian), conveyed through the very thin channel of translations from Arabic. We thus have a first explanandum: *Acculturation in the Midi does not involve the surrounding (Latin) majority culture but passes via translations from the Arabic.*[7]

This is quite odd, certainly not following the classic pattern of an acculturation process. To this we have to add another intriguing oddity. This is the striking temporal proximity and parallelism of the Arabic-to-Hebrew knowledge transfer and its Arabic-to-Latin counterpart, itself a part of the so-called Renaissance of the twelfth century. The Arabic-to-Latin translation movement started at the beginning of the twelfth century, when it centered around Petrus Alfonsi and Adelard of Bath, and it lasted until the end of the century, reaching a peak with the work of Gerard of Cremona and Gundissalinus in Toledo. The Arabic-to-Latin translation activity thus either preceded the Arabic-to-Hebrew translation movement by a few decades or was simultaneous with it. We should therefore ask: How can the striking parallelism and contemporaneity of the intellectual evolutions in the Jewish and the Christian societies be explained? This is a second explanandum: *The acculturation process within Jewish Provence is contemporaneous with the Latin-to-Arabic translation movement.* Now it seems clear that there was no direct causal relationship between the two movements: there are virtually no Latin-to-Hebrew translations of philosophical literature until the end of the thirteenth century, and Jewish scholars in Provence are strikingly unaware of Scholastic philosophy.[8] It thus seems clear that the Arabic-to-Hebrew translation movement was not a *direct* response to the Arabic-to-Latin translations and the rise of Scholastic philosophy. The question then remains: are these developments related, and how? Unless we wish to content ourselves by invoking the elusive Zeitgeist, the historian's treacherous temptation, this question is open, and we have yet to come to grips with the tantalizing parallelism and the near simultaneity of the cultural changes in the Christian majority culture and in Provençal Judaism.

To the two explananda already mentioned, we can now add a third explanandum, also related to the Latin majority culture. This is *the absence of acculturation in the regions known in Hebrew as Tsarfat and Ashkenaz.* As is well-known, this geographical area was the center of the highly intellectualist Tosafist activity involving numerous individuals.[9] The Tosafists were consistently uninterested in and, indeed, hostile to science and philosophy: even Maimonides' *Guide* never found favor there, as highlighted by the role played by the French rabbis in the Maimonidean controversy of 1231.[10] Now the Tosafist and the Provençal Jewish cultures were both embedded in the same majority culture whose language was Latin, to which neither had significant access. The two cases are therefore comparable and we must ask: can we identify factors that brought about the acculturation process in Provence but were not operative in the north?

The Italian Peninsula is a sui generis case. The acculturation process there was hybrid inasmuch as it involved translations into Hebrew from both Arabic and Latin. In Italy, in other words, acculturation was along two parallel channels, following two dissimilar patterns: one operated, as in the Islamic context, with respect to the immediately environing majority culture, while the other operated, as in Provence, with respect to the distant Arabic culture.[11]

We have thus identified a small set of related problems: Why did acculturation processes having the majority culture as their source develop in all Islamic settings but usually not in Christian contexts (except in Italy)? Is the

Arabic-to-Hebrew translation movement in Provence connected to the contemporaneous Arabic-to-Latin translation movement and, if so, how? What are the dynamics underlying the Provençal and Italian acculturation processes, which had for their source not the surrounding majority culture but a distant culture whose resources were mostly centuries old and required translation? Why did the acculturation process not spread from Provence to Tsarfat and Ashkenaz? Why did a double-track acculturation (Arabic-to-Hebrew and Latin-to-Hebrew) develop in Italy but nowhere else? Questions are easier posed than answered. In what follows I will do no more than propose a tentative and partial answer to a subset of these questions.

I suggest a two-tiered explanation (without implying that there were no other factors at work). The Jewish philosophical culture evolved, at least in part, as a response to the challenge of specifically *rationalist* Christian polemics against Judaism: Jewish scholars needed a comparable, that is, philosophical, body of knowledge to rebut rationalist critique. Jewish awareness of this challenge and the need to respond to it were modulated by the types of social communication with the gentile environment, which in turn depended on the Jewish-Christian relations in each region.

The Emergence of Jewish Philosophical Culture and the Challenge of Rationalist Christian Theology

My first suggestion is that although the Jewish culture in the Midi did not respond to the twelfth-century Arabic-to-Latin translation movement itself, it did react to one of the *consequences* of the rise of Latin philosophy. I have in mind the increasing use of philosophical modes of argumentation in the interreligious debates of the twelfth century. The late Amos Funkenstein has underscored the importance of the new genre of philosophically informed arguments in twelfth-century Christian anti-Jewish polemics.[12] These are arguments that draw on reason and invoke scientific ideas and concepts in order to show that fundamental ideas of Judaism run against what one knows through philosophy. Such arguments were advanced notably by Jewish converts who had an intimate knowledge of the Jewish sources. The most prominent among these was certainly Petrus Alfonsi (formerly Moshe ha-Sefaradi), who also played an important role in the early Arabic-to-Latin translation movement. Alfonsi composed his *Dialogus* (or *Dialogui*) *contra judaeos* after his conversion in 1106, probably only in the later 1120s, in Toledo.[13] This interior dialogue between Alfonsi's former self (Moyses) and his present Christian self (Petrus) addresses itself to the educated reader and endeavors to show that the Christian belief has much more to recommend itself than mere scriptural evidence, that is, that it is grounded in philosophy and natural science. Judaism, in contrast—and this is one of Alfonsi's main lines of attack—entertains anthropomorphic notions of God that are incompatible with reason. Indeed, Alfonsi's conversion itself must be understood as following from scientific and philosophical considerations.[14]

This *rationalist* Christian criticism of Judaism is clearly a consequence of the appropriation of rationalist science and philosophy in Latin culture. Petrus Alfonsi is an emblematic figure of this concomitance of knowledge transfer and rationalistically grounded polemic against Judaism. Similar critiques, however, were voiced by other authors as well. Jewish scholars, for their part, responded both defensively, by seeking to invalidate the Christian arguments, and offensively, by showing that fundamental Christian dogmas are incompatible with reason.

The first step of my argument is as follows: The *specifically rationalist challenge* to Judaism issuing from the majority culture created among Jewish scholars a need to respond to it in its own, that is, rationalist, terms. Just as in the early tenth century Saadya Gaon understood that Judaism must adapt to the evolution of theology in the majority Muslim culture and therefore (among other reasons) accommodate the rationalist thought in which it was grounded, so also certain leading Jewish thinkers in Provence realized that in order to rebut the rationalist Christian critique they must acquire intellectual tools comparable to those used by their adversaries. This need was also nourished by a more general sense of Jewish intellectual inferiority vis-à-vis the novel Christian science and learning. The confrontation with the new intellectual tools of the majority culture thus created a need for the acquisition of works in the rationalist tradition. "Acquisition" here obviously presupposes translation into Hebrew, and the natural objects for translation were the Judeo-Arabic works of religious philosophy. Thus, a first step in my argument is: *The Arabic-to-Hebrew translation movement is not a* direct *response to the Arabic-to-Latin translations but to the new rationalist genre of anti-Jewish polemics that emerged in their wake.*

Corroborating evidence for this thesis can be found in two major polemical works that were written by Jews in Provence concurrently with the beginning of the Arabic-to-Hebrew translations. These are *Milḥamot ha-Shem* by Jacob b. Reuben, who wrote his book in 1170, following a sojourn probably in Gascony, in the Midi, and *Sefer ha-Berit*, written in Narbonne at the very same time by Joseph Qimḥi (1105–70). We will now see that the two works draw heavily on rationalist thought, thus confirming that the interreligious debate in fact created a need for rationalist intellectual tools of the kind described above; moreover, they tell us which specific works were identified by contemporaries as offering these intellectual tools.

I begin with Jacob b. Reuben.[15] A perusal of *Milḥamot ha-Shem* shows that Jacob derived his knowledge of Sefardi Jewish writings exclusively from sources available in Hebrew;[16] thus, his intellectual needs can be taken as representative for those of contemporary Provençal intellectuals. Jacob describes his work as having been triggered by a long series of discussions with a Christian priest, whom he describes as a friend learned in logic and in all philosophical sciences (pp. 4–5). Scholars agree that Jacob's descriptions reflect historical reality and are not fictional. The debates are expressly characterized as free ("speak as you will, and do not fear me," the priest tells the author; p. 5), although Jacob understandably feels more at ease to express his defense of Judaism than his critique of Christian beliefs (which, he says, he would have preferred to keep to himself out of fear).[17] Insight into Jacob's social context is offered by his remark that he visited the priest regularly in order to learn from him "wisdom" (*bi-heyoti ragil lilmod mimenu ḥokhmah va-daʿat*; p. 5). The Christian scholar introduces the Jewish neophyte to both philosophy and theology and Jacob indeed acquired surprisingly good knowledge of both: he freely draws on philosophical arguments and at times uses *laʿazim* for philosophical terms—palpable witnesses to the instruction received in the vernacular.[18] Jacob's familiarity with Christian scriptures and theology (as well as with Latin) is evinced by the fact that his work includes Hebrew translations of sections from the New Testament and from an anti-Jewish polemical work by Gilbert Crispin.[19] Jacob reports that in the course of his religious discussions with his Christian mentor he soon felt inferior: in order not to suffer defeat in the debates he sought succor in the writings of the earlier Jewish scholars that he manifestly did not know before (*natati libbi lishmoʿa u-lehavin u-leḥappes ve-latur teshuvot li-meshuvotav kefi sikhli u-khefi asher yoruni gedolim mimeni le-yamim va-ʿatiqim me-ḥokhmah u-mi-daʿat*; p. 6; *le-hashiv lakhem be-ḥokhmati . . . la-ʿarokh teshuvot neged ha-meshuvot*; p. 23). Jacob indeed says that the aim of his work is to use his now "purified" intellect to "answer you [Christians] according to my wisdom" and thereby "refine the truth and cleanse the doctrine" (p. 23). The author's rationalist frame of mind is evident at every turn: he refers to knowledge that becomes evident from "all the books of metaphysics [lit., the divine science]" confirmed by "the teachings of our intellect" (p. 13) and refers to what is "truly known to all scholars relying on the intellect and what is evident to all rational souls" (p. 33).

Jacob b. Reuben's intellectual evolution is emblematic of that of the entire Provençal Jewish community. When he arrived at Gascony he was familiar only with traditional Jewish learning. The discussions with the priest both made him aware of the existence of philosophical thought and created a need for Jewish philosophical literature in Hebrew that would allow him to confront his teacher on his own ground. The little we know of Jacob's biography thus aptly demonstrates how the interreligious debates in a free ambiance created a need for Hebrew versions of philosophical works.

This need can be defined with greater precision. Since the question of the Trinity was naturally one of the main subjects of disagreement (see, e.g., pp. 7ff.), it was natural for Jacob to devote particular attention to the notion of the unity of God. Indeed, the Jewish protagonist is called the Unifier (*ha-meyaḥed*), his Christian opponent is qualified only as the Denier (*ha-mekhaḥed*). Jacob thus opens his work by stating that "apodictic proofs, made evident through the intellect," which he learned from earlier (Jewish) scholars, establish that the deity is an entity whose Unity is incomparable to any other unity (pp. 3–4). One of these unnamed scholars can be identified as Baḥya ibn Paquda: Jacob in fact draws on Judah Ibn Tibbon's very recent Hebrew translation of the first Gate of *Duties of the Hearts* that was completed less than a decade earlier (1161).[20] We now realize that the translations of Baḥya's lofty work responded to a number of needs at the same time: in addition to other explicit and implicit motives,[21] there was also the context of interreligious theological debates. R. Meshullam b. Jacob's enthusiasm for the Gate on the Unity of God may thus have been nurtured not only by the intrinsic nobility of the proof of divine unity but also by its usefulness in the Jewish-Christian polemic.

Jacob b. Reuben explicitly names a number of earlier Jewish scholars on whose works he draws. The one most frequently mentioned is Saadya Gaon. This is the case especially in the Twelfth Gate of *Milḥamot ha-Shem*, discussing the Messiah, in which Saadya is quoted and referred to repeatedly either as "the great sage" (*he-ḥakham ha-gadol*) or as "ha-Gaon."[22] Writing in 1170, more than a decade before Judah Ibn Tibbon was to translate *Beliefs and Opinions* (1186), Jacob used the earlier so-called paraphrastic translation of this work.[23] In the present context, the noteworthy fact is that Jacob found Saadya's composition useful for his needs in the Jewish-Christian debate inasmuch as it supplied him with effective arguments and intellectual tools. This usefulness, together with the deficiencies of the flowery but imprecise language of the paraphrastic version (which must have become particularly glaring when seen against Judah Ibn Tibbon's new philosophical Hebrew), possibly induced some scholars in the Midi to seek a new translation. It would thus seem that the interreligious debate supplied at least one reason why scholars in Lunel would ask Judah Ibn Tibbon for a modern Hebrew translation of this particular work. (In the absence of a translator's introduction, we have no direct knowledge of the precise circumstances and considerations that led him to translate this book.) We recall that Petrus Alfonsi had borrowed some arguments from Saadya; ironically, the use of this—rationalist—source by converts indirectly created the need for those who set out to rebut them to draw on the same source.

Other Jewish thinkers in the rationalist tradition whose Hebrew works Jacob used and mentioned explicitly are: Abraham bar Ḥiyya, also described as *he-ḥakham ha-gadol*;[24] Joseph b. Meir Ibn Zabara;[25] Abraham Ibn Ezra, on whose Bible commentaries Jacob drew implicitly;[26] *Sefer Nestor ha-komer* (The Book of Nestor the Priest), a ninth-century anti-Christian polemical work translated from Arabic into Hebrew in the middle of the twelfth century;[27] and Isaac Israeli's (lost) Pentateuch exegesis.[28] Drawing on all these Hebrew sources, and on the instruction received from his Christian friend, Jacob b. Reuben acquired a remarkable mastery of the philosophical mode of thought. Remembering that Jacob was writing in 1170, not even a decade after Judah Ibn Tibbon completed his first translation, we realize that the level of philosophical instruction in Provence, including scholars' ability to express philosophical ideas in Hebrew, was clearly quite remarkable after the middle of the century.

Similar conclusions follow from Joseph Qimḥi's *Book of the Covenant*.[29] Having been raised in al-Andalus before fleeing the Almohad persecutions to Narbonne, Qimḥi naturally had a command of Arabic culture, notably philosophy, on which he could draw for the purposes of his anti-Christian polemics. His explicit purpose is to justify the Jewish faith on the basis of "reason . . . understanding and knowledge,"[30] precisely what Petrus Alfonsi sought to do for Christian belief a few decades earlier. His entire treatise is indeed informed by the philosophical mode of thought: "That 'logic rejects most of what you sayest' is a cry which reverberates throughout the *Book of the Covenant*, be it in connection with a syllogistic refutation of a Christian dogma or in the context of the denunciation of a Christological interpretation of a biblical passage," Frank Talmage wrote.[31] This work, too, was written (at the request of a student) to satisfy a twofold need: to bring together texts and arguments affording "refutations against the heretics and deniers who polemize against our faith"[32] so as to bring them back to the covenant;[33] and "increase [i.e., strengthen] the faith in the God of Israel."[34] As a scholar imbued with the Sefardi Arabic literature that he had internalized in his youth, Qimḥi did not perceive a need to refer to specific authorities to buttress his philosophical arguments. For that reason, he is less valuable than Jacob b. Reuben as an informant of the intellectual needs of autochthonous Provençal scholars. It is therefore particularly significant to find that he, too, silently borrows one of his arguments directly from Baḥya ibn Paquda's *Duties of the Hearts*,[35] a work that, we recall, he himself had translated into Hebrew. Qimḥi thus confirms that this work was particularly useful in the context of the rationalist Christian-Jewish debate.[36]

We thus see that Jewish participants in the interreligious polemics, which at that time and in that region were rationally grounded, drew on the relevant available Jewish philosophical literature. Particularly noteworthy is the fact that Jacob b. Reuben and Joseph Qimḥi drew on Hebrew versions of Saadya's *Beliefs and Opinions* and Baḥya's *Duties of the Hearts*. This testifies to the usefulness of these two works for polemical purposes. The case of Saadya's *Beliefs and Opinions* is particularly telling: in 1170 Jacob b. Reuben uses faute de mieux the awkward paraphrastic version, but a decade later this translation is already replaced by Judah Ibn Tibbon's.

The argument so far can be summarized as follows: In the Midi, the environment of polemic generated a *need* for philosophical proficiency and hence for philosophical literature in Hebrew. The Jewish culture in the Midi responded not to the twelfth-century Arabic-to-Latin translation movement itself but to the resultant increasing use of philosophical modes of argumentation in the interreligious debates of the twelfth century. To counter gentile challenges, Jewish scholars needed a counterculture, as it were, a culture that would be both comparable to the culture of the host society and an alternative to it: this was the Judeo-Arabic culture, translated into Hebrew.[37]

This argument yields the following corollary: The fact that the philosophical culture in Provence rose in close temporal proximity to the Arabic-to-Latin translation movement now appears as natural. The Jewish need for philosophy is a response to the introduction of philosophical modes of argumentation into theology, itself one aspect of the Renaissance of the twelfth century, of which the translation movement was an essential component. Although the Jews did not in any form partake of the intellectual evolution of the majority culture, they were affected by one of its aspects, namely the rationalization of theology, whence the concomitance of both developments.

* * *

This suggestion now raises a new query. My account implies that the Arabic-to-Hebrew translation of philosophical texts should be correlated with the distribution of rationalist Christian theology. But this is *not* the case. For Christian thought and theologians were distributed evenly in southern and northern Europe. Indeed, the centers of Christian rationalist learning were in the north rather than in the south, in Paris rather than in Lunel. According to the account suggested here, we would therefore expect Jews in the north to be at least as affected by the rationalization of Christian theology as those in the south. But, as we will now see, the opposite is the case: the Arabic-to-Hebrew translation movement began in Provence but never took root in the north (Tsarfat and Ashkenaz).

Religious Polemics in Northern Europe: The Absence of Appeal to Philosophy

The character of the Jewish-Christian religious polemics in the Midi on the one hand and in Tsarfat-Ashkenaz on the other is very dissimilar. The Hebrew books for polemical purposes composed in the north, written only in the middle of the thirteenth century, are *Sefer Vikkuaḥ Rabbi Yeḥiʾel mi-paris* of 1240, *Sefer Yosef ha-meqanneʾ*, and *Sefer Niṣṣaḥon yashan*, the two latter having been written soon after the first.[38] Germane to our purpose is the fact that, contrary to the two Provençal works considered, these three compositions are based almost exclusively on proof texts: there is virtually no appeal (by either the Christian or the Jewish protagonists) to philosophy and science. It is important to note that the Jewish authors did not draw on philosophical arguments (for either offensive or defensive purposes) even when they were within reach: Daniel J. Lasker has remarked that although the old paraphrastic version of Saadya's *Beliefs and Opinions* was known in Ashkenaz in the twelfth century, the (correctly translated) arguments against the Trinity were not used in Ashkenazi polemical literature. Similarly, when in the thirteenth century Ashkenazi scholars became acquainted with *Sefer Nestor ha-komer*, they ignored its philosophical argumentation.[39] Again in the thirteenth century, the author of *Sefer Niṣṣaḥon yashan*, although aware of philosophical arguments, deliberately refrained from using them.[40] Clearly, in the north, Jews (and, in fact, Christians too) shunned the use of philosophical arguments for polemical purposes.

This striking indifference of the northern authors to anything philosophical can be further illustrated by *Sefer Yosef ha-meqanne*ʾ. The author, R. Josef Official, writes that some have argued that the phrase "in our image, in our resemblance" (*be-ṣalmenu ki-demutenu*; Gen. 1:26) implies that the deity has a (human) figure (*demut*) and "real" limbs, a claim they have corroborated with further scriptural proofs invoking God's head, mouth, ears, and so forth. Now Official's concern here is not a possible criticism of Judaism as anthropomorphic, but rather that this construal of the deity threatens to lend support to Christianity: "the ones in disarray [*ha-mevohalim*] said: 'He [God] might as well be a man [*ma ḥaser she-loʾ haya adam*]?'" an argument that can be used to give a rational account of Incarnation. In response, Official writes: "I will now reply by what I have found in the name of Rabbenu Saadya [Gaon], in the name of Rabbenu Nissim, and [in the names] of [Salomon] Ibn Gavirol and [Abraham] Ibn Ezra, who attended to *ṣelem* and *demut*."[41] The noticeable thing is that Official is completely uninterested in the issue of anthropomorphism, which was so central to all the authors he names with whose works and thoughts he was apparently acquainted: he seems entirely indifferent to their problématique and devotes to the entire point a sum total of thirteen lines, saying that the meaning of the biblical text can be "solved in a number of ways" (*u-peshaṭ ha-miqraʾ yesh liftor be-khamah ʿinyanim*). Official, we see, is not in the least concerned by the threat of anthropomorphism, nor by the theological question of how one should construe the deity. Rather, his aim is only to avert the potential support to Christianity of the verse from Genesis (if interpreted literally), and he does so in typical midrashic fashion, where a number of alternative interpretations can be adduced simultaneously. Joseph Qimḥi, to cite only one example, from a book that was also written for polemical purposes and not as a philosophical treatise, seriously considered the question regarding in which aspect man "resembles" the deity and gave it a rationalistic explanation.[42]

Religious polemics in the north were based on proof texts only, then, with a marked indifference to arguments "according to reason." But why did the rationalist arguments not make any inroads in these debates? The question is important in our context inasmuch as, according to the above analysis, such a development might have created a need for religious-philosophical literature among Jewish scholars in the north. It is not that in the north there were no contacts between Jewish and Christian scholars. On the contrary: Jews were aware of Christian critique of Judaism. Research on biblical exegesis in northern France has shown that informal exchanges over exegesis took place in northern Europe as early as the eleventh century and that Jewish writers responded to Christian exegesis in their biblical commentaries: this is the case already with Rashi, as well as with R. Samuel b. Meir (Rashbam) and his circle.[43] In Tsarfat and Ashkenaz Jewish scholars also debated with their Christian counterparts no less than in the south: "debate was a central phenomenon in the social and intellectual life of medieval Ashkenazic Jewry," David Berger wrote.[44] Assuming now that the churchmen in the north were as rationalistically educated as their counterparts in the south—after all, the University of Paris, founded in 1200, was a most significant intellectual center—the question arises why the debates in the north were limited to altercations in which the only modes of proofs were those grounded in Scripture or the Talmud.[45] Although there are similarities between the Christian and the Jewish respective institutions of higher learning (pointed out, e.g., by the late Israel Ta-Shma), the latter, unlike the former, excluded the scientific disciplines that occupied a central place in the former.[46] The question is, why?

In short, our initial account of the factors that triggered the appropriation process of the Hebrew rationalist literature implied that that appropriation should be evenly distributed throughout northern and southern Europe. Since this is not the case, our account needs to be refined.

Interreligious Violence and Jewish-Christian Cultural Contacts

We must indeed introduce here a further crucial variable. The fact that Christian theologians developed a rationalist theology does not imply they drew on it in their exchanges with Jewish scholars. Whether and to what extent Jews were confronted with a rationalist critique of Judaism depended on the patterns of communication between them and their respective host societies. Different social conditions would determine whether Jews were aware of the rationalist criticism of Judaism and felt a need to respond to it. The hypothesis that the need for the rationalist body of knowledge resulted (inter alia) from the rationalist theological criticism of Judaism needs to be complemented with the idea that that need was modulated according to Jewish scholars' familiarity with that criticism and the possibility of reaction to it. The latter, obviously, depended on the type of social communication and interaction between Jews and Christians at different places. My suggestion thus is as follows: The Jewish need for a rationalist body of knowledge was modulated according to Jewish scholars' *need to respond* to Christian critique. Rationalist arguments were required only where interaction was relatively free.

Here a "paradigm" describing Jewish-gentile relationships in the Middle Ages put forward by Mark R. Cohen proves extremely helpful. Cohen's is a sophisticated analysis of levels and types of social interaction between medieval Jews and their various host societies, relating differences in violence toward medieval Jews to the Jews' social positions in the respective societies.[47] I will mention only the most pertinent points.

Cohen juxtaposes Islam with the northern, mainly Germanic, version of Christendom, chosen as an extreme ideal type allowing for a clarifying contrast with Islam. The main variables that emerge as explanans for the differences in anti-Jewish violence engendered in the two societies are: the differences in the institutionalized attitudes of the two religions; the differences in the legal positions of the Jews; the differences in Jews' economic roles in both societies; and the respective places of Jews in the two hierarchical social orders. Under the last heading Cohen introduces sociological and anthropological ideas on hierarchies and marginality. The major point to emerge is that in northern Christendom Jews, the only aliens around, were excluded from the social order, viz. through conversion, expulsion, or destruction. In Islam, by contrast, Jews were one minority group among many and their status of *dhimmī* offered them a niche in the social order: although inferior to that of the Muslims, it gave them long-term stability and protection. Cohen summarizes his theoretical matrix by saying that "the paradigm that emerges from the comparative study of Christian-Jewish and Muslim-Jewish relations in the Middle Ages . . . claims that anti-Jewish violence is related, in the first instance, to the totalitarianism of religious exclusivity."[48]

Cohen's theory proves its fruitfulness and solidity in that it also elegantly accounts for differences in violence toward Jews within different *Christian* settings. Cohen points out that "Mediterranean Latin Christendom offered a much more hospitable surrounding to Jews than the northern reaches of Europe. Jewish communities of the south were less segregated from Christians, and their economic activities varied. In southern Europe, also, the stronger legacy of the Roman legal traditions contributed to the relative security of the Jews as compared with their status in the northern communities, where Roman law was virtually forgotten in the early Middle Ages. Additionally, whereas in the north political unity was accompanied by intensified degradation of the Jew-as-alien, the absence of regional political unification in the south afforded Jews with a greater free space. It was only after the conquest of southern France by the French monarchy that some of the anti-Jewish oppression characteristic of northern European Christendom began to appear in these annexed lands."[49]

So far Cohen's account. What is truly striking about it in the present context is this: The very same lands that manifested less violence toward the Jews (namely the Islamic settings, followed by the Midi and Italy) are exactly those that witnessed the emergence of a scientific-philosophical Jewish culture. By contrast, the lands in which violence was endemic—Tsarfat and Ashkenaz—are those in which rationalist thought found no acceptance. We thus have a second tantalizing connection between the majority society and the evolution inside the Jewries. But how does this connection work? Why should violence toward Jews be inversely correlated with Jewish "zest and gusto" for philosophical translations?

I submit that the character of the intercommunity communication, and with it the character of the interreligious polemics, was shaped by the social situations of greater or lesser tolerance toward Jews in different settings depicted by Cohen. These communication situations in turn shaped the need for the rationalist intellectual tools and thus account in part for the observed differences in the appeal to rationalist modes of argumentation in the north and in the south. Consider why.

In the Midi Jews had an inferior status, but they were not outcasts—they were integrated in society. This allowed Jews and Christians to socialize and communicate, and there is ample evidence that Jewish dignitaries and intellectuals interacted with their Christian counterparts.[50] This context of relatively peaceful communication created social situations for free religious exchanges. Some were not polemical at all, as when Christians sought the advice of Jewish scholars on the Hebrew Bible.[51] Other exchanges included reciprocal criticism but in a relatively serene atmosphere. These were not yet public debates but encounters that took place in any number of informal circumstances.[52] It is these open exchanges that confronted Jews with the recent rationalist critique of the unsophisticated Jewish belief system. Numerous incidental remarks in Jewish Bible commentaries testify to Jewish awareness of Christian Bible exegesis and thus of these informal intellectual exchanges.[53] Debates with converts from Judaism were particularly challenging because they were familiar with the Jewish literary corpus: R. Joseph Qimḥi's *Sefer ha-Berit*, for example, was written as a response to converts ("the children of the impudent among our people").[54] As already suggested, these situations of intellectual debates in a relatively free atmosphere created social situations for religious exchanges "according to reason" and hence a *need* for rationalist intellectual tools. These new intellectual tools were required in order to allow Jewish scholars to rebut the Christian criticism with the very same means, viz., logic and philosophy; at the same time, turned inward, they allowed the Jews in the Midi to refine their theology and rid it of the conceptions that had come under Christian attack. The challenge confronting the Jewish communities in the Midi was thus to rehearse, as it were, the process of cultural transformation that had taken place in Islamic cultural settings two centuries earlier. In sum: in an atmosphere of free intellectual exchanges, Jews needed a culture *comparable* to the majority culture that could at the same time be posited as a Jewish *alternative* to it. Such a culture could not be derived from Talmud study alone.

Consider now the corresponding situation in Ashkenaz and Tsarfat. "[O]ne of the most striking characteristics of the *Niṣṣaḥon Vetus* and other Ashkenazic polemics of this period is their aggressiveness, vigor, and vituperation," David Berger has observed.[55] It stands to reason that this type of harsh and antagonistic communication is a consequence of the relationships between the two populations. In the north, Jews were socially separated from the environing society, with regular outbursts of anti-Jewish violence. Hence communication consisted of aggressive altercations rather than intellectual exchanges "according to reason." The very nature of the social context in the north, where barriers were high and animosity great, made an exchange of rational arguments unlikely. We should indeed keep in mind that all these debates were oral, with real, flesh-and-blood persons facing one another. In communication situations that are always oral, the feelings of resentment, hate, fear, and aversion that the opponents harbor toward one another play an important role. Owing to the orality of the polemics, therefore, the overall social context impacted with particular vigor on the communication patterns. In the north, then, a historical situation similar to that that had existed in Provence in the second half of the twelfth century never existed: whereas in the south the occasionally vehement expression of the Jewish position was compatible with the appeal to rationality, the debates in the north, by their very social context, seem to have excluded an exchange of rational arguments. This goes some way toward explaining the noted differences between the north and the south. One contributing reason is the fact that in the north the debates began only in the thirteenth century: at that time, the character of Jewish-Christian polemics against Judaism changed in the south as well, becoming more violent and acrimonious, with the appeal to reason being replaced by an appeal to the authority of proof texts.

This brings us to the following suggestion: as a result of the absence of philosophical argumentation, no demand for an alternative yet comparable culture that could be opposed to Christian theology emerged in the north. In the north, Jewish intellectuals were not called upon to defend their faith by the tools of rationalism, and they felt no need to seek rationalist learning. The scholars in Ashkenaz and Tsarfat thus responded to the hostile environment by ignoring it, devoting themselves exclusively to their own, autochthonic culture, that of the Talmud.

It hardly needs to be restated that this factor operated within a large historical context. The absence of acculturation in the north is an integral part of an overall picture that awaits treatment by historians. This is among the most intriguing phenomena of medieval Jewish cultural history, and the preceding preliminary remarks have only the ambition to highlight the problem rather than to offer a solution to it.[56]

The situation in Italy was essentially analogous to that in Provence: violence toward Jews was low, making the exchange of philosophical arguments possible. As already noted, some Jewish scholars were indeed in close contact with their Christian counterparts and translated philosophical books from Latin into Hebrew while others translated books from Arabic. The reasons for this exceptional situation cannot be explored here.[57] In the present context, the salient point is that the contacts with Christian intellectuals produced among Jews the need to appropriate a comparable philosophical culture for themselves: here, too, it seems, it was the interaction with the gentile environment that triggered the introduction of the "alien sciences" into the Jewish culture. (Contrary to the situation in Provence, the contact with the host culture did not occur via religious discussions.) This Jewish philosophical culture developed in Hebrew and in Hebrew only: it was intended as an alternative to the Latin philosophical culture. In Italy, too, therefore, we can construe the function of the Jewish philosophical lore as that of serving as a culture that is both comparable to the environing one and a Jewish alternative to it.

Conclusion

In this essay the following cultural phenomena have been identified and partially explained:

- the rapid appropriation of philosophy, albeit specifically Jewish philosophy, in Provence during the second half of the twelfth century;
- the temporal and geographical proximity of the Renaissance of the twelfth century and the introduction of Greco-Arabic learning into

Jewish culture in the Midi, especially the near simultaneity of the Arabic-to-Latin and the Arabic-to-Hebrew translation movements;

the fact that in contrast to the analogous processes in the Islamic settings, the acculturation in Europe did not involve borrowing from the majority culture;

the fact that the Jewish culture in Tsarfat and Ashkenaz remained consistently shut to a similar acculturation.

To account for these phenomena, the following suggestions have been put forward:

Latin philosophy and science did not impact *directly* on the Jewish culture. Rather, the influence of Latin rationalist culture on Judaism was transmitted via rationalist theology and its use of rationalist tools in religious polemic.

This rationalist theological challenge to Judaism created a need for a *comparable*—that is, rationalist—Jewish religious philosophy that could meet the majority culture on its own ground. At the same time, to vouchsafe Jewish identity, this culture also had to be an *alternative* to the majority culture. This need was an important (although not the sole) cause for the emergence of the Arabic-into-Hebrew translation movement. This explains the contemporaneity of the Arabic-to-Latin and Arabic-to-Hebrew translation movements.

The challenge to Judaism was modulated according to the character of social contacts between Jews and Christians: the lower the social boundaries, the greater the need for a comparable, rationalist culture. Consequently, acculturation was strongest where violence was lowest: in the Midi and in Italy, the rationalist culture flourished.

In Tsarfat and Ashkenaz, the high social boundaries excluded interreligious polemics "according to reason," and no need for a philosophic culture ensued. This is one reason (among many) why rationalist learning found only feeble acceptance in the north.

Let me end with a disclaimer. It has not been my intention to propose a monocausal explanation, to suggest that the rise of the Arabic-to-Hebrew translation movement was triggered solely by interreligious polemics. What I have attempted to do is to identify one factor that played a role in spurring the translations of philosophical works: these were the spearhead of the translation movement but not the sole motivating factor. Other bodies of knowledge were also transferred from Arabic into Hebrew, notably Halakhah, Hebrew grammar, and even, believe it or not, belles lettres. The formation of a complete picture of how all these pieces of the puzzle fit together and at the same time fit into a overall historical context of material, social, and cultural realities yet awaits.

CHAPTER 10

Fusion Cooking in an Islamic Milieu

Jewish and Christian Jurists on Food Associated with Foreigners

DAVID M. FREIDENREICH

> The fact that Maimonidean writing is so often characterized, in Ben Jonson's phrase, by "a newness of sense and antiquity of voice" is the crucial determinant, eclipsing the formalization of genetic-literary relationships. His literary and conceptual apparatuses are purposely fused. Proper study of the *Mishneh Torah* thus necessitates tireless sleuthing, a deliberate and disciplined search for sources, together with an ever-deepening empathy for the modes of abstraction and conceptualization. In the final analysis, however, the attempt to uncover and understand "Maimonides' mind" must be paramount, for the originality of the "Maimonidean mind" was ensconced in the smooth anonymous texture of the work.[1]

The principle that intellectual activity is shaped by the milieu in which it occurs receives strong confirmation in medieval philosophical literature by Jews and Christians who lived in lands dominated by Islamic culture. Sarah Stroumsa vividly depicts the intellectual marketplace in these lands as a whirlpool whose current transports and transforms ideas irrespective of the religious community in which they originate: "Like colored drops falling into a whirlpool, new ideas were immediately carried away by the stream, coloring the whole body of water while changing their own color in the process."[2] Because Christian and Jewish philosophers were full participants in what scholars have dubbed "the Islamic philosophical tradition," their works cannot be fully understood in isolation from that broad intellectual tradition. These philosophers were, in a sense, "Islamic" as well as Jewish or Christian; the confession-specific terminology commonplace in modern scholarship is inadequate when it comes to capturing the complexity of this medieval reality.

Our profession-specific terminology is similarly inadequate, as medieval "philosophers" in the Islamic world engaged in a range of intellectual activities that transcends modern disciplinary boundaries. Among these activities is the study of law. In contrast to philosophy, law in premodern Islamic lands is a genre of thought beholden to an explicitly confessional intellectual tradition. If the medieval marketplace of ideas can be likened to a whirlpool, the currents of legal thought can be said to flow in narrow channels bounded according to individual religious communities—at least in theory. We shall see that the reality is somewhat more complicated. Legal literature, moreover, is "traditional" not only in its appeal to sources from a single normative tradition but also in its conservative rhetoric. The authority of a work of law derives in no small measure from its claim of fidelity to the normative tradition in which it grounds itself. Ideas from outside that confessional tradition lack normative authority.

Some of the most prominent medieval intellectuals were both active participants in the transconfessional Islamic intellectual marketplace and masters of the law within the circumscribed chambers of the Jewish or Christian—or Islamic, in the narrow sense of the term—house of study. This essay examines the work of two such masters, Gregorius Barhebraeus and Moses Maimonides, each of whom draws on ideas and models from his Islamic milieu in the course of codifying Christian or Jewish law. The essay focuses on a pair of passages about restrictions governing food associated with adherents of foreign religions, laws that express conceptions regarding the distinctiveness of one's own religious community.[3] These passages reflect the intermingling of ideas derived from both confessional and transconfessional intellectual traditions. Analysis of the confluence of these distinct currents reveals the minds of these jurists at work. To shift our metaphorical vocabulary from the realm of water to that of food, these case studies show our jurists to be cooks who employ a wide range of locally available ingredients and draw on both ancestral and regional recipes to create their own brand of intellectual fusion cuisine.

This essay endeavors to uncover the principles of fusion cooking employed by Barhebraeus and Maimonides, which is to say the ways in which these jurists select and utilize both elements native to their own legal tradition and elements derived from their Islamic milieu in the formulation and expression of explicitly Christian or Jewish norms. Its emphasis on the thought processes that underlie legal texts, what Isadore Twersky refers to in the epigraph as the "Maimonidean mind," stands at the core of what William Ewald calls "comparative jurisprudence." Ewald uses this term to describe the study of law from a culture other than one's own in order to obtain knowledge of how participants in that legal system think about their own law (as opposed to, say, in order to obtain information about the contents of a foreign system's laws regarding any given subject). Ewald's approach emphasizes that law is "a cognitive phenomenon, . . . not just a set of rules or a mechanism for the resolution of disputes, but a style of thought, a deliberate attempt, by people in their waking hours, to interpret and organize the social world: not an abstract structure, but a conscious, ratiocinative activity. So viewed, law becomes part of a larger framework of cognition, and it both shapes and reflects the metaphysics and the sensibilities of the age."[4] The principles of fusion cooking this essay identifies, therefore, are also relevant for understanding non-legal intellectual activity within the medieval Islamic world including, I suspect, the intellectual activity of non-philosophers.

In order to understand how Barhebraeus and Maimonides fuse elements from distinct intellectual traditions within a single coherent cognitive framework, we first need to be able to identify the source of each element. Ewald offers a helpful technique for accomplishing this task. In order to demonstrate the fundamental differences between modern German law and the classical Roman law on which it is based, Ewald imagines what a sixth-century Roman law student, "Romulus," would make of the nineteenth-century German law code and the way it is studied and applied. The aspects of German law that Romulus would fail to understand are, by definition, influenced by sources other than Roman law itself.[5]

This essay engages in a similar exercise, namely the reading of law codes in the company of individuals familiar with only one of the intellectual traditions in which our medieval jurists participate. First, we will examine Barhebraeus's *Ktābā d-Hudāye* in the company of "Muhammad," an imaginary Muslim jurist well versed in the Shāfiʿī legal tradition but ignorant of canon law. Having examined how an outsider might have reacted to a Christian law code, we will then examine the way in which an insider did in fact understand a Jewish law code. We will read a passage from Maimonides' *Mishneh Torah* alongside Solomon Ibn Adret, a medieval scholar from outside the

Islamic world fluent in Rabbinic literature but unfamiliar with Maimonides' intellectual milieu.

Both case studies demonstrate the degree to which these law codes draw not only on Christian or Jewish ideas but also on those of Islamic origin. The *Ktābā d-Hudāye* and the *Mishneh Torah* are thus "Islamic" in the broad sense of that term (what Marshall G. S. Hodgson dubs "Islamicate"). The passages we will examine, however, simultaneously give voice to the distinctly Christian and Jewish nature of these codes; indeed, both authors would bristle at the suggestion that their works contain "Islamic" ideas. The essay concludes by examining this apparent paradox, with particular attention to a key element of Islamic thought that Barhebraeus and Maimonides deem inappropriate for inclusion in their works. Our texts, I will suggest, capture an important facet of the way medieval intellectuals conceptualized the borders between their respective religious traditions.

* * *

The scholar commonly known in the West as Gregorius Barhebraeus was born in 1225/26 in Melitene, a town in eastern Anatolia; his patronymic, Bar ʿEbrāyā, may reflect the family's origins in the town of ʿEbrā, just across the nearby Euphrates.[6] Barhebraeus was a polymath whose dozens of works include texts on theology, philosophy, history, grammar, and medicine, among other topics. Barhebraeus was fluent in Arabic—he translated a philosophical treatise by Ibn Sīnā into his native Syriac—and he was evidently quite familiar with the scholarship of his Islamic milieu, both "secular" and "religious" (to use two more contemporary terms ill suited for medieval realities). Barhebraeus served as Maphrian of the Syrian Orthodox Church, the second-highest position in the ecclesiastical hierarchy, from 1264 until his death in 1286. It was during this period that he composed his *Ktābā d-Hudāye* (Book of Directions), the most comprehensive Syrian Orthodox code of law; Western scholars often refer to this work as the *Nomocanon* of Barhebraeus.

Early Orientalists already recognized the considerable influence of Islamic intellectual currents on Barhebraeus's works in general and on the *Ktābā d-Hudāye* in particular. As Carlo Alfonso Nallino made clear in the 1920s, the structure and much of the content of this work parallels that of the *Kitāb al-Wajīz* by the Shāfiʿī philosopher-jurist Muḥammad ibn Muḥammad al-Ghazālī (d. 1111).[7] Nallino's conclusions have been widely accepted without serious reconsideration of the evidence.[8] In a recent dissertation on the subject, Hanna Khadra affirms that Barhebraeus relies on a law code by al-Ghazālī but asserts that this code was not *Kitāb al-Wajīz*, the shortest of al-Ghazālī's three codes, but rather the midsized *Kitāb al-Wasīṭ*.[9] Reading the work of Nallino and Khadra, one might readily conclude that the chapters on civil and criminal law in the *Ktābā d-Hudāye* constitute little more than Islamic law translated into Syriac and that, with respect to these subjects, Barhebraeus functions as a wholesale importer of originally non-Christian ideas. Our imaginary Shāfiʿī companion, Muhammad, would beg to differ.

If Muhammad were given an Arabic translation of the *Ktābā d-Hudāye*, he would have no trouble navigating this work: Barhebraeus employs the same organizational structure developed by al-Ghazālī for his own law codes. This parallel structure holds not only at the level of chapter subjects but even within many chapters, including the one we will examine, "On slaughter, hunting, and distinctions among foods."[10] "There are four elements of slaughter," Barhebraeus writes at the start of this chapter: "the person performing the act of slaughter, the animal being slaughtered, the instrument used for slaughter, and the act of slaughter"; the author proceeds to address each element in turn.[11] This organizational structure, unparalleled in earlier Christian works of law, matches precisely the way in which al-Ghazālī discusses this subject matter.[12] It is clear that Barhebraeus expresses his ideas about the laws governing animal slaughter—and, as Nallino and Khadra demonstrate, laws regarding other subjects as well—within a framework established by his Muslim counterpart.

Nallino asserts that Barhebraeus imports not only the framework of his discussion of laws regarding animal slaughter from al-Ghazālī but also the entirety of its contents; this assertion apparently rests in no small measure on a mistaken assumption that there is no native Christian tradition of dietary regulations.[13] Muhammad, however, would actually find himself in unfamiliar territory. According to al-Ghazālī, the act of slaughter may be performed by "any mentally competent Muslim or *kitābī*," which is to say, any adherent of a religion based on a divinely revealed scripture (the Qur'an, the Gospels, or the Torah). Al-Ghazālī emphasizes that Jews and Christians may slaughter animals for Muslim consumption but that Zoroastrians and idolaters may not. He proceeds to address borderline cases involving Zoroastrians: What if the butcher is the offspring of a religiously mixed marriage? What if a Muslim and a Zoroastrian are partners in the act of slaughter or go hunting together? After thus elaborating upon the requirement that the butcher adhere to a divinely revealed religion, al-Ghazālī explains that the requirement of mental competence excludes madmen and children who have not reached the age of rational discernment; acts of slaughter performed by discerning youths and by the blind, however, are permissible. Barhebraeus, in contrast, stipulates that butchers "must be mentally competent Christian laypersons."

Muhammad would recognize the requirement of mental competence, which Barhebraeus also stipulates excludes young children and madmen. He would likely scratch his head upon encountering the requirement that the butcher not be a priest or deacon, as Islamic law does not recognize the existence of clergy as a professional category bound by distinctive restrictions. What would most confuse our Muslim jurist in Barhebraeus's discussion of these laws, however, is the requirement that the butcher be a Christian. Sunnis uniformly hold that Muslims may, in principle at least, eat the meat of animals slaughtered by any adherent of a divinely revealed religion, in accordance with the Qurʾanic dictum, "the food of those who were given the Book is permitted to you" (Q. 5.5). This verse, moreover, also declares that "your food is permitted to them," which is to say that God has permitted Jews and Christians to eat the meat of animals slaughtered by Muslims. Why, then, does Barhebraeus limit the performance of animal slaughter to Christian butchers? On the basis solely of his own Islamic legal tradition, Muhammad would be unable to comprehend this passage of the *Ktābā d-Hudāye*.

Barhebraeus explains that "our Holy Fathers prohibited eating the meat of animals slaughtered by members of other faiths, especially by pagans—that is, idolaters and Zoroastrians. The meat of animals slaughtered by Jews is worse than the meat of animals slaughtered by Muslims because [Jews] deceive the minds of believers. Nevertheless, Paul, the Apostle of God, ruled regarding times of scarcity for believers that they may eat anything sold in the marketplace without inquiring." The contents of this passage are distinctively Christian. Concern about meat slaughtered by pagans, especially in idolatrous contexts, appears in the New Testament (Acts 15:29; see also 1 Cor. 10:14–21) and in the Syrian Orthodox *Synodicon*, a collection of legal texts whose contents may have been known to Barhebraeus.[14] Jacob of Edessa (d. 708), a renowned Syrian Orthodox authority, prohibits Christians from eating meat slaughtered by pagans in non-idolatrous contexts but, on the authority of Paul, freely permits such behavior in cases of necessity.[15] In an especially stern responsum, Jacob also prohibits Christians from consuming food and drink prepared by Jews, excepting only cases of pressing need.[16] Al-Ghazālī's law codes, in contrast, make no distinction between the food of

Jews and Christians or, for that matter, their meat and meat prepared by a Muslim.[17]

Barhebraeus's fusion of an organizational structure drawn from the Islamic legal tradition and norms drawn from the Christian legal tradition would be readily apparent to a Shāfiʿī law student reading an Arabic translation of the *Ktābā d-Hudāye*. If Muhammad were to compare Barhebraeus to a cook, he might say that Barhebraeus employs a traditionally Islamic recipe but uses distinctly Christian ingredients. What Muhammad would fail to realize, because he lacks the proper perspective to notice this fact, is that Barhebraeus employs distinctively Islamic ingredients in this passage as well. Barhebraeus distinguishes "pagans—that is, idolaters and Zoroastrians"—from Jews and Muslims and declares that the prohibition of non-Christian meat applies "especially" to the former category. This distinction, which lies at the core of Islamic comparative religion in general and Islamic law regarding animal slaughter in particular, is unknown to many earlier Syrian Orthodox authorities, who equate Muslims and pagans in their legal writings.[18] Barhebraeus's specific reference to Zoroastrians, whom earlier Christian authorities simply refer to as "pagans,"[19] also appears to reflect the influence of a distinctively Islamic pattern of thought. Recall that al-Ghazālī, like many of his Muslim counterparts, treats Zoroastrians as the paradigmatic exemplar of foreigners whose act of slaughter renders meat prohibited for Muslim consumption. Barhebraeus's stipulation that the butcher must be mentally competent may also constitute an "Islamic ingredient" in the *Ktābā d-Hudāye*, although there is certainly nothing confessional, or even especially original, about this regulation.[20]

In short, Barhebraeus not only uses the structure of an Islamic law code to organize his avowedly Christian legal text but also employs legal material of both Christian and Islamic origins. Barhebraeus must have made a conscious decision to appropriate the organizational structure used by al-Ghazālī for his own code. Whether he noticed the subtle ways in which Islamic ideas about foreign religions shaped his own is less certain. Either way, Barhebraeus claims that his legal statements stand in perfect accord with those of "the Holy Fathers" and "Paul, the Apostle of God"; nowhere in the *Ktābā d-Hudāye* does Barhebraeus acknowledge his debts to al-Ghazālī or any other Muslim figure.[21] If pressed on this issue, Barhebraeus would likely deny that the ideas he adopts from texts by Muslims are distinctively "Islamic," just as he would dispute the notion that the "Islamic philosophical tradition" in which he participates is Islamic in any confessional sense of the term.

Barhebraeus, master of the Christian legal tradition he inherited, is also a man of his times, and the ideas of his majority-Muslim intellectual milieu are his own. These ideas shape the very categories in which Barhebraeus thinks about traditional Christian laws regarding animal slaughter and regarding non-Christians more broadly. The *Ktābā d-Hudāye*, therefore, gives voice to ideas of non-Christian origin. By doing so anonymously and by fusing these ideas with those found within the Christian legal tradition, Barhebraeus implies—and, it appears, believes—that these "Islamic" ideas are of a piece with the ideas expressed by earlier Christian authorities. Twersky's observation that "the originality of the 'Maimonidean mind' was ensconced in the smooth anonymous texture" of the *Mishneh Torah*, a text "characterized, in Ben Jonson's phrase, by 'a newness of sense and antiquity of voice,'" applies admirably to Barhebraeus and the *Ktābā d-Hudāye* as well. Attention to the ideas Barhebraeus selects for inclusion in his law code and the manner in which he fuses them together reveals the mind of this "Islamic" Christian jurist at work.

* * *

Moses Maimonides (1138–1204), like Barhebraeus, was a scholar of philosophy, theology, and medicine, an active participant in the Islamic intellectual marketplace who was recognized in his lifetime and beyond as a leading legal authority within his own religious community. Raised in Spain under the Almohad regime, Maimonides ultimately moved to Cairo, where he wrote the *Mishneh Torah* (Repetition of the Torah, ca. 1180), regarded as one of the most important and influential systematic codes of Rabbinic law.[22] Maimonides, like Barhebraeus, integrates ingredients of Islamic origin into his code; failure to appreciate the source of these ingredients can result in a misunderstanding of Maimonides' ideas.[23] The *Mishneh Torah*'s discussion of wine associated with non-Jews is a case in point, as we shall see by reading a passage from this discussion alongside Solomon Ibn Adret (d. 1310), a prominent Rabbinic authority who lived in Christian Spain.[24]

As Maimonides explains, "Wine that has been offered in idolatrous libation is prohibited for the derivation of benefit, and one who drinks any amount of it deserves lashes for violating a Biblical precept." Talmudic Sages, he continues, ruled that "All wine which a gentile has touched is prohibited lest he offered it in libation, because gentiles constantly think about idolatry."[25] Not only does the Talmud forbid Jews from consuming wine touched by gentiles, Jews also may not derive benefit from such wine—for instance, by selling it or watering their plants with it—even if the wine in question was made by a Jew. The stringency of the wine taboo reflects the Sages' uncompromising opposition to idolatry, as well as their presumption that gentiles must think about idolatry at least as much as the Sages dwell on their own religion. This prohibition against deriving benefit from wine touched by gentiles is unrelated to the Rabbinic prohibitions against drinking with or consuming various foods prepared by non-Jews, prohibitions Maimonides believes are designed to prevent social and, ultimately, sexual intercourse between Jews and gentiles.[26]

Talmudic Sages, it is important to note, presume that all gentiles are idolaters and ascribe no legal significance to the differences between Christians, Zoroastrians, and adherents of traditional Greco-Roman religion. Only wine associated with a monotheistic "resident alien" (*ger toshav*) is exempt from the Talmudic prohibition against the derivation of benefit. In the Babylonian Talmud, discourse about resident aliens is hypothetical: the Sages presumed that no actual community of gentiles qualified as resident aliens. Maimonides, however, defines Muslims as resident aliens and thus transforms practical law regarding the derivation of benefit from wine associated with gentiles:

> The wine of a "resident alien"—one who accepts the seven Noahide laws [among which is the prohibition of idolatry], as we have explained—is prohibited for consumption but permitted for the derivation of benefit; one may leave [Jewish] wine alone with him temporarily but may not store it in his possession. The same applies to all gentiles who are not idolaters, like these Muslims: their wine is prohibited for consumption but permitted for benefit, as all the Geonim taught. Christians, however, are idolaters, and their ordinary wine is prohibited for benefit.[27]

Maimonides' statement about the status of wine associated with Muslims appears to fit comfortably within the Rabbinic legal tradition. After all, it summarizes the Talmud's statement about resident aliens (bAZ 64b) and makes reference to the teachings of the Geonim, heads of the Babylonian Rabbinic academies during the eighth through the eleventh centuries. In fact, as we shall see, Maimonides expresses a radically different understanding of this law than do his predecessors.

Solomon Ibn Adret, among the most influential medieval authorities on the subject of Rabbinic dietary regulations, saw nothing out of the ordinary in this passage from the *Mishneh Torah*. In his own discussion of foreign wine, Ibn Adret summarizes Maimonides' statement as follows:

> A resident alien, as we have said, does not render wine prohibited for benefit by touching it; similarly, the wine he makes is permissible for benefit. On the basis of this precedent, the Geonim permitted the derivation of benefit from wine touched by those Muslims, as they are not idolaters. The wine of all [gentiles] who are not idolaters may not be consumed on account of their daughters, as the first decree [regarding foreign wine] prohibited only consumption and did so on account of their daughters, as I explained above. The prohibition against deriving benefit [from foreign wine], which a subsequent court promulgated out of concern regarding libations, applies only to idolatrous gentiles who offer libations, not to those who are not idolaters.[28]

Although Ibn Adret does not refer to Maimonides by name, his reliance on the *Mishneh Torah* is evident from his discussion of the resident alien, his assertion that the Geonim applied the resident alien precedent to Muslims, and his definition of Muslims as "not idolaters." Each of these elements is unusual within medieval Rabbinic literature, and the combination cannot be coincidental.

Ibn Adret defines gentiles whose wine is exempt from the prohibition against benefit as those who do not offer idolatrous libations, and he cites Muslims as the paradigmatic example of this class of non-Jews. Ibn Adret understands the *Mishneh Torah* to make the following pair of claims, which he treats as effectively equivalent:

1. Because Muslims are not idolaters, the Geonim permit deriving benefit from wine touched by Muslims on the basis of the Talmudic dictum permitting the derivation of benefit from wine associated with resident aliens.
2. Because Muslims do not offer wine libations, the Talmudic prohibition against deriving benefit from foreign wine does not apply to Muslims.

On close inspection, however, it becomes apparent that these claims are not at all equivalent: the first relates to Islamic beliefs while the second relates to Islamic practices. Neither claim, moreover, appears in the *Mishneh Torah*. The second statement reflects the opinion of the Geonim but is not expressed in the *Mishneh Torah*, while the logic underlying the first statement is not Geonic but rather is original to Maimonides.

Ibn Adret's statement that the Geonim regarded Muslims as analogous to resident aliens is incorrect: Geonic responsa regarding Muslim wine make no reference to the resident alien precedent or, for that matter, to the notion that Muslims are not idolaters. Rather, the responsa that permit deriving benefit from wine touched by Muslims do so on the grounds that Muslims, unlike other gentiles, do not offer wine libations. In the words of the eleventh-century Hayya (Hai) Gaon, "It is clear that wine is not at all associated with their worship and they consider it to be sinful. Therefore we do not hold stringently in this matter and are not concerned about the potential of libation." This leniency does not apply to wine touched by Christians "because they do offer wine libations."[29] Geonim preserve the prohibition against consuming wine touched by Muslims by appeal to a Talmudic statement that this prohibition applies even to wine touched by a newborn idolater, someone who clearly does not offer libations either (bAZ 57a). If Jews may not drink wine touched by a newborn idolater, the Geonim argue, surely they may not drink wine touched by an adult Muslim.[30] Responsa regarding wine touched by Muslims, moreover, make clear that the Geonim consider Islam to be a form of idolatry; in the words of Naḥshon Gaon, "Muslims are idolaters without realizing it."[31]

Maimonides, who acknowledges the Geonic use of the newborn analogy in one of his own responsa, makes no reference in the *Mishneh Torah* to this analogy or, for that matter, to wine libations.[32] The *Mishneh Torah* focuses not on the ritual practices of non-Jews but on their beliefs. Unlike his Geonic predecessors, Maimonides declares in no uncertain terms that Muslims "are not idolaters." Maimonides affirms this point in a responsum to Obadiah the convert: "Those Muslims are not idolaters at all. Idolatry has long since been torn from their lips and their hearts, and they ascribe unity to God, the exalted, in a fitting and flawless manner."[33] Emphasizing the monotheistic nature of Islam, Maimonides compares Muslims to resident aliens rather than newborn idolaters. Maimonides' condemnation of Christianity as idolatrous is similarly grounded in Christian belief rather than Christian practices.[34]

Maimonides states, accurately, that the Geonim agree with his ruling on the status of wine touched by Muslims (i.e., that Jews may benefit from it but not drink it). Maimonides does not claim that the Geonim would endorse the method by which he reached this position, namely by appeal to the resident alien precedent. He may well hope, however, that many of his readers would fail to notice the originality of the *Mishneh Torah* on this point: this passage exemplifies the "newness of sense and antiquity of voice" that modern scholars have observed in Maimonides' careful use of anonymity in his writing.

Ibn Adret is among those who fail to notice Maimonides' originality. Carried along by the current of the Rabbinic legal tradition, Ibn Adret mistakenly assumes that Maimonides, like his Geonic predecessors (and European counterparts), is interested in what gentiles do rather than what they believe. Ibn Adret embraces the *Mishneh Torah*'s unprecedented analogy of Muslims and resident aliens, perhaps because French Tosafists found a fatal flaw in the Geonic equation of Muslims and newborns.[35] He fails, however, to appreciate the implication of Maimonides' analogy, namely that monotheism or the lack thereof constitutes a valid criterion for establishing legal distinctions among different groups of non-Jews. This failure to understand Maimonides should alert us to the possibility that the *Mishneh Torah* draws here on ideas that stem not from the Rabbinic legal tradition but from Maimonides' Islamic intellectual milieu.[36]

Maimonides, unlike either his Talmudic and Geonic predecessors or his European contemporaries and successors, grants legal significance to the differing beliefs associated with different gentile religions. The criterion Maimonides uses to classify foreigners—either truly monotheistic or idolatrous—corresponds with the standard advanced by Muḥammad Ibn Tūmart, the ideological founder of the movement aptly named "Almohad": *al-muwaḥḥidūn*, those who insist upon the oneness of God. Ibn Tūmart asserted that recognition of God's non-anthropomorphic unity derives purely from logical reasoning, not from divine revelation; it is, therefore, both accessible to and incumbent upon all humanity.[37] The Almohads, who employed theological tenets as rallying cries for their political movement, imposed their brand of pure monotheism upon all of their subjects, Maimonides among them, and required them to memorize Ibn Tūmart's credal statements.[38] Sarah Stroumsa has identified a number of ways in which Maimonides' works, including the *Mishneh Torah*, reflect Almohad ideas.[39] It would seem that Maimonides also embraced the following Almohad notions: that strictly non-anthropomorphic monotheism constitutes a fundamental characteristic in the classification of humanity, that monotheism is accessible to those who have not received God's true revelation, and that the difference between monotheists and non-monotheists bears legal significance. These ideas are distinctly Islamic, as opposed to universally philosophical or traditionally Jewish, components of the intellectual milieu in which Maimonides lived and thought. Nevertheless, they are integral to Maimonidean theology and to Maimonides' conception of non-Jews. For this reason, these ideas prompt Maimonides to interpret the received Rabbinic legal tradition regarding the wine of non-Jews in an original manner.

Maimonides holds that the distinction between monotheists and idolaters is of legal significance but recognizes that this distinction does not coincide with the traditional Jew-gentile dichotomy. Consequently, Maimonides feels the need to carve out a special place for monotheistic gentiles within Rabbinic law and to adjust the prohibition against foreign wine accordingly. The impetus for this task derives from factors outside the Rabbinic legal tradition, but Maimonides accomplishes it within that tradition's narrow boundaries by means of his creative reapplication of the resident alien precedent found in the Talmud itself. Like Barhebraeus, Maimonides adopts ideas from his Islamic intellectual milieu, fuses them with ideas native to his own legal tradition, and expresses the resulting conception of religious foreigners and their food through a judicious combination of anonymity and references to authoritative predecessors, a combination that masks the newness of this conception. Analysis of this passage from the *Mishneh Torah* reveals Maimonides as a master of intellectual fusion cooking, an "Islamic" yet thoroughly Jewish jurist.

* * *

Both Barhebraeus and Maimonides think about their own Christian and Jewish legal traditions in a manner that reflects their internalization of aspects of the Islamic milieu in which they lived. They employ patterns of thought that originated among Muslim intellectuals and adapt traditional laws to accommodate their own Islamically influenced ideas about religious foreigners. Their fusion of confessional and transconfessional ingredients reflects the degree to which the *Ktābā d-Hudāye* and the *Mishneh Torah* are "Islamic" codes of law, in the broad sense of that adjective.

One who imagines Jewish, Christian, and Islamic thought to exist within discrete domains might say that Barhebraeus and Maimonides are smugglers of intellectual goods across the borders separating these intellectual traditions one from the next. This conception of interaction among Jews, Christians, and Muslims prompts Nallino's analysis of "Islamic law in the Syrian Christian *Nomocanon* of Barhebraeus," as well as Abraham Geiger's famous question, "What

Did Mohammed Take from Judaism?" and it remains commonplace in contemporary scholarship. The metaphor of smuggled ideas, however, is problematic or, at the very least, deeply ironic. After all, the passages we have examined reveal our jurists as guardians of communal borders who endorse a form of social segregation as a means of preserving their community's distinctive identity.

Daniel Boyarin describes the founders of what became orthodox Christianity and Rabbinic Judaism as border guards who unwittingly function as the smugglers of ideas across the boundary they seek to protect.[40] Barhebraeus and Maimonides, however, appear to be aware of the role that ideas of Islamic origin play in their work. Barhebraeus's decision to employ al-Ghazālī's organizational structure for the *Ktābā d-Hudāye* must have been conscious. Maimonides' awareness that his Almohad-influenced conception of Islam differs from that of his Geonic predecessors is evident in the fact that he seeks out a new Talmudic proof text to underpin this conception. If our philosopher-jurists knowingly smuggled ideas across the very border they guarded, we would expect them to offer some sort of justification for their activity, yet they do not. The reason for this silence, I would suggest, is that Barhebraeus and Maimonides define "Islamic" in a different manner than the one to which modern academics are accustomed.

Academics tend to define as "Islamic" the ideas, practices, phenomena, and so forth that originate among avowed Muslims. The medieval intellectuals we have examined in this essay, however, do not share our concern about the question of origins but rather focus on the essence of the ideas they encounter. For Barhebraeus and Maimonides alike, ideas that are (or can become) compatible with the Christian or Jewish intellectual tradition are, ipso facto, Christian or Jewish. It is this orientation toward ontology rather than genealogy that underpins the whirlpool-like intellectual marketplace in which these philosophers participated, an environment in which ideas, constantly in flux, could easily cross confessional boundaries. Ibn Tūmart's conception of monotheism, from Maimonides' perspective, is not "Islamic," it is true; al-Ghazālī's approach to legal codification, Barhebraeus might say, is not "Islamic," it is useful. As Ivan G. Marcus observes in his study of medieval Ashkenazic Jewry, "Jews absorbed into their Judaism aspects of the majority culture and understood the products to be part and parcel of their Judaism."[41] Within the ontologically oriented paradigm embraced by medieval intellectuals like Maimonides and Barhebraeus, only ideas that conflict with the Jewish or Christian intellectual tradition are "Islamic." We should not be surprised that such ideas are absent from the *Mishneh Torah* and *Ktābā d-Hudāye* alike. An example of such a narrowly "Islamic" idea, namely the concept of "People of the Book," illustrates this point.

Recall that al-Ghazālī, who in this respect is representative of the Sunni legal tradition as a whole, permits without reservation Muslim consumption of meat from animals properly slaughtered by a Jewish or Christian butcher. Al-Ghazālī does so on the basis of the fact that this butcher is a *kitābī*, someone who adheres to a religion set forth in a divinely revealed scripture. Whereas most Sunni laws regarding non-Muslims emphasize the inferiority of *dhimmīs* to their Muslim overlords, the law regarding meat prepared by Jews and Christians elevates People of the Book above other non-Muslims within a multi-tiered confessional hierarchy.[42] The parity between Scripturists and Muslims with respect to the act of animal slaughter renders Jews and Christians "Islamic" in a limited sense: they, too, adhere to a religion set forth by God through the agency of an authentic apostle. Maimonides and Barhebraeus refuse to embrace this notion of limited parity among the so-called People of the Book and, indeed, reject the concept of "People of the Book" itself.[43]

Maimonides maintains the traditional distinction between Jews and non-Jews expressed in Rabbinic prohibitions against gentile food. Jews, he allows, may derive benefit from Muslim wine because Islam is monotheistic. Nevertheless, Jews still may not drink the wine of Muslims nor may they consume a host of other foodstuffs prepared by gentiles, Muslims included, "lest Jews intermingle with them in ways that result in marriage."[44] Jews must maintain their distinctive identity within the broader society irrespective of the theology embraced by non-Jews. Maimonides, moreover, accords Muslims a relatively elevated status among non-Jews on account of their monotheistic beliefs, not their adherence to a "Book." As Ibn Tūmart and his followers emphasized, recognition of God's absolute unity may be obtained by means of logical reasoning alone, without the aid of a divine revelation. This conception of rational monotheism, consistent with scripture but ultimately not derived from scripture, is evident in the opening chapter of the *Mishneh Torah* as well.[45] It enables Maimonides to acknowledge the legitimacy of Islamic theology even while rejecting Islam's claim to receipt of a divine revelation. Emphasis on strict monotheism also allows him to reject the legitimacy of Christian theology while acknowledging Christian acceptance of the authentic revelation that is the (Jewish) Bible. Maimonides holds that possession of an authentic scripture does not affect one's legal status, although it does enable Jews to persuade Christians of their erroneous beliefs by means of scriptural disputation.[46]

Barhebraeus, like Maimonides, embraces in a limited fashion the Islamic notion of a multi-tiered confessional hierarchy, but he, too, refuses to adopt the Sunni stance that this abstract notion should be expressed through the permission of food prepared by certain types of religious foreigners. Barhebraeus offers no rationale for the prohibition of meat from animals slaughtered by Muslims beyond the generic prohibition of foreign meat articulated by "our Holy Fathers." In doing so, Barhebraeus follows the traditional Syrian Orthodox practice of equating Muslims and pagans for normative purposes even while he acknowledges the differences between these categories. Barhebraeus does justify his especially strong condemnation of meat prepared by Jewish butchers. Jews, he explains, "deceive the minds of believers," apparently through their claims regarding the meaning of scripture; Barhebraeus seems to agree with Maimonides that scriptural disputation gives Jews an opportunity to best Christians.[47] Because Jewish dietary practices directly challenge Christian beliefs about scripture, Barhebraeus and other Christian authorities imagine Jewish food to be especially threatening to the Christian faithful. Muslims, one should note, do not pose a comparable threat to Christians precisely because they are *not* "People of the Book" in any relevant sense of the term.

Al-Ghazālī and other Sunni jurists, in contrast, do not perceive distinctively Jewish (or Christian) practices as threatening to Islamic truth claims. Rather, Muslim acceptance of meat that Jews slaughter in accordance with the strict rules God imposed upon the Israelites serves an Islamic agenda by enabling Muslim polemicists to gloat about the relative leniency of the Qurʾan, which permits a wider range of meat than does the Torah.[48] The limited legitimacy Muslim authorities accord Judaism and Christianity, moreover, reinforces Qurʾanic claims that God's final revelation builds upon and supersedes the Torah and the Gospels. "People of the Book," in the Qurʾan and in medieval thought, is a distinctly Islamic conception that serves a confessionally specific purpose.

Both Maimonides and Barhebraeus, for different reasons, reject the limited legitimation of other religious traditions implicit in this conception as "Islamic," foreign to their own Jewish or Christian beliefs. Each gives voice instead to a distinctly Jewish or Christian conception of humanity, albeit one that reflects the internalization of ideas that originated among Muslim intellectuals. Maimonides' world, like that of the Talmudic Sages, consists of Jews and gentiles, but Maimonides distinguishes monotheistic gentiles from idolaters in a manner foreign to his predecessors. Like the Church Fathers of antiquity, Barhebraeus perceives a world made up of Christians, gentiles, and

Jews and expresses particular concern about the last of these categories; Barhebraeus, however, also distinguishes between Jews and Muslims on the one hand and idolaters on the others.

As academic scholars, we may profitably view these medieval intellectuals and their codes of law as "Islamic" in certain respects, but we should not forget that our authors did not think about their own work in this manner. If we ascribe confessional adjectives to ideas on the basis of their origins, Barhebraeus and Maimonides function simultaneously as smugglers and as border guards, selectively introducing ideas of Islamic origin into the circumscribed confines of Christian or Jewish legal thought. This metaphor, however, emphasizes the presence of a border that our authors did not perceive in the same way we do. Perhaps, therefore, the metaphor of fusion cooking is more helpful: our authors, masters of multiple culinary traditions, selectively and creatively utilize the ingredients and resources at their disposal to create a banquet for members of their own religious community that is both soothingly traditional and refreshingly contemporary. The choices made by our cooks reflect their simultaneous commitment to their respective communities' intellectual heritage on the one hand and to the truth and value of many ideas that originate within their Islamic intellectual milieu on the other. Neither, however, would call the latter set of ideas "Islamic."

NOTES

INTRODUCTION

I thank David Freidenreich for his generous editing and suggestions, as well as Jonathan Decter for his comments on an earlier draft of this essay. I also thank an anonymous reader of this volume for useful comments.

1. For a detailed discussion of a variety of approaches and terminologies used in the discussion of "border crossings" in the context of Islam, see James E. Montgomery, "Islamic Crosspollinations," in *Islamic Crosspollinations: Interactions in the Medieval Middle East*, ed. Anna Akasoy, James E. Montgomery, and Peter E. Pormann (Cambridge: Gibb Memorial Trust, 2007), 148–93.

2. Daniel Boyarin, *Border Lines: The Partition of Judaeo-Christianity* (Philadelphia: University of Pennsylvania Press, 2004), 1–2.

3. Nevertheless, rife during the Islamic period was the accusation of duplicity in religion—secretly holding Manichaean, Zoroastrian, or, in a later period, Ismaʿili or Jewish beliefs while outwardly professing Islam. On such accusations put forth by Muslims, see Bernard Lewis, "The Significance of Heresy in Islam," in *Islam in History: Ideas, People, and Events in the Middle East* (Chicago: Open Court, 2001), 275–94, esp. 285–87. From the other side of the question, on the sincerity of Jews living in the medieval Islamic world who converted to other religions, see Sarah Stroumsa, "On Jewish Intellectuals Who Converted to Islam in the Early Middle Ages," in *The Jews of Medieval Islam: Community, Society, Identity*, ed. Daniel Frank (Leiden: Brill, 1995), 179–97. Crypto-Judaism also existed under the Almohads in Morocco: see S. D. Goitein, *A Mediterranean Society*, 5 vols. (Berkeley: University of California Press, 1967–93), 2:300, 591n3. Regarding the lines between Judaism and Christianity, it is important to note that Shlomo Pines believed that certain groups of Judeo-Christians continued to exist well into the Islamic period. See the articles collected in Shlomo Pines, *Studies in the History of Religion*, ed. Guy G. Stroumsa (Jerusalem: Magnes Press, 1996), 4:211–380.

4. Marshall G. S. Hodgson, *The Venture of Islam: Conscience and History in a World Civilization*, 3 vols. (Chicago: University of Chicago Press, 1974).

5. See, e.g., Richard Bulliet, "Review of *Venture of Islam*," *Journal of the American Oriental Society* 98.2 (1978): 157–58; Edmund Burke, "Islamic History as World History:

Marshall Hodgson, *The Venture of Islam*," *International Journal of Middle East Studies* 10.2 (1979): 241–64; and John Wansbrough, "Review of *The Venture of Islam*," *Bulletin of the School of Oriental and African Studies* 40.1 (1977): 169–70.

6. See Ira M. Lapidus, *A History of Islamic Societies*, 2nd ed. (Cambridge: Cambridge University Press, 2005), 3–9. Lapidus explicitly acknowledges Hodgson. Lewis raises similar issues in his discussion of the word "Islam," without reference to Hodgson. Bernard Lewis, *Jews of Islam* (Princeton, N.J.: Princeton University Press, 1984), 4–6.

7. On Goitein's view of the Mediterranean as a unifying and unified entity, culturally, socially, and economically, see Joel Kraemer, "Goitein and His *Mediterranean Society*" [Hebrew], *Zemanim* 34–35 (1990): 6–17.

8. For discussion of Goitein as historiographer and his evolving view of the relationship between Islam and Judaism, see Gideon Libson, "Hidden Worlds and Open Shutters: S. D. Goitein Between Judaism and Islam," in *The Jewish Past Revisited: Reflections on Modern Jewish Historians*, ed. David N. Myers and David B. Ruderman (New Haven, Conn.: Yale University Press, 1998), 163–98.

9. See, e.g., Américo Castro, *La realidad histórica de España*, 3rd ed. (Mexico: Editorial Porrúa, 1966), 429–35; Castro, *España en su historia: Cristianos, moros y judios* (Buenos Aires: Editorial Losada, 1948), 206–14. Castro uses the terms "tolerancia" and "convivencia" in his discussions of the interactions between religions during the Muslim period in Iberia.

10. See Steven M. Wasserstrom, *Between Muslim and Jew: The Problem of Symbiosis Under Early Islam* (Princeton, N.J.: Princeton University Press, 1995), 3–7.

11. A. I. Sabra, "The Appropriation and Subsequent Naturalization of Greek Science in Medieval Islam," *History of Science* 25 (1987): 223–43; Dimitri Gutas, *Greek Thought, Arabic Culture: The Graeco-Arabic Translation Movement in Baghdad and Early ʿAbbâsid Society* (New York: Routledge, 1998).

12. See, e.g., Claire Sponsler, "In Transit: Theorizing Cultural Appropriation in Medieval Europe," *Journal of Medieval and Early Modern Studies* 32.1 (2002): 17–39.

13. See the discussion in Jonathan P. Decter's chapter in this volume.

14. Ivan Marcus, *Rituals of Childhood: Jewish Culture and Acculturation in Medieval Europe* (New Haven, Conn.: Yale University Press, 1996).

15. Hava Lazarus-Yafeh, *Intertwined Worlds: Medieval Islam and Bible Criticism* (Princeton, N.J.: Princeton University Press, 1992), 6–7.

16. Sabra, "The Appropriation and Subsequent Naturalization of Greek Science in Medieval Islam," 228.

CHAPTER 1. OBSERVATIONS ON THE BEGINNINGS OF JUDEO-ARABIC CIVILIZATION

An early version of this essay was delivered at a conference entitled "The Jews of Medieval Islam," which was convened at the Institute of Jewish Studies, University College London, in the summer of 1992. As a rule, translations of biblical quotations are given here according to *Tanakh: A New Translation of the Holy Scriptures According to the*

Traditional Hebrew Text (Philadelphia: Jewish Publication Society, 1985); translations of Qur'ān verses are according to A. J. Arberry, *The Koran Interpreted* (Oxford: Oxford University Press, 1964). I wish to express my gratitude to an anonymous reviewer whose erudite and helpful suggestions contributed toward the improvement of this chapter.

1. Cf. Chaim Rabin, "'Arabiyya," *Encyclopaedia of Islam,* 2nd ed., 1:565a, with further references. Al-Samaw'al's Jewish affiliation has been questioned in modern scholarship: see T. Bauer, "Al-Samaw'al," *Encyclopaedia of Islam,* 2nd ed., 8:1041–42.

2. This would include the philosophical works of Isaac Israeli and Solomon Ibn Gabirol. It has usually been accepted that the philosophical works of Da'ūd b. Marwān al-Muqammaṣ (ninth century) also belong to this category, namely that they do not contain any specifically Jewish elements. However, see Sarah Stroumsa, *Dāwūd ibn Marwān al-Muqammiṣ's Twenty Chapters* (Leiden: Brill, 1989), 30–32, where fragments of the *Twenty Discourses* (*'Ishrūn maqāla*) that had been considered lost clearly contain such elements; see also pp. 15–16 on the chronology of Ibn al-Muqammaṣ.

3. See Joshua Blau and Simon Hopkins, "Judaeo-Arabic Papyri—Collected, Edited, Translated and Analysed," *Jerusalem Studies in Arabic and Islam* 9 (1987): 87–160 (also Joshua Blau, *Studies in Middle Arabic and Its Judaeo-Arabic Variety* [Jerusalem: Magnes Press, 1988], 401–74), especially pp. 90–91 (404–5) on the chronology of the earliest documents in Judeo-Arabic. While the possibility of dating the earliest documents to the eighth century is mentioned there cautiously, it is mentioned absolutely affirmatively in Joshua Blau, *The Emergence and Linguistic Background of Judaeo-Arabic*, 3rd ed. (Jerusalem: Ben-Zvi Institute, 1999), 241–43.

4. Abraham S. Halkin, "Judaeo-Arabic Literature," in *The Jews*, ed. Louis Finkelstein, 3rd ed. (New York: Harper and Brothers, 1960), 1116–48; Blau, "Judaeo-Arabic Literature," *Encyclopaedia Judaica*, 1st ed., 10:411–23. Hava Lazarus-Yafeh, "Judaeo-Arabic Culture," *Encyclopaedia Judaica Year Book, 1977–78* (Jerusalem: Keter Publishing House, 1979), 101, suggests an even earlier date: "We are dealing here with that particular body of Jewish religious writings of all types, written in the shadow of Islam, usually in Arabic, but in Hebrew characters, during the period from before Saadiah Gaon until after the days of Maimonides and his son Abraham, i.e., from approximately the 8th century to the end of the 13th century."

5. Izhak Hasson, "Remarques sur l'inscription de l'epoque de Muawiya a Hammat Gader," *Israel Exploration Journal* 46.1–2 (1996): 97–101; Joshua Blau, "The Transcription of Arabic Words and Names in the Inscription of Muawiya from Hammat Gader," *Israel Exploration Journal* 46.1–2 (1996): 102.

6. See a list of such inscriptions in Chaim Rabin, "'Arabiyya: (ii) The literary language," *Encyclopaedia of Islam,* 2nd ed., 1:564; Nikita Eliseef, "Namāra," *Encyclopaedia of Islam,* 2nd ed., 7:945b; see also Irfan Shahīd, "Philological Observations on the Namâra Inscription," *Journal of Semitic Studies* 24 (1979): 33–42; and James A. Bellamy, "A New Reading of the Namārah Inscription," *Journal of the American Oriental Society* 105 (1985): 31–51.

7. About Christian materials, see Jane Dammen McAuliffe, *Qur'anic Christians* (Cambridge: Cambridge University Press, 1992).

8. Genesis 9:25–27.

9. Josephus, *Antiquities*, I.iii.1, English translation in Josephus, *Jewish Antiquities*, ed. and trans. H. St. J. Thackeray (London: Loeb Classical Library, 1930), 4:35, which also relates that Noah tried to convince people to improve their thoughts and acts.

10. See Louis Ginzberg, *The Legends of the Jews* (Philadelphia: Jewish Publication Society, 1947), 1:153–54, 5:74–75 nn19–20.

11. "It was only Noah He saved, the preacher of righteousness" (2 Pet. 2:5). The text does not quote the contents of Noah's preaching. The referential style indicates that the theme was known to the audience. See also Ginzberg, *Legends of the Jews*.

12. See Suras 11, 23, 26, and 71.

13. Qur'ān 10:90–92, cf. Jacob Z. Lauterbach, *Mekilta de-Rabbi Ishmael: A Critical Edition with an English Translation, Introduction and Notes* (Philadelphia: Jewish Publication Society, 1933–35), 1:163; *Pirke de-Rabbi Eliezer*, chapter 43.

14. Qur'ān 58:2–3, 33:4.

15. Joseph Schacht, *The Origins of Muhammadan Jurisprudence* (Oxford: Clarendon Press, 1950), 165, 203.

16. See al-Ṭabarī, *Jāmiʿ al-bayān*, 28:7.

17. Mishnah *Nedarim* 2:1.

18. Yerushalmi *Nedarim* 2:1, 37b.

19. Mordecai Margulies, *Hilkhot Erets Yisrael min ha-Geniza* (Jerusalem: Mosad Ha-Rav Kook, 1973), 81.

20. See the bibliographical survey of articles on Judeo-Arabic in Georges Vajda, "Études judéo-arabes," *Revue des Études Juives* 139.1–3 (1980): 41–44.

21. Norman Calder, "From Midrash to Scripture: The Sacrifice of Abraham in Early Islamic Tradition," *Le Muséon* 101 (1988): 375–402.

22. Ibn Manṣūr, *Mukhtaṣar Taʾrīkh Dimashq li-Ibn ʿAsākir*, 28 (Dimashq: Dār al-Fikr, 1989), 99–100. A nearly complete edition of the full text of Ibn ʿAsākir's work was published in 1995–2000 by Dār al-Fikr (Beirut) in eighty volumes. However, some parts are still missing, including the biography of Joshua.

23. *Pirke de-Rabbi Eliezer*, chapter 52 (quoted also in *Yalquṭ Shimʿoni*, II, sec. 22); cf. Ginzberg, *Legends of the Jews*, 4:10–11, 6:178n40.

24. See, e.g., *Leviticus Rabbah*, ed. Mordecai Margulies, 3rd ed. (New York: Jewish Theological Seminary of America Press, 1993), 756–57 (chapter 33).

25. Al-Ṭabarī, *Jāmiʿ al-bayān*, 21:67–68; to be sure, in the tradition quoted there, two organs feature: the tongue and the heart.

26. Ignaz Goldziher, "Ueber Bibelcitate in muhammedanischen Schriften," *Zeitschrift für Allttestamentlische Wissenaschaft* 13 (1893): 317, quoted by Hava Lazarus-Yafeh, *Intertwined Worlds: Medieval Islam and Bible Criticism* (Princeton, N.J.: Princeton University Press, 1992), 119n28.

27. The earliest and most explicit source regarding the Greek pun is *Pesikta de-Rav Kahana* (perhaps sixth century), ed. Bernard Mandelbaum (New York: Jewish Theological Seminary of America Press, 1987), 246–47 (chapter 14), where the Greek word is mentioned. It is then quoted in many later sources. The pun suggested here, which is based on a phonetic resemblance between biblical Hebrew and Arabic, may be compared to a pun in the Qur'ān

(Sura 4:46); see Reuven Firestone, "The Failure of a Jewish Program of Public Satire in the Squares of Medina," *Judaism* 46.4 (1997): 439–52. However, the pun discussed here seems to reflect an attempt to elucidate, in a popular or even homiletic way, a difficult and rare word in the biblical text. The pun discussed by Firestone, as interpreted by him, reflects an attempt by the Jews of al-Madīna to challenge and ridicule Muḥammad's authority. Firestone's interpretation assumes (or is conditioned by) a close relationship between the Qurʾānic text, its chronology (established by Theodor Nöldeke on the basis of Islamic tradition), and Muḥammad's biography.

28. Al-Ṭabarī, *Jāmiʿ al-bayān*, 21:91–93.

29. "God is He that created the heavens and the earth, and what between them is, in six days."

30. See further Qurʾān 22:47, 97:3.

31. Heinrich Speyer, *Die biblischen Erzählungen im Qoran* (repr.; Hildesheim: G. Olms, 1961), 24–25.

32. Ibid., 449, 455.

33. It seems related to Qurʾān 22:47 but not to 32:5.

34. *Genesis Rabbah* 6:6, 8:2 (ed. Theodor-Albeck, 45–46, 57).

35. Al-Ṭabarī, *Jāmiʿ al-bayān*, 23:76.

36. D. 65/685, cf. Etan Kohlberg, "Sulaymān b. Ṣurad," *Encyclopaedia of Islam*, 2nd ed., 9:826.

37. *Genesis Rabbah* 38:13 (ed. Theodor-Albeck, 364), according to which the one punished for his arrogance by death in Nimrod's furnace was Haran, Abraham's youngest brother and Lot's father.

38. A. Díez-Macho, *Neophyti* 1 (Madrid-Barcelona: Consejo Superior de Investigaciones Científicas, 1968), 1:60–61, 524 (English).

39. The final version of this study is still in preparation.

40. *Unzila al-qurʾān ʿalā sabʿa aʿruf*; for the sources, see A. T. Welch, "Qurʾān," *Encyclopaedia of Islam*, 2nd ed., 5:408; al-Ṭabarī, *Jāmiʿ al-bayān*, 1:11–29.

41. *Midrash Tanḥuma* (Warsaw), pericope Shemot, #25.

42. On the issue in Islam in general, see Daniel Gimaret, *Les noms divins en Islam* (Paris: Cerf, 1988), 85–94. In Judaism *shem rabbah* is mentioned in bSan 60a; *shma rabbah we-qaddisha* is mentioned in Pseudo-Jonathan ad Numbers 31:8. There, the Targum adduces a story about how Phinehas combated Balaam's witchcraft by means of the "Great and Holy Name" and brought him down from the sky in order to kill him with his sword (in a parallel passage in ySan 10:2, Phinehas uses the High Priest's frontlet, probably because it had the holy name inscribed on it). See also Jacob Lassner, *Demonizing the Queen of Sheba: Boundaries of Gender and Culture in Postbiblical Judaism and Medieval Islam* (Chicago: University of Chicago Press, 1993), 109–12 ("The Mightiest Name of God").

43. *Pirke de-Rabbi Eliezer*, chapter 3.

44. In Judaism, see Bavli *Qiddushin* 71a (name of forty-two letters); *Genesis Rabbah* 44:19 (ed. Theodor-Albeck, 442), and in Islam, Gimaret, *Noms divins*, 88–89; cf. Lawrence Harvey Schiffman, "The Forty-Two Letter Divine Name in the Aramaic Magic Bowls," *Bulletin of the Institute of Jewish Studies* 1 (1973): 97–102.

45. On the development of the phenomenon in Judaism and its background in antiquity, see Ephraim E. Urbach, *The Sages* (Cambridge, Mass.: Harvard University Press, 1987), 733–40.

46. This definition is used here instead of the more common term "mainstream Judaism," which I find difficult to define adequately.

47. A detailed analysis of the Sura is beyond the scope of the present study. For references to studies of the Sura, see Rudi Paret, *Der Koran: Kommentar und Konkordanz* (Stuttgart: Kohlhammer, 1979), 530, 555, including a brief discussion regarding the contents and language of the Sura.

48. *The Liturgical Poems of Rabbi Yannai According to the Triennial Cycle of the Pentateuch and the Holidays*, ed. Zvi Meir Rabinovitz (Jerusalem: Mosad Bialik, 1985), 388, #84/2, line 1 [Hebrew]; the translation is mine. I am indebted to Simon Hopkins for advice on the translation of this line. On the chronology of Yannai and the background of this poem, see p. 51; for further discussion and interpretation, cf. Joseph Yahalom, "Paradox in Late Antique Jewish Poetry," *Jewish Studies in a New Europe* (Proceedings of the Fifth Congress of Jewish Studies in Copenhagen, 1994), ed. Ulf Haxen et al. (Copenhagen: C. A. Reitzel, Det Kongelige Bibliotek, 1998), 886–905; Yahalom, *Poetry and Society in Jewish Galilee of Late Antiquity* (Jerusalem, Tel-Aviv: Yad Ben-Zvi and Ha-Kibbuts ha-Me'uḥad, 1999), 197–210 [Hebrew].

49. See John E. Wansbrough, *Quranic Studies: Sources and Methods of Scriptural Interpretation* (Oxford: Oxford University Press, 1977), 14, 18.

50. Al-Ṭabarī, *Jāmiʿ al-bayān*, 15:156.

51. Cf. Margaret Schlüter and Hans Georg von Mutius, *Synopse zur Hekhalot-Literatur*, ed. Peter Schäfer (Tübingen: Mohr, 1981), §§ 77 (pp. 38–39), 388 (pp. 164–65).

52. Cf. Lassner, *Queen of Sheba*, 135–37.

53. Cf. Lazarus-Yafeh, "Judaeo-Arabic Culture," 101–2: "Two periods can be clearly distinguished in the interrelationship of Judaism and Islam. During the first period—the 7th and maybe also the 8th centuries—Judaism, more than any other religion and culture, left a decisive impact on Islam, a new religion in the process of consolidation. In the second period—probably from the 8th century, and in particular from the 9th century onward—Islam, which had become a rich and variegated culture, profoundly influenced Jewish culture. Consequently, the interrelationship of these two cultures may be regarded as a closed circle, a rare phenomenon in cultural relationships." It is difficult to see how these two linear developments, moving in two opposite directions, can form "a closed circle."

54. See Joshua Blau, "Judaeo-Aramaic and Judaeo-Arabic: Why Judaeo-Arabic Did Not Become a Language of Prayer in the Synagogue," in *Jews and Judaism in the Second Temple, Mishna and Talmud Period: Studies in Honor of Shmuel Safrai*, ed. Isaiah Gafni et al. (Jerusalem: Yad Yizhak Ben-Zvi, 1993), 389–91 [Hebrew].

55. The explanation suggested in this essay has been mentioned by Lassner, *Queen of Sheba*, 125–26. Norman Calder suggested this line of argumentation with respect to the legal terminology and theory; see the quotation at the end of this essay.

56. To be sure, A. S. Yahuda, "A Contribution to Qur'ān and Ḥadīth Interpretation," in *Ignace Goldziher Memorial Volume*, vol. 1, ed. Samuel Loewinger and Joseph

Somogyi (Budapest: Globus, 1948), 280–308, is a serious attempt at discussing Qurʾān and early *ḥadīth* as one corpus. The question has also been asked separately with respect to historiography: see F. Rosenthal, "The Influence of Biblical Tradition," in *Historians of the Middle East*, ed. Bernard Lewis and P. M. Holt (London: Oxford University Press, 1962), 35–45. On pp. 35–39, Rosenthal discusses the influence of the biblical idea of history on Muḥammad. Rosenthal is of course committed to the connection between the Qurʾān, historical tradition, the biography of Muḥammad, and the limited environment of Arabia. He accepts the ascription of biblical materials in the papyri published by Nabia Abbott to Wahb b. Munabbih and Kaʿb al-Aḥbār (who died outside Arabia; p. 41). It is worth quoting Rosenthal's statement on p. 43: "Unless it can be shown that a given story cannot have come to the Muslims from Jewish or Christian sources, the Judaeo-Christian tradition remains the most likely source of origin in particular for all the older material."

57. Speyer, *Die biblischen Erzählungen*, 463, 492.

58. Cf. Hava Lazarus-Yafeh, "Tawrāt," *Encyclopaedia of Islam,* 2nd ed., 10:393–95; Lazarus-Yafeh, *Intertwined Worlds*, 114–15; Camilla Adang, "Torah," *Encyclopaedia of the Qurʾān*, 5:300–311.

59. A similar question may be asked regarding Christian materials in the Qurʾān and early Muslim traditions. Some modern students of Christian Arabic in fact argue for the existence of Arabic Bible translations prior to Islam (Bernhard Levin, *Die griechisch-arabische Evangelien-Übersetzung: Vat. Borg. ar. 95 und Ber. Orient. oct. 1108* [Uppsala: Almqvist & Wiksells Boktryckeri, 1938]). Most scholars, however, agree that there is no sound evidence for the existence of such translations before the second half of the eighth century. See Joshua Blau, "Sind uns Reste arabischer Bibelübersetzungen aus vorislamischerzeit erhalten geblieben?" *Le Muséon* 86 (1973): 67–72 (Blau, *Studies*, 291–96). Lazarus-Yafeh, *Intertwined Worlds*, 115, quotes from Abū Nuʿaym al-Iṣfāhānī, *Ḥilyat al-awliyāʾ* (Beirut: Dār al-Kitāb al-ʿArabī, 1985), 1:375, a story by Mālik b. Dīnār (d. 131/748–49) about a library of a monastery near Baṣra that contains translations of books from the Bible; p. 381 contains an Arabic translation of Psalm 1; cf. the statement of Joshua Blau, *A Grammar of Christian Arabic: Based Mainly on South-Palestinian Texts from the First Millennium* (Louvain: Secretariat du Corpus SCO, 1966–67), 1:20n7: "It stands to reason that some works copied in the ninth/tenth century were composed as far back as the eighth (and perhaps the seventh?) century." Be that as it may, the standing of Christian traditions was somewhat different than that of Jewish ones: They never attained that well-defined status in Muslim tradition that is expressed by the term *Isrāʾīliyyāt.*

60. On the Aramaic haggadic/midrashic paraphrases (such as Pseudo-Jonathan) and their relationship to more or less literal Aramaic translations, see Avigdor Shinan, *The Embroidered Targum* (Jerusalem: Magnes Press, 1992), especially chapter 2 [Hebrew], with references to additional publications . See also I. J. Mandelbaum, "Early Jewish Exegesis of Ex. 32: A Study of Targum Pseudo-Jonathan" (master's thesis, Oxford University, 1979). The author concludes on p. 122 that "Ps-J may be regarded as firmly connected to contemporary targumic and rabbinic exegesis, on the one hand, but as forming fresh interpretations from this exegesis, on the other."

61. Dimitri Gutas, *Greek Thought, Arabic Culture: The Greco-Arabic Translation Movement in Baghdad and Early ʿAbbāsid Society (2nd–4th/8th–10th Centuries)* (London: Routledge, 1998), esp. 136–41.

62. The late professor Shlomo Pines used to quote this information orally, on various occasions; I have no textual reference for this information.

63. Or made various editorial alterations or paraphrases. The texts in question include, for example, the translation of part of Aristotle's *Metaphysics* by Usṭāth, or of the *Theology* ascribed to Aristotle by ʿAbd al-Masīḥ b. ʿAbdallāh b. Naʿīma al-Ḥimṣī (ʿAbd al-Raḥmān Badawī, *Ufluṭīn ʿind al-ʿArab* [Cairo: Maktabat al-Nahḍa al-Miṣriyya, 1955], introduction); see Gutas, *Greek Thought*, 145, quoting Gerhard Endress, "The Circle of al-Kindī," in *The Ancient Tradition in Christian and Islamic Hellenism: Studies on the Transmission of Greek Philosophy and Sciences Dedicated to H. J. Drossaart Lulofs on His Ninetieth Birthday*, ed. Gerhard Endress and Remke Kruk (Leiden: Research School CNWS, School of Asian, African, and Amerindian Studies, 1997), 52–58. See also F. Rosenthal, "Al-Kindī and Ptolemy," *Studi Orientalistici in Onore di Giorgio Levi della Vida* (Roma: Instituto per l'Oriente, 1956), 2:436–56.

64. See G. Strohmaier, "Ḥunayn b. Isḥāq," *Encyclopaedia of Islam*, 2nd ed., 3:578–81; cf. Gutas, *Greek Thought*, 179; according to him, Ḥunayn could have found enough Greek manuscripts in locations within the political boundaries of Islam.

65. M. J. Kister, "Ḥaddithū ʿan Banū Isrāʾīl," *Israel Oriental Studies* 2 (1972): 215–39.

66. See Lassner, *Queen of Sheba*, 121.

67. It should be noted that Ignaz Goldziher, *Muhammedanische Studien* 2 (Halle: Max Niemeyer, 1890), 137 (English trans.: Samuel M. Stern, *Muslim Studies* [London: George Allen and Unwin, 1971], 131), quoted this tradition also from Jāḥiẓ, *Bayān* (Cairo, 1332 AH [1913/4]), 1:192, as a "secular" tradition. Goldziher discussed the matter again in *Die Richtungen der islamischen Koranauslegung* (1920; Leiden: Brill, 1970), 58 (English trans.: Wolfgang H. Behn, *Schools of Koranic Commentators* [Wiesbaden: Harrassowitz, 2006], 38), in relation to early exegetes who relied heavily on Jewish and Christian materials. The role of converts in the "Islamization" of Jewish traditions is also emphasized by Lassner, *Queen of Sheba*, 122–25; see also Bernard Lewis, *The Jews of Islam* (Princeton, N.J.: Princeton University Press, 1984), 67–106.

68. See Robert G. Hoyland, *Arabia and the Arabs: From the Bronze Age to the Coming of Islam* (London: Routledge, 2003), 78–83, 198–247, and passim; see also David J. Wasserstein, "Why Did Arabic Succeed Where Greek Failed? Language Change in the Near East After Muhammad," *Scripta Classica Israelica* 22 (2003): 257–72, and the response of Robert Hoyland, "Language and Identity: The Twin Histories of Arabic and Aramaic (and: Why Did Aramaic Succeed Where Greek Failed?)," *Scripta Classica Israelica* 23 (2004): 183–99.

69. This town was later known by its Arabic name al-Anbār (present-day Fallūja).

70. Aharon Oppenheimer, *Babylonia Judaica in the Talmudic Period* (Wiesbaden: Ludwig Reichert, 1983), especially pp. 366–67.

71. Medina was not the only Jewish community in the northwestern part of the Arabian Peninsula; see Haim Z. Hirschberg, "Arabia," *Encyclopaedia Judaica*, 2nd ed., 2:294–96.

72. See Irfan Shahīd, "Ṭayyiʾ," *Encyclopaedia of Islam,* 2nd ed., 10:402–3. Shahīd mentions that "Ṭayyiʾ played an important role in pre-Islamic times, and its name became the generic one for the Arabs in the Syriac sources, *ṭayyāyē* (West Syriac pronunciation, *ṭayōyē*)." He does not, however, make any mention of the numerous references to this generic name in Rabbinic sources.

73. The common view is that this term reflects the name of the Roman province Arabia, the southern part of Transjordan, which was populated mainly by Nabateans but also Arab tribes. The many lexicographic explanations in Rabbinic sources that quote usages "in Arabia" are sometimes based on Arabic words and sometimes in other languages, mostly Nabatean; see *Leviticus Rabbah* vol. 1, p. 9:7, and many references in the notes to parallels and to former studies; and Michael Sokoloff, *A Dictionary of Jewish Palestinian Aramaic of the Byzantine Period*, 2nd ed. (Ramat-Gan: Bar Ilan University Press; Baltimore: Johns Hopkins University Press, 2002), s.v. "*ṣ.w.ḥ.*"

74. Cf. Moshe Gil, "The Authorities and the Local Population," in *The History of Jerusalem: The Early Muslim Period, 638–1099*, ed. Joshua Prawer and Haggai Ben-Shammai (Jerusalem: Yad Izhak Ben-Zvi; New York: New York University Press, 1996), 111, who discusses the regulations that were aimed at discriminating against the "protected people" (*ahl al-dhimma*) in various aspects of daily private and communal life. According to Gil, "the kernel of these regulations is found in the letters of capitulation made with the local population." Chronologically, this means the first century of the Islamic era. Such agreements made with the people of the districts of Damascus-Palestine (*al-Shām*) mention, among others, prohibitions on Jews and Christians to use Arabic (script?) in the inscriptions of their seals and to study Qurʾān. It seems reasonable that the assumption underlying the decrees is that the people concerned would resort precisely to the practices mentioned, were it not for these prohibitions. It may thus indicate that Jews or Christians did in fact switch to Arabic already in the Umayyad period at the latest.

75. On Wahb b. Munabbih, see Raif Georges Khoury, "Wahb b. Munabbih," *Encyclopaedia of Islam,* 2nd ed., 11:34; and Gordon D. Newby, "The Drowned Son: Midrash and Midrash-Making in the Qurʾan and *Tafsir*," in *Studies in Islamic and Judaic Traditions*, ed. William M. Brinner and Stephen D. Ricks (Atlanta: Scholars Press, 1986), 30n7. Lazarus-Yafeh, *Intertwined Worlds,* 112, discusses the possibility that authors of collections of *qiṣaṣ al-anbiyāʾ* (by al-Kisāʾī, al-Thaʿālibī) used some kind of an Arabic paraphrase of biblical stories, like Aramaic translations. She refers there to a number of more or less literal translations in al-Ṭabarī, *Taʾrīkh,* 1:167, 636, 639–40, 658; al-Ṭabarī, *Tafsīr,* ad Qurʾān 21:83 (al-Ṭabarī, *Jāmiʿ al-bayān*, 17:57–69); these passages are quoted as traditions on the authority of Wahb, but this is not mentioned by Lazarus-Yafeh. She discusses the question whether Ibn Qutayba could have access to the Hebrew text of the Bible, but the question is not relevant if we consider that there were Judeo-Arabic translations in the format used by Ibn Qutayba. See also Michael Pregill, "Isrāʾīliyyāt, Myth, and Pseudepigraphy: Wahb b. Munabbih and the Early Islamic Versions of the Fall of Adam and Eve," *Jerusalem Studies in Arabic and Islam* 34 (2008): 215–84, esp. 215–22, who describes the approach of modern scholarship in ascribing a pivotal role in the absorption of Jewish materials in early Islamic sources to such converts in terms of "consensus" and "basic axiom" and intends to reevaluate this approach.

76. Some of them have been edited by Raif Georges Khoury, *Wahb b. Munabbih*, vols. 1–2 (Wiesbaden: O. Harrassowitz, 1972; *Codices Arabici antique*, Bd. 1).

77. A tradition about Job is recorded in al-Ṭabarī, *Jāmiʿ al-bayān*, 17:65 (ad Qurʾān 21:83) in the name of "Wahb b. Munabbih al-Yamānī and others of the people of the early books (*wa-ghayruhu min ahl-al-kutub al-uwal*)"; see also D. J. Halperin and Gordon Newby, "Two Castrated Bulls: A Study in the Haggadah of Kaʿb al-Aḥbār," *JAOS* 102 (1982): 631–38.

78. In addition to various eschatological popular, magical, or astrological, works in Arabic entitled *Kitāb Danyāl*, see G. Vajda, "Daniyāl," *Encyclopaedia of Islam*, 2nd ed., 2:112–13.

79. Josef Horovitz, *Koranische Untersuchungen* (Berlin: Walter de Gruyter, 1926), 91.

80. Like the case of Isḥāq; Horovitz, *Koranische Untersuchungen*, 90.

81. Horovitz refers to Martin Hartmann, *Der islamische Orient*, vol. 2, *Die arabische Frage* (Leipzig: Rudolf Haupt, 1909), 620, who says that Muḥammad had in mind an actual ethnic ("völkische") group.

82. One could add 2:40 as well.

83. Horovitz, *Koranische Untersuchungen*, 153–54.

84. The issue of the chronology of the Qurʾān is beyond the scope of the present study. Suffice it to say that the chronology that is rather widely current in Western Islamic studies since Nöldeke is not to be taken for granted.

85. Indeed, Uri Rubin, *Between Bible and Qurʾān* (Princeton, N.J.: Princeton University Press, 1999), 2, thinks that the term *Banū Isrāʾīl* normally denotes "the others," i.e., all non-Muslim monotheists, while those groups are "sometimes" called *Yahūd* or *Naṣārā*; see also p. 60 and elsewhere.

86. See, e.g., Cynthia Baker, "When Jews Were Women," *History of Religions* 45 (2005): 114–34 (I am indebted to David Freidenreich for this reference); and Peter J. Tomson, "The Names Israel and Jew in Ancient Judaism and in the New Testament," *Bijdragen* 47 (1986): 120–40, 266–89. As is evident from the title, Tomson aims to compare the use of the names "in ancient Jewish texts with their use in the New Testament." Consequently he is committed to "early" Jewish texts that are contemporaneous with the New Testament or close to that. Tomson published his study when efficient search tools had not been as available and accessible as they are now, which may have affected the results of his investigation.

87. Thus Baker, "When Jews Were Women," 123, quotes an example from Mishnah *ʿAvodah Zarah* 2:1: "A daughter of Israel may not assist a Gentile woman in childbirth, but a Gentile woman may suckle the child of a daughter of Israel." But a parallel text is quoted in a *barayta* (i.e., "early" Palestinian?) in the Babylonian Talmud, *ʿAvodah Zarah* 26a, that says, "A Jewess [*yehudit*] may assist a heathen/Aramean woman in childbirth for payment."

88. It may be interesting to note that in Onkelos on Exodus 1–10 (only there, not in Genesis or in Exodus 21) the Hebrew term *ʿIvri* is translated consistently by *Yehuday* (or inflected forms according to gender and number). A similar translation is found in Jonah 1:9.

89. Al-Bukhārī, *Ṣaḥīḥ* (Cairo: Maktabat al-Mashhad al-Ḥusaynī, n.d.), 9:193; see also 6:25, where it is adduced in the context of *tafsir* on Qurʾān 2:136. This tradition is quoted by Lazarus-Yafeh, *Intertwined Worlds*, 120, with references to other sources; she

renders *yufassirūnaha* as "translate and explain," which is acceptable, since the root *f.s.r.* in the second form has a variety of meanings, including interpretations of every imaginable size or format.

90. The ascription to Abū Hurayra is not of much relevance here.

91. He died in 870 CE; his compilation dates therefore from roughly the middle of the ninth century.

92. See the discussion of Goldziher, *Muhammedanische Studien*, 2:234–36 (English trans.: 2:216–18).

93. *Teshuvot Rav Naṭronai Bar Hilai Gaon*, ed. Robert Brody (Jerusalem: Ofeq Institute, 1994), 152–54 (see parallel sources in the footnotes); see also *Otzar ha-Geonim*, ed. Benjamin M. Lewin, vol. 5: *Megilla* (Jerusalem: The Hebrew University Press Association, 1932), 30–31. Naṭronai did, however, allow informal study of Bible interpretations in that language.

94. See Tsvi Langerman, "Eimatai nosad ha-luaḥ ha-yehudi," *Asufot* 1 (1987): 159–68.

95. See Fuat Sezgin, *Geschichte des arabischen Schrifttums*, vol. 5: *Mathematik* (Leiden: Brill, 1974), 228–41; vol. 6: *Astronomie* (Leiden: Brill, 1978), 140–43; J. Vernet, "Al-Khʷārazmī," *Encyclopaedia of Islam*, 2nd ed., 4:1069–71; and Gutas, *Greek Thought*, index, s.v. "al-Ḫwārizmī, Muḥammad ibn Mūsā."

96. See Joshua Blau, "On a Fragment of the Oldest Judaeo-Arabic Bible Translation Extant," *Genizah Research After Ninety Years: The Case of Judaeo-Arabic*, ed. Joshua Blau and Stefan C. Reif (Cambridge: Cambridge University Press, 1992), 31–39.

97. See Neil Danzig, *Introduction to Halakhot Pesuqot* (New York: Jewish Theological Seminary of America Press, 1993) [Hebrew]; and Robert Brody, *The Geonim of Babylonia and the Shaping of Medieval Jewish Culture* (New Haven, Conn.: Yale University Press, 1998), 217–23.

98. From a later period one finds statements of R. Hay Gaon concerning villagers who are not knowledgeable or accurate in the text of the Hebrew Scripture. See *Otzar ha-Geonim*, ed. Benjamin M. Lewin, vol. 1: *Berakhot* (Haifa, 1928), 114.

99. Albeit so far quite briefly, in my "Between Ananites and Karaites: Observations on Early Medieval Jewish Sectarianism," *Studies in Muslim-Jewish Relations* 1 (1992): 19–29.

100. See the discussion in my essay "The Rabbinic Literature in Seʿadya's Exegesis: Between Tradition and Innovation," in *Heritage and Innovation in Medieval Judaeo-Arabic Culture* (Proceedings of the Sixth Conference of the Society for Judaeo-Arabic Studies), ed. Joshua Blau and David Doron (Ramat-Gan: Bar-Ilan University Press, 2000), 33–69, esp. pp. 37, 68 [Hebrew].

101. Geiger's work appeared in English translation by F. M. Young, *Judaism and Islam* (Madras, 1898; repr., Tel-Aviv: Zohar, 1969; New York: Ktav, 1970). See Jacob Lassner, "Abraham Geiger: A Nineteenth-Century Jewish Reformer on the Origins of Islam," in *The Jewish Discovery of Islam*, ed. M. Kramer (Tel-Aviv: Moshe Dayan Center, 1999), 103–36 (an appraisal of Geiger's work, including a description of the historical circumstances of Young's English translation).

102. Norman Calder, "Sharīʿa," *Encyclopaedia of Islam,* 2nd ed., 9:322 (I thank Miriam Goldstein for drawing my attention to this quote). Calder refers to the works of

Wansbrough: *Quranic Studies* and *The Sectarian Milieu: Content and Composition of Islamic Salvation History* (Oxford: Oxford University Press, 1978).

CHAPTER 2. *Shurūṭ ʿUmar*

1. Antoine Fattal, *Le statut légal des non-musulmans en pays d'Islam* (Beirut: Dar el-Machreq, 1958), 103. The italics are mine.

2. Shlomo Dov Goitein, *A Mediterranean Society*, vol. 2, *The Community* (Berkeley: University of California Press, 1971), 287–88.

3. Moshe Gil, *A History of Palestine, 634–1099* (New York: Cambridge University Press, 1992), 159.

4. See Fattal, *Statut légal,* 97–101; Abū Yūsuf Yaʿqūb, *Kitāb al-kharāj* (Cairo: Al-Maṭbaʿa al-Salafiyya, 1302), 127; *Chronique de Michel le Syrien*, ed. Jean Baptiste Chabot (1899–1910; Bruxelles: Culture et civilisation, 1963), 2:489. Fattal, *Statut légal,* 98, cites the twelfth-century jurist al-Kasānī, as well as Christian writers, who also attribute the invention of the *ghiyār* to ʿUmar b. ʿAbd al-ʿAzīz.

5. See Milka Levy-Rubin, "The Date and Ideology Behind the Emergence of the *Ghiyār* Code," in *Non-Muslims in the Early Islamic Empire: From Surrender to Coexistence* (Cambridge: Cambridge University Press, 2011), 88–98.

6. See Milka Levy-Rubin, "*Shurūṭ ʿUmar* and Its Alternatives: The Legal Debate on the Status of the *Dhimmīs,*" *Jerusalem Studies in Arabic and Islam* 30 (2005): 170–207. Daniel E. Miller, "From Catalogue to Codes to Canon: The Rise of the Petition to ʿUmar Among Legal Traditions Governing Non-Muslims in Medieval Islamicate Societies" (Ph.D. diss., University of Missouri–Kansas City, 2000), with which I became acquainted only in 2007, comes to a similar conclusion regarding the existence of several competing codes. See chapter 3, "Developing the Catalogue," 86–114. I would like to thank Professor Mark Cohen for referring me to this work.

7. This accords with the opinion of Daniel Miller, who also noted the connection between the two but presumes that it was al-Mutawakkil's decrees that brought about the rise in the popularity of the *shurūṭ* (Miller, "From Catalogue to Codes to Canon," 204–5). I would prefer to say that al-Mutawakkil's restrictions were likely based on an existing document and that there is no reason to doubt that this document was a version of *shurūṭ ʿUmar.*

8. See Arthur S. Tritton, *The Caliphs and Their Non-Muslim Subjects* (London: Oxford University Press, 1930); Fattal, *Statut légal.*

9. The most important works on this subject are Tritton, *Caliphs*; Eliyahu Strauss (Ashtor), "The Social Isolation of Ahl al-Dhimma," *Études Orientales à la mémoire de Paul Hirschler*, ed. O. Komlos (Budapest: J. Kertész, 1950), 73–94 (reprinted in *The Medieval Near East: Social and Economic History* [London: Variorum, 1978]); Fattal, *Statut légal*; Albrecht Noth, "Abgrenzungsprobleme zwischen Muslimen und Nicht-Muslimen—Die 'Bedingungen ʿUmars (*aš-Šurūṭ al-ʿumariyya*)' unter einem anderen Aspekt gelesen," *Jerusalem Studies in Arabic and Islam* 9 (1987): 290–315; Mark R. Cohen, "What Was the Pact of ʿUmar? A Literary-Historical Study," *Jerusalem Studies in Arabic and Islam* 23 (1999): 100–157.

10. See Andrew Palmer et al., *The Seventh Century in West-Syrian Chronicles* (Liverpool: Liverpool University Press, 1993), 169–70. The conflict over the public display of the cross by Christians is discussed by Sidney H. Griffith in "Images, Islam and Christian Icons," *La Syrie de Byzance à l'Islam VIIe–VIIIe siècles: Actes du Colloque international Lyon—Maison de l'Orient Méditerranéen Paris—Institut du Monde Arabe 11–15 Septembre 1990*, ed. Pierre Canivet and Jean-Paul Rey-Coquais (Damascus: Institut Français de Damas, 1992), 121–38.

11. See Dionysius of Tell Mahrē in Palmer, *Seventh Century*, text no. 12, AG 1015, 78; see also Palmer's reference to *Chronique de Michel le Syrien,* 447, ll. 17–20, who reports an order to remove all crosses in the same context.

12. See n. 32 below.

13. Daniel C. Dennett, *Conversion and the Poll Tax in Early Islam* (Cambridge, Mass.: Harvard University Press, 1950), 78–84.

14. Abū Yūsuf, *Kitāb al-kharāj*, 127–28; ʿAbd al-Razzāq al-Ṣanʿānī, *Al-muṣannaf*, vol. 6 (Beirut: Dar al-Qalam, 1972), 61, no. 10004; Abū ʿUbayd al-Qāsim b. Sallām, *Kitāb al-amwāl* (Cairo: Al-Maktaba al-Tijāriyya al-Kubrā, 1353 AH), 53, no. 137; Ibn ʿAbd al-Ḥakam, *Sīrat ʿUmar b. ʿAbd al-ʿAzīz* (Cairo: Dar al-Faḍīla, 1994), 160; see also Levy-Rubin, "The Date and the Ideology Behind the Emergence of the *Ghiyār* Code."

15. Abū Yūsuf, *Kitāb al-kharāj*, 127; see also ʿAbd al-Razzāq al-Ṣanʿānī, *Al- muṣannaf*, vol. 6, 61, no. 10004.

16. Michael the Syrian, *Chronique*, 2:489; ʿAbd al-Razzāq al-Ṣanʿānī, *Al-muṣannaf*, vol. 6, 61, no. 10004.

17. Michael the Syrian, *Chronique*, 2:489.

18. See Fattal, *Statut légal,* 185–86, citing Abū ʿUbayd, *Kitāb al-amwāl*, 95; al-Ṭurṭushī, *Sirāj al-mulūk* (Cairo, 1289 AH), 138; Muḥammad b. Jarīr al-Ṭabarī, *Taʾrīkh*, ed. M. J. de Goeje II, 1371–72 (translated in *The History of al-Ṭabarī*, vol. 24, *The Empire in Transition,* trans. and annot. D. S. Powers [Albany: State University of New York Press, 1989], 101). See also Levy-Rubin, "*Shurūṭ ʿUmar,*" 176–79.

19. See ʿAbd al-Razzāq al-Ṣanʿānī, *Al-muṣannaf*, vol. 6, 19–20; compare with vol. 10, 319–20.

20. Tritton, *Caliphs*, 42–43.

21. See ibid., 102, adducing evidence in favor, and Michael the Syrian, *Chronique,* who claims that ʿUmar forbade tithes and bequests to churches.

22. See Levy-Rubin, "The Date and the Ideology Behind the Emergence of the *Ghiyār* Code."

23. See ʿAlī b. al-Ḥasan Ibn ʿAsākir, *Taʾrīkh dimashq* (Beirut: Dār al-Fikr, 1995), 34:236–59; and Jamāl al-Dīn Abū al-Ḥajjāj Yūsuf al-Mizī, *Tahdhīb al-kamāl fī asmāʾ al-rijāl* (Beirut: Muʾassasat al-Risāla, 1992), 17:12–18.

24. Abū Yūsuf, *Kitāb al-kharāj*, 127–28.

25. The usual term is *zunnār*, the term used by Abū Yūsuf himself in the previous paragraph describing the prohibitions of his day. The use of the term *minṭaqa,* which is later reserved for military and honorary belts, may point to the early date of this tradition, before a clear distinction was made between these two terms. On this distinction see my

Non-Muslims in the Early Islamic Empire: From Surrender to Coexistence (Cambridge: Cambridge University Press, 2011), 154–57.

26. See Abū Yūsuf, *Kitāb al-kharāj*, 127–28.

27. Theophanes, *Chronographia*, ed. Carl de Boor (Leipzig: Teubner, 1883–85), 431 (English translation: *The Chronicle of Theophanes Confessor*, trans. with introduction and commentary by Cyril Mango and Roger Scott [Oxford: Blackwell, 1997], 596).

28. Theophanes, *Chronographia*, 439 (Mango, *Chronicle*, 607).

29. Theophanes, *Chronographia*, 446 (Mango, *Chronicle*, 616); see also Jean Baptiste Chabot, ed., *Incerti auctoris chronicon anonymum pseudo-Dionysianum vulgo dictum* (Louvain: L. Durbecq, 1933), 104–5 (trans.: 123–24).

30. Theophanes, *Chronographia*, 430 (Mango, *Chronicle*, 595).

31. See n. 10.

32. See Aḥmad b. Yaḥya al-Balādhurī, *Kitāb futūḥ al-buldān*, ed. M. J. de Goeje (Leiden: Brill, 1866), 193; al-Jahshiyārī, *Kitāb al-wuzarāʾ wa-ʾl-kuttāb* (Cairo: Maṭbaʿat Ḥanafī, 1938), 38–40. Both of these sources make a clear connection between the Arabization of the administration and the ousting of prominent non-Muslims from the administration, although of course practically this goal was much harder to achieve. See also A. A. Duri, "Diwān," *Encyclopaedia of Islam*, 2nd ed., 2:324; Gerald R. Hawting, *The First Dynasty of Islam* (New York: Routledge, 2000), 63–65. There are many traditions relating how ʿUmar b. al-Khaṭṭāb adamantly prohibited the employment of non-Muslims in government offices; even if this were indeed true, this was definitely unfeasible at the time. For a survey on this issue, see Fattal, *Statut légal*, 240–63.

33. Theophanes, *Chronographia*, 430 (Mango, *Chronicle*, 594). The name is miswritten in the text as Salim. Ṣāliḥ was governor of Egypt until 757/8 CE.

34. Al-Ṭabarī, *Taʾrīkh*, III, 712–13 (translated in *The History of al-Ṭabarī*, vol. 30, *The ʿAbbāsid Caliphate in Equilibrium*, trans. and annot. C. E. Bosworth [Albany: State University of New York Press, 1989], 89–93).

35. See ibid., 712, 89–91; al-Azdī, *Taʾrīkh al-mawṣil*, ed. A. Ḥabība (Cairo: Muʾassasat Dār al-Taḥrīr, 1967), 311; Tritton, *Caliphs*, 117–18; Fattal, *Statut légal*, 100–101.

36. See Milka Levy-Rubin, *The Continuatio of the Samaritan Chronicle of Abūʾ ʾl-Fatḥ al-Sāmirī al-Danafī* (Princeton, N.J.: Darwin Press, 2002), 90.

37. See al-Ṭabarī, *Taʾrīkh*, III, 1389–92 (translated in *The History of al-Ṭabarī*, vol. 34, *Incipient Decline*, trans. and annot. Joel L. Kraemer [Albany: State University of New York Press, 1989], 268).

38. ʿAbd al-Raḥmān b. ʿAlī b. Muḥammad b. al-Jawzī, *Al-muntaẓam fī taʾrīkh al-muluk wa-ʾl-umam* (Beirut: Dār al-Kutub al-ʿIlmiyya, 1992), 13:82; Jamāl al-Dīn abī al-Maḥāsin Taghrī Birdi, *Al-nujūm al-ẓāhira fī mulūk miṣr wa-ʾl-qāhira*, ed. Gautier H. A. Juynboll (Leiden: Brill, 1861), 174–75. M. Belin, "Fetoua sur la condition des *dhimmīs*," *Journal Asiatique*, 4th ser., 18 (1851): 455, reports that al-Muqtadir forbade the employment of *dhimmīs* in the government, gave an order to dismiss all *dhimmīs* already employed, and went as far as executing one such *dhimmī* employed by the *ḥājib* Yūnus. Fattal, *Statut légal*, 103, reports that Muḥammad al-Ikhshīd enforced a similar set of rules but does not cite the actual source.

39. Aḥmad b. ʿAlī Al-Maqrīzī, *Ittiʿāẓ al-ḥunafāʾ bi-akhbār al-ʾumūr al-fāṭimiyīn al-khulafāʾ* (Cairo: Al-Majlis al-aʿlā li-ʾl-Shuʾūn al-Islāmiyya, 1967), 1:132; Tritton, *Caliphs*, 54, 120, 130, and passim.

40. On the restrictions of al-Ḥākim, see Yaacov Lev, "Persecutions and Conversion to Islam in Eleventh-Century Egypt," *Asian and African Studies* 22 (1988): 80–83.

41. Al-Ṭabarī, *Taʾrīkh*, III, 1419 (34:128).

42. See also Ibn al-Jawzī, *Al-muntaẓam*, 11:222–23. I thank Prof. Yaacov Lev for kindly sharing with me these references to Ibn al-Jawzī's *Muntaẓam*.

43. Ibid., 238.

44. Ibid., 265.

45. Ibid., 270.

46. Yassā ʿAbd al-Masīḥ and Oswald H. E. Burmester, eds., *History of the Patriarchs of the Egyptian Church by Sawīrus ibn al-Muqaffāʿ*, vol. 2, part 1 (Cairo: Institut français d'archéologie orientale, 1943), 6.

47. *The Chronography of Abū ʾl Faraj Known as Bar-Hebraeus*, trans. Ernest A. Wallis Budge (Oxford: Oxford University Press, 1932), 1:141.

48. Levy-Rubin, *Continuatio*.

49. Ibid., 91–93.

50. See Yedida K. Stillman and Paula Sanders, "Ṭirāz," *Encyclopaedia of Islam*, 2nd ed., 10:534.

51. According to al-Ṭabarī, this served as the distinguishing sign for the lower strata of society, who did not wear special mantles and hoods. The higher strata were distinguished, according to him, by the honey color of their clothes; al-Ṭabarī, *Taʾrīkh*, III, 1389, 1392 (34:89–90, 93).

52. See al-Ṭabarī, *Taʾrīkh*, III, 1389 (34:89–90).

53. See ibid., 1390 (34:90): "In addition, he ordered that their graves be made level with the ground so as not to resemble the graves of the Muslims" (34:91).

54. See ibid., 1390 (34:90); al-Ṭabarī calls these idols *ṣuwar shayāṭīn*, i.e., images of devils. The reason given for this is cited by Ashtor, "Social Isolation," 80: "if the houses of the *Dhimmīs* will not bear distinctive signs the beggars approaching them will beg Allāh's mercy upon them and his forgiveness for their sins, and this—say the theologians—is absolutely forbidden." This was surely a restriction that was meant to be derogatory, since both *shayṭān* and *wathan* are definitely negative terms.

55. The word used here is the Hebrew word *goy*—literally a man belonging to a different faith, a non-Jewish person—in Samaritan script.

56. Al-Ṭabarī, *Taʾrīkh*, III, 1419 (34:127).

57. See Ibn ʿAsākir, *Taʾrīkh dimashq*, 2:175–77, 179; Muḥammad b. Abī Bakr Ibn Qayyim al-Jawziyya, *Aḥkām ahl al-dhimma*, vol. 2, ed. Ṣubḥi al-Ṣāliḥ (Damascus: Matbaʿat Jāmiʿat Dimashq, 1961), 659, 661–62; *shurūṭ al-naṣārā* in Cohen, "What Was the Pact of ʿUmar?" 137–39, 142, 146.

58. Al-Ṭabarī, *Taʾrīkh*, III, 1393 (34:93–94); Cohen, "What Was the Pact of ʿUmar?" 151.

59. Al-Ṭabarī, *Taʾrīkh*, III, 1393 (34:93–94).

60. Abū Yūsuf, *Kitāb al-kharāj*, 96.

61. ʿArīb b. Saʿd al-Qurṭubī, *Ṣilat taʾrīkh al-Ṭabarī*, ed. M. J. de Goeje (Leiden: Brill, 1965), 30.

62. Ibid.

63. See Ibn Qayyim al-Jawziyya, *Aḥkām ahl al-dhimma*, 1:212–42; for Ibn al-Naqqāsh, see M. Belin, "Fetoua sur la condition des *dhimmīs*," *Journal Asiatique*, 4th ser., 18 (1851): 417–516, esp. 440–55; vol. 19 (1852/2): 97–140.

64. See Levy-Rubin, *Continuatio*, 103–4; ms. p. 251.

65. The word used here is *nabīdh*; this is an alcoholic drink usually made of raisins or dates. It could, however, also mean "wine expressed from grapes"; see E. W. Lane, *Arabic–English Lexicon* (1863; Cambridge: Islamic Texts Society Trust, 1984), 2757.

66. Michael the Syrian, *Chronique*, 2:489; *Chronicon ad annum christi 1234 pertinens*, ed. and trans. Jean Baptiste Chabot (1916; Louvain: L. Durbecq, 1952/3), text, 1:307–8 (trans.: 239); Agapius b. Maḥbūb, *Kitāb al-ʿunwān*, ed. and trans. Alexandre Vasiliev, *Patrologia Orientalis*, vol. 8, part 3 (Turnhout: Brepols, 1971), 502–3.

67. Theophanes, *Chronographia*, 399 (Mango, *Chronicle*, 550).

68. Muḥammad b. Idrīs al-Shāfiʿī, *Kitāb al-umm* (Beirut: Dār al-Kutub al-ʿIlmiyya, 1993), 4:281, 283.

69. See, e.g., Ibn Qayyim al-Jawziyya, *Aḥkām ahl al-dhimma*, 2:659, 661–62.

70. Levy-Rubin, *Continuatio*, 102–6, ms. pp. 251–53.

71. Regarding the enforcement of *ghiyār* regulations under his rule, see Alexander Scheiber, "A New Fragment of the Life of Obadiah, the Norman Proselyte," *Kiryat Sefer* 30 (1954–55): 93–98.

72. See text and note 63 above.

73. See, e.g., Fattal, *Statut légal*, 102–10; and Mark R. Cohen, *Under Crescent and Cross: The Jews in the Middle Ages* (Princeton, N.J.: Princeton University Press, 1995), 62–68.

74. On al-Ḥākim, see n. 40 above; regarding Salāḥ al-Dīn, see ʿAbd al-Masīḥ and Burmester, *History of the Patriarchs of the Egyptian Church by Sawīrus ibn al-Muqaffaʿ*, vol. 3, part 2 (Cairo: Institut Français d'Archéologie Orientale, 1968), 97–98 (trans.: 164–66).

CHAPTER 3. THINKERS OF "THIS PENINSULA"

1. Among modern scholars, see, e.g., Muḥammad Ibrāhīm al-Fayyūmī, *Taʾrīkh al-falsafa al-islāmiyya fī al-maghrib wa-ʾl-andalus* (Beirut: Dār al-Jīl, 1997), 6.

2. See Ibn Ḥazm, *Risāla fī Faḍl al-andalus wa-dhikri rijālihā*, in *Rasāʾil Ibn Ḥazm al-andalusī*, ed. Iḥsān ʿAbbās (Beirut: Al-Muʾassasa al-ʿArabiyya liʾl-Dirāsāt wa-ʾl-Nashr, 1981), 2:186–87; and Ibn Ṭumlūs, *Kitāb al-madkhal ilā ṣināʿat al-manṭiq*, ed. Miguel Asín-Palacios (Madrid: Al-Maṭbaʿa al-Ubayriqa, 1916), 9–12. Al-Maqqarī is quoted in Solomon Munk, *Mélanges de philosophie juive et arabe* (Paris: Nouvelles Éditions, 1955), 309–458, reprinted as Solomon Munk, *Des principaux philosophes arabes et de leur doctrine* (Paris: Vrin, 1982), 334.

3. See David H. Baneth, "Judah Halevi and al-Ghazali," *Kenesset* 7 (1941–42): 311–29 [Hebrew].

4. See Shlomo Pines, "Shī'ite Terms and Conceptions in Judah Halevi's *Kuzari*," *Jerusalem Studies in Arabic and Islam* 2 (1980): 165–261; Ehud Krinnis, "The Idea of Chosen People in *al-Kitāb al-khazārī* and Its Sources in Imāmī Shī'ism" (Ph.D. diss., Ben Gurion University, 2007) [Hebrew]; and Diana Lobel, *Between Mysticism and Philosophy: Sufi Language of Religious Experience in Judah Ha-Levi's "Kuzari"* (Albany: State University of New York Press, 2000).

5. See Amos Goldreich, "On Possible Arabic Sources for the Distinction Between Duties of the Heart and Duties of the Body," *Te'uda* 6 (1988): 179–208 [Hebrew].

6. See, e.g., Shlomo Pines, "Translator's Introduction: The Philosophic Sources of the *Guide of the Perplexed*," in Moses Maimonides, *The Guide of the Perplexed*, trans. Pines (Chicago: University of Chicago, 1963), lvii–cxxxiv; Alfred L. Ivry, "The Guide and Maimonides' Philosophical Sources," in *The Cambridge Companion to Maimonides*, ed. Kenneth Seeskin (Cambridge: Cambridge University Press, 2005), 58–81; and Steven Harvey, "Medieval Sources of Maimonides' *Guide*," *Bulletin de Philosophie Médiéval* 46 (2000): 283–87.

7. See, e.g., Dominique Urvoy, "The Ulamā' of al-Andalus," in *The Legacy of Muslim Spain*, ed. Salma K. Jayyusi (Leiden: Brill, 1992), 849–75. Urvoy suggests that "the Christians and Jews of Spain . . . caused traditional factors to predominate within Islam itself on their conversion, and from this springs the 'deliberate conservatism, even archaising,' character which Lévy-Provençal regards as the characteristic quality of Andalusian Islam" (849). Miguel Cruz Hernández, *Historia del pensamiento en el mundo islámico*, 3 vols., especially vol. 2, *El pensamiento de al-Andalus (siglos IX–XIV)* (Madrid: Alianza, 1996).

8. Although, as Dimitri Gutas has shown, their involvement in the translation movement was less dominant than hitherto believed; see Gutas, *Greek Thought, Arabic Culture: The Graeco-Arabic Translation Movement in Baghdad and Early 'Abbasid Society (2nd–4th/8th–10th Centuries)* (London: Routledge, 1998); and Sarah Stroumsa, "Philosophy as Wisdom: On the Christians' Role in the Translation of Philosophical Material to Arabic," in *Exchange and Transmission Across Cultural Boundaries: Philosophy and Science in the Mediterranean World*, ed. Haggai Ben-Shammai, Shaul Shaked, and Sarah Stroumsa (Jerusalem: Israel Academy of Sciences and Humanities, forthcoming).

9. A translation movement that appeared in Spain in the twelfth century led in the opposite direction, transmitting the Muslim heritage (via Jewish converts who translated the Arabic to Castilian) to the Latin-speaking Christians; see José L. Abellán, *Historia crítica del pensamiento español*, vol. 1, *Metodología, introducción general* (Madrid: Espasa-Calpe, 1979), 198, 210–18. On the role of Jews as transmitters of the Arabic philosophical lore to the West, see also Munk, *Des principaux philosophes arabes*, 335, 439.

10. See Dominique Urvoy, *Pensers d'al-Andalus: La vie intellectuelle à Seville et Cordoue au temps des empires berbères (fin XIe siècle–débuts XIIIe siècle)* (Toulouse: Presses Universitaires de Mirail,1990), 29, 33. See also Bernard F. Reilly, *The Contest of Christian and Muslim Spain* (Oxford: Blackwell, 1992), 17–18.

11. Ann Christys, *Christians in al-Andalus (711–1000)* (Richmond: Curzon, 2002), 23.

12. According to Reilly, *The Contest of Christian and Muslim Spain*, 14–15, the Jewish community was "the most literate community of the peninsula," which may explain their disproportionate representation in written sources. A similar situation, where the philosophy that was out of favor in Islam found refuge among the Jews, is commonly depicted concerning the end of the twelfth century, with the translation of philosophical texts from Arabic to Latin; see Munk, *Des principaux philosophes arabes*, 335.

13. The specific, independent character of Andalusian thought is often downplayed by scholars. See, e.g., Abellán, *Historia crítica del pensamiento español,* 181, who admits the existence of autonomous elements but insists on Oriental influence and generally regards Andalusian philosophy as "but a continuation of the topics and problems which occupied Islamic thought as a whole."

14. See E. I. J. Rosenthal, ed. and trans., *Averroes' Commentary on Plato's "Republic"* (Cambridge: Cambridge University Press, 1956), 97. The Arabic original is not extant, and the medieval Hebrew translation reads *meḥozenu.* Aḥmad Shaḥlān, who reconstructed the Arabic from the Hebrew, suggests *ṣaqʿinā*; see *Al-Ḍarūrī fī'l-siyāsa: Mukhtaṣar kitāb al-siyāsa li-aflāṭūn* (Beirut: Markaz Dirāsāt al-Waḥda al-ʿArabiyya, 1998), 195. For the Commentary on *Meteorology*, see Abū al-Walīd ibn Rushd, *Talkhīṣ al-āthār al-ʿulwiyya*, ed. Jamāl al-Dīn al-ʿAlawī (Beirut: Dār al-Gharb al-Islāmī, 1994), 103–4 ("*hādhihi al-jazīra*").

15. See Moses ibn Ezra, *Kitāb al-muḥāḍara wa'l-mudhākara*, ed. Montserrat Abumalham Mas (Madrid: Consejo Superior de Investigaciones Científicas, Instituto de Filología, 1985), 1:59.

16. See Joshua Blau, "'At Our Place in al-Andalus,' 'At Our Place in the Maghreb,'" in *Perspectives on Maimonides: Philosophical and Historical Studies*, ed. Joel L. Kraemer and Lawrence V. Berman (Oxford: Oxford University Press, 1991), 293–94.

17. See, e.g., the structure of Josef van Ess's *Theologie und Gesellschaft im 2. und 3. Jahrhundert Hidschra: Eine Geschichte des religiösen Denkens im frühen Islam*, 6 vols., especially vol. 4 (Berlin: Walter de Gruyter, 1997), 259–76. On the question of the existence of an Andalusian philosophical school, see Lawrence I. Conrad, "The World of Ibn Ṭufayl," in *The World of Ibn Ṭufayl: Interdisciplinary Perspectives on Ḥayy ibn Yaqẓān*, ed. Lawrence I. Conrad (Leiden: Brill, 1996), 12–13.

18. See, e.g., J. Guttmann, *Philosophies of Judaism: The History of Jewish Philosophy from Biblical Times to Franz Rozenzweig*, trans. D. W. Silverman (New York: Anchor, 1964); and C. Sirat, *A History of Jewish Philosophy in the Middle Ages* (Cambridge: Cambridge University Press, 1985).

19. That is to say, the dominant culture of the Islamicate world, which, although reflecting the heavy influence of Islam, was also shared by non-Muslim communities.

20. See Sarah Stroumsa, "Ibn Masarra and the Beginnings of Mystical Thought in al-Andalus," in *Wege mystischer Gotteserfahrung: Judentum, Christentum und Islam*, ed. Peter Schäfer (Munich: Oldenbourg, 2006), 97–112. For a comprehensive study of Ibn Masarra, see Sarah Stroumsa and Sara Sviri, *The Beginnings of Mystical Philosophy in al-Andalus: Ibn Masarra and His Writings* (Leiden: Brill, forthcoming).

21. Guichard advocates "la necécessité ou la légitimité d'une utilisation—la plus prudente possible—de sources moins directes et immédiatements exploitables que les

sources arabes, défaut ou en complément de celles-ci." See Pierre Guichard, *Les musulmans de Valence et la reconquête (Xie–XIIIe siècles)* (Damascus: Institut français du Damas, 1990–91), 1:11.

22. Ṣā'id al-Andalusī, *Ṭabaqāt al-umam,* ed. Ḥayāt Bū 'Alwān (Beirut: Dār al-Ṭalī'ah, 1985), 162–63. For another English translation, see Sema'an I. Salem and Alok Kumar, *Science in the Medieval World: The "Book of the Categories of Nations" by Ṣā'id al-Andalusi* (Austin: University of Texas Press, 1991), 191.

23. See David J. Wasserstein, *The Rise and Fall of the Party-Kings: Politics and Society in Islamic Spain, 1002–1086* (Princeton, N.J.: Princeton University Press, 1985), 194; Wasserstein, "The Muslims and the Golden Age of the Jews in al-Andalus," in *Dhimmis and Others: Jews and Christians and the World of Classical Islam*, ed. Uri Rubin and David J. Wasserstein, Israel Oriental Studies 17 (Winona Lake, Ind.: Eisenbrauns, 1997), 179–93.

24. Wasserstein ("The Muslims and the Golden Age," 186, 194) doubts that Ḥasdāy attained particularly high rank in the service of the Umayyads. Ṣā'id's terminology *khādim*, however, seems to me to suggest exactly such high rank; see also Eliyahu Ashtor, *The Jews of Moslem Spain* (Philadelphia: Jewish Publication Society, 1984), 3:79.

25. Ṣā'id al-Andalusī, *Ṭabaqāt al-umam*, 203–4. For an English translation of this passage, see Wasserstein, "The Muslims and the Golden Age," 189–92. See also J. Finkel, "An Eleventh Century Source for the History of Jewish Scientists in Mohammedan Lands (Ibn Ṣā'id)," *Jewish Quarterly Review*, n.s., 18 (1927–28): 45–54. The same information, with very similar formulations, appears in Ibn Abī Uṣaybi'a's entry on Ḥasdāy ibn Isḥāq; see his *'Uyūn al-anbā' fī ṭabaqāt al-aṭibbā'*, ed. Nizār Riḍā (Beirut: Maktabat al-Ḥayāt, n.d), 498. Ibn Abī Uṣaybi'a also mentions Ḥasdāy in his entry on Ibn Juljul, *'Uyūn al-anbā'*, 493–95. This may mean that for his information on Ḥasdāy, Ibn Abī Uṣaybi'a depended on Ibn Juljul. Ṣā'id also mentions Ibn Juljul, and he may well have depended on this source, too. One may then wonder whether Ibn Juljul was also one of the sources used by the twelfth-century Abraham Ibn Daud (see note 27 below).

26. See, e.g., Wasserstein ("The Muslims and the Golden Age," 194), who establishes the connection between Ṣā'id's stories about the importation of books and the fact that Ḥasdāy "in thus cutting the umbilical cord with Iraq, was acting in concert with his employer, the caliph of Cordoba." Wasserstein estimates that "the Jewish revolution of fourth/tenth century Spain is a sub-set of the overall Iberian separatist revolution of that period." See also David J. Wasserstein, "The Library of al-Ḥakam II al-Mustanṣir and the Culture of Islamic Spain," *Manuscripts of the Middle East* 5 (1990–91): 99–105, esp. 103. See also Gerson D. Cohen, "The Story of the Four Captives," *Proceedings of the American Academy of Jewish Research* 29 (1960–61): 55–131, esp. 115–16; Jacob Mann, *Texts and Studies in Jewish History and Literature* (Cincinnati: Hebrew Union College Press, 1931), 1:111–12; and J. Vahid Brown, "Andalusi Mysticism: A Recontextualization," *Journal of Islamic Philosophy* 2 (2006): 69–101, esp. 71–72.

27. Ibn Daud, *A Critical Edition with a Translation and Notes of the Book of Tradition (Sefer ha-Qabbalah)*, ed. Gerson D. Cohen (Philadelphia: Jewish Publication Society, 1967), 66/48.

28. See Christys, *Christians in al-Andalus*, 109–17.

29. Ṣā'id al-Andalusī, *Ṭabaqāt al-umam*, 163–64.

30. Among them the library of the vizier of Zuhayr, the Slav ruler of Almeria (d. 1038), which is said to have contained 400,000 volumes; see Wasserstein, "The Library of al-Ḥakam II," 99. On libraries in al-Andalus, see also Julián Ribera y Tarragó, "Bibliófilos y bibliotecas en la españa musulmana," in *Disertaciones y opúsculos* (Madrid: E Maestre, 1928), 1:181–228. Ṣā'id's account of al-Manṣūr's censorship falls within what Roger Collins depicts as "a framework of interpretation that sees the history of Spain as a whole being best represented by a pattern of long periods of isolationism and exclusivity on the part of the peninsula in relation to the outside world, punctuated by a succession of shorter, rather hectic, phases of catching up, in the course of which Spain becomes almost uncritically receptive of outside influences." See Roger Collins, *The Arab Conquest of Spain, 710–797* (1989; Oxford: Blackwell, 1994), 11.

31. See, e.g., Alain de Libera, *La philosophie médiévale* (Paris: Presses Universitaires de Paris, 1993), 143.

32. It is interesting to note, for comparison, the attempt of Christian monarchs in thirteenth-century Spain to supervise and control what Jews read. In 1255 a royal patent of rights forbade Jews to read or to own books that contravened Jewish law; see Nahem Ilan, "The Jewish Community in Toledo at the Turn of the Thirteenth Century and the Beginning of the Fourteenth," *Hispania Judaica Bulletin* 3 (2000): 65–95, esp. 81–82. As noted by Ilan (p. 75), the Jews of that period played a decisive role as cultural intermediaries between the Muslims and the Christians. Rather than an interest in defending Jewish orthodoxy, as suggested by Ilan, the patent was probably meant to block the passing of uncensored material (including translations of philosophy and science) to the Christians.

33. The observation that the Jews were "useful intermediaries" in the cultural process is made by Wasserstein, *Party-Kings*, 192.

34. But according to Miguel Cruz Hernández, "La crítica de Averroes al depotismo oligarquico andalusi," in *Ensayos sobre la filosofía en al-Andalus*, ed. Andrés Martínez-Lorca (Barcelona: Editorial Anthropos, 1990), 110, 110n5, it is not true that the party-kings supported the development of Andalusi thought after al-Manṣūr. On the continued philosophical activity in the *ṭa'ifa* period, see also Manuela Marín, "Los Reinos de Taifas—Teología y filosofía," in Ramón Menéndez Pidal, *Historia de España* VIII, ed. María Jesús Viguera (Madrid: Espasa Calpe, 1994), 4:528–30, on p. 530.

35. See Ibn Bājja, *Rasā'il falsafiyya li-Abī Bakr ibn Bājja: Nuṣūṣ falsafiyya ghayr manshūra*, ed. Jamāl al-Dīn al-'Alawī (Beirut: Dār al-Bayḍā', 1983), 78–79; Ṣā'id al-Andalusī, *Ṭabaqāt al-umam*, 205–6 (English trans.: 81–82). See also Eliyahu Ashtor, "Ḥisday ibn Ḥisday, Abū al-Faḍl," *Encyclopaedia Judaica*, 1st ed., 8:533; Miquel Forcada, "Ibn Bājja and the Classification of the Sciences in al-Andalus," *Arabic Sciences and Philosophy* 16 (2006): 287–307, esp. p. 294. On the paramount importance of Saragossa for Jewish philosophy in al-Andalus, see Wasserstein, "The Muslims and the Golden Age," 192; and Joaquín Lomba Fuentes, *La filosofía Islamica en Zaragoza* (Zaragosa: Diputación General de Aragón, Departamento de Cultura y Educación, 1987).

36. See Shlomo Pines, "La dynamique d'Ibn Bājja," *Mélanges Alexandre Koyré* (Paris: Hermann, 1964), 1:442–68, reprinted in *The Collected Works of Shlomo Pines* (Jerusalem:

Magnes, 1986), 2:440–68; Juan Vernet, *La transmisión de algunas ideas científicas de oriente a occidente y de occidente a oriente en los siglos XI–XIII* (Rome: Unione internazionale degli instituti di archeologia storia e storia dell'arte in Roma, 1992), 25–31; and Forcada, "Ibn Bājja and the Classification of the Sciences in al-Andalus," 296.

37. Forcada, "Ibn Bājja and the Classification of the Sciences in al-Andalus," 295.

CHAPTER 4. TRANSLATIONS IN CONTACT

1. This verse was quoted by St. Jerome in his letter to Pammachius on "The Best Method of Translating." Philip Schaff and Henry Wace, eds., *A Select Library of Nicene and Post-Nicene Fathers of the Christian Church*, vol. 6, *St. Jerome: Letters and Select Works* (1893; Grand Rapids, Mich.: Eerdmans, 1979), letter 57, p. 114.

2. For a detailed study of "literal" versus "free" biblical translations, see James Barr, *The Typology of Literalism in Ancient Biblical Translations* (Göttingen: Vandenhoeck and Ruprecht, 1979); Sebastian Brock's extensive studies of Greek and Syriac biblical translations: *The Bible in the Syriac Tradition*, 2nd rev. ed. (Piscataway, N.J.: Gorgias Press, 2006); "Aspects of Translation Technique in Antiquity," *Greek, Roman, and Byzantine Studies* 20.1 (1979): 69–87 (reprinted in Brock, *Syriac Perspectives on Late Antiquity* [London: Variorum, 1984], III); and "Translating the Old Testament," in *It Is Written: Scripture Citing Scripture*, ed. Donald A. Carson and Hugh G. M. Williamson (Cambridge: Cambridge University Press, 1988), 87–98; as well as Eugene A. Nida, *Toward a Science of Translating: With Special Reference to Principles and Procedures Involved in Bible Translating* (Leiden: Brill, 1964).

3. Barr, *Typology of Literalism*, 5, 7, and section III (pp. 20–49).

4. Nida, *Toward a Science of Translating*, 12; Barr, *Typology of Literalism*, 5.

5. The questions why and when this tradition of literal biblical translation developed into "free" or "reader-oriented," especially with regard to the end of the European Middle Ages, have already been adequately answered by Brock, *The Bible in the Syriac Tradition*, 11–12.

6. Brock, *The Bible in the Syriac Tradition*, 12. Nida, *Toward a Science of Translating*, 12, remarks, regarding the Latin translations, that some of them were "apparently rather haphazard."

7. Aquila's translation of the Hebrew Old Testament into Greek in the early second century CE has been described as "a painfully literal translation" that displays "absurd literalism" and "barbarous Greek." See Nida, *Toward a Science of Translating*, 12, 23.

8. The Latin Vulgate may also display this tendency, for although St. Jerome (in his letter to Pammachius on "The Best Method of Translating," 113) defends the method of "sense for sense" that he and others had employed in translating various writings, he also remarks that translating the Scriptures demands another method: "For I myself not only admit but freely proclaim that in translating from the Greek (except in the case of the holy scriptures where even the order of the words is a mystery) I render sense for sense and not word for word." Bruce M. Metzger, *The Early Versions of the New Testament* (Oxford: Clarendon Press, 1977), 323, has described the Old Latin version of the New Testament as

"totally lacking in polish, often painfully literal, and occasionally even of dubious Latinity."

9. It is interesting to note that the Ethiopic version of the Old Testament (based on the Septuagint and composed in the fifth or sixth century) is also marked by literality, to the point of having sections that seem to be a word-for-word translation of the *Hebrew* text. See Michael A. Knibb, *Translating the Bible: The Ethiopic Version of the Old Testament* (Oxford: Oxford University Press, 1999), 60. As Knibb remarks, this is "perhaps merely a reflection of the fact that the Ethiopic is a literal translation of what is itself quite a literal translation" (as well as the fact that there are some similarities between the Hebrew and Ethiopic vocabularies).

10. Sebastian Brock, "Towards a History of Syriac Translation Technique," *Studies in Syriac Christianity* (Aldershot: Variorum, 1992), X, 1–14.

11. See, e.g., Moshe Zucker, *Rav Saadya Gaon's Translation of the Torah* [Hebrew] (New York: Jewish Theological Seminary of America Press, 1959), 1–7; Joshua Blau, "Arabic Translations," in *Bible Translation: An Introduction*, ed. Chaim Rabin [Hebrew] (Jerusalem: Bialik Institute, 1984), 157–58.

12. Joshua Blau and Simon Hopkins, "On Early Judaeo-Arabic Orthography," *Zeitschrift für arabische Linguistik* 12 (1984): 9–27 [*Studies in Middle Arabic and Its Judaeo-Arabic Variety* (Jerusalem: Magnes Press, 1988), 381–400]; Joshua Blau, "On a Fragment of the Oldest Judaeo-Arabic Bible Translation Extant," in *Genizah Research After Ninety Years*, ed. Joshua Blau and Stefan C. Reif (Cambridge: Cambridge University Press, 1992), 31–39.

13. It is nearly certain that these written translations were preceded by oral translations.

14. Blau and Hopkins, "Orthography"; Joshua Blau and Simon Hopkins, "Ancient Bible Translations to Judeo-Arabic" [Hebrew], *Peʿamim* 83 (2000): 4–14.

15. Blau, "Fragment," 32; Simon Hopkins, "On the Vorlage of an Early Judaeo-Arabic Translation of Proverbs," *Jerusalem Studies in Arabic and Islam* 27 (2002): 372–73.

16. Hopkins, "Vorlage," 371–72.

17. Zucker, *Translation*, 43.

18. English translation according to the King James Version.

19. Hopkins, "Vorlage," 370. For more examples of this kind of blunder, see p. 371.

20. Rina Drory, *The Emergence of Jewish-Arabic Literary Contacts at the Beginning of the Tenth Century* [Hebrew] (Tel-Aviv: Ha-Kibbuts ha-Meʾuḥad, 1988), 122–23; Sarah Stroumsa, "The Impact of Syriac Tradition on Early Judaeo-Arabic Bible Exegesis," *ARAM* 3.1–2 (1991): 83–96.

21. Influence of the Syriac on Judeo-Arabic Bible translations goes even further than this: Babylonian Hebrew vocalization, as also found in manuscripts containing Judeo-Arabic biblical translations, is clearly derived from the Syriac system of points. See Gotthelf Bergsträsser, *Hebräische Grammatik*, 1 Teil (Leipzig: Verlag von F. C. W. Vogel, 1918), 54–55; Paul E. Kahle, *The Cairo Geniza* (Oxford: Basil Blackwell, 1959), 65.

22. Joshua Blau and Simon Hopkins, "On Aramaic Vocabulary in Early Judaeo-Arabic Texts Written in Phonetic Spelling," *Jerusalem Studies in Arabic and Islam* 32 (2006): 433–71.

23. Ibid., 443–45.

24. Ibid., 446–71. To these examples add also the word *jamalūn* as a translation of the Hebrew *attiq* (Ezek. 42:3) mentioned by Haggai Ben-Shammai in his review of Meira Polliack and Sasson Somekh, "Two Hebrew-Arabic Biblical Glossaries from the Cairo Geniza" [Hebrew; *Peʿamim* 83 (2000): 15–47], *Peʿamim* 88 (2001): 124–38, on pp. 125–30.

25. See Colin F. Baker and Meira Polliack, *Arabic and Judaeo-Arabic Manuscripts in the Cambridge Genizah Collections: Arabic Old Series (T-S Ar. 1a-54)* (Cambridge: Cambridge University Press, 2001), #3152, p. 229.

26. Edward W. Lane, *Arabic-English Lexicon* (London: Williams and Norgate, 1867), 3:924.

27. The glossary in MS T-S Ar.31.245 very often does not follow the order of the verses.

28. This is according to the JPS translation. Another common translation is "righteous": see Ludwig Koehler and Walter Baumgartner, *The Hebrew and Aramaic Lexicon of the Old Testament* (Leiden: Brill, 1995), 2:482; Saadya translates *ṯiqāt* ("trustworthy, honest").

29. This is according to the King James Version.

30. See Koehler and Baumgartner, *Lexicon*, 2:483.

31. Lane, *Arabic-English Lexicon*, 3:1026.

32. Al-Jawharī (d. 1000 CE), *Tāj al-lugha wa-ṣaḥāḥ al-ʿArabiyya* (Būlāq, 1282 AH), 2:130, refers to it as *muʿarrab*; Ibn Manẓūr (d. 1311 CE), *Lisān al-ʿArab* (Beirut: Dār Ṣādir, 1956), 10:403, quotes al-Layth's remark that this word is considered to be *dakhīl*. Both also mention Ibn Durayd's claim that this is a genuine Arabic word.

33. This is on the authority of al-Azharī.

34. Robert Payne Smith, *Thesaurus Syriacum* (Oxford: Clarendon, 1879), 1:465, 471. As Payne Smith remarks, *bukhnā* translates the words *ezraḥ* (Exod. 12:48, 49) and *ger* (Exod. 12:19; Josh. 8:33) in the Peshitta. Payne Smith (p. 465) brings the Arabic renderings of this word, of which two match those of the glossary: *al-dahāqīn al-rātiba. Bunkā*, in addition to the above-mentioned meaning, is also "base, station, or candlestick," very close to the Hebrew *ken* which is at the basis of all four renderings.

35. Michael Sokoloff, *A Dictionary of Jewish Babylonian Aramaic of the Talmudic and Geonic Periods* (Ramat-Gan: Bar-Ilan University Press; Baltimore: Johns Hopkins University Press, 2002), mentions the word *bunkā* but only with the meaning of "base, basis, place, garden bed."

36. See, e.g., Meira Polliack, "Major Trends in Karaite Biblical Exegesis in the Tenth and Eleventh Centuries," in *Karaite Judaism*, ed. Meira Polliack (Leiden: Brill, 2003), 365.

37. Leon Nemoy, *Karaite Anthology* (New Haven, Conn.: Yale University Press, 1952), 83, remarks that Yefet's translation was "done in a most literal manner, often in violation of the rules of Arabic grammar." Meira Polliack, *The Karaite Tradition of Arabic Bible Translation* (Leiden: Brill, 1997), 40, describes Yefet's translation as "slavish and ungrammatical."

38. Geoffrey Khan, *Karaite Bible Manuscripts from the Cairo Genizah* (Cambridge: Cambridge University Press, 1990); Haggai Ben-Shammai, "Hebrew in Arabic Characters: Qirqisānī's View," in *Studies in Judaica, Karaitica and Islamica Presented to L. Nemoy* (Ramat-Gan: Bar-Ilan University Press, 1982), 115–26; Hopkins, "Vorlage," 373.

39. MS Inst. B217, fol. 164v.

40. Cf. Haggai Ben-Shammai, "Between Ananites and Karaites: Observations on Early Medieval Jewish Sectarianism," *Studies in Muslim-Jewish Relations* 1 (1993): 19–29; Moshe Gil, "The Origins of the Karaites," in *Karaite Judaism*, ed. Polliack, 73–118.

CHAPTER 5. CLAIMS ABOUT THE MISHNA IN THE *EPISTLE* OF SHERIRA GAON

Thanks to Drs. David Freidenreich, Miriam Goldstein, and Joseph Lowry for prodding me to clarify my thinking about this subject. Profound thanks to them, too, and to Nicholas Harris for correcting errors. Those that remain are mine alone.

1. This work exists in two recensions that circulated in "French" and "Sephardi" lands. Both recensions appear in the critical edition by Benjamin M. Lewin, *Iggeret Rav Sherira Gaon* (Haifa: Itzkovsky, 1921). My translations are based on the "French" recension, which recent scholars of Geonica regard as the one that better reflects geonic cultural assumptions. See, e.g., Yaakov Sussman, "'*Torah she-be-ʿal peh'—peshuta ke-mashmaʿa*," in *Meḥqere Talmud* 3, *Muqdash le-zikhro shel Prof. E. E. Urbach*, ed. Yaakov Sussman and David Rosenthal (Jerusalem: Magnes Press, 2005), 234n26 (and 214n18); Y. N. Epstein, *Mevoʾot le-Sifrut ha-amoraim* (Jerusalem: Magnes Press, 1963), 610–15; and Moshe Berr, "ʿIyyunim le-Iggeret Sherira Gaon," *Shenaton Bar Ilan* 4–5 (1967): 181–96. Where I have opted for a word or phrase that is not in the "French" recension provided by Lewin, my choice is nonetheless in one of the cited "French" variants. Such instances are indicated in the notes.

2. "Those Early Ones [who flourished] up to the death of Rabbi [Judah the Patriarch, ca. 200 CE] did not recite in one [single] formulation, but rather, they explained it as we, today, explain matters and the like to our students." Lewin, *Iggeret*, 51–52.

3. The first surviving attempt at chronological arrangement of informants is the *Seder tannaʾim ve-amoraʾim*, composed after 885. See Robert Brody, *The Geonim of Babylonia and the Shaping of Medieval Jewish Culture* (New Haven, Conn.: Yale University Press, 1998), 274–77.

4. See Yonah Frenkel, *Darko shel Rashi be-ferusho la-Talmud ha-Bavli* (Jerusalem: Magnes Press, 1980), chapter 2. See also Talya Fishman, *Becoming the People of the Talmud* (Philadelphia: University of Pennsylvania Press, 2011), chapter 4.

5. On the place of Sherira's *Epistle* in Maimonides' historiography, see Fishman, *Becoming the People*, chapter 2.

6. See, e.g., the prefaces to Menaḥem ha-Me'iri's *Bet ha-beḥira*, composed in thirteenth-century Provence, and to Menaḥem ben Zeraḥ's *Tsedah la-derekh*, composed in fourteenth-century Spain.

7. In *Kuzari* 3:67, Halevi writes about the Mishna: "Its traditions are so reliable that no suspicion of invention could be upheld. Besides this, the Mishna . . . is greatly distinguished by terseness of language, beauty of style, excellence of composition and the comprehensive employment of homonyms, applied in a lucid way, leaving neither doubt nor obscurity. This is so striking that everyone who looks at it with genuine scrutiny must be aware that a mortal

man is incapable of composing such a work without divine assistance." English translation by Hartwig Hirschfeld, *Book of Kuzari* (London: G. Routledge; New York: Dutton, 1905), 106. This passage is noted in Moshe Perlmann, "Samau'al al-Maghribi, *Ifham al-Yahud*: Silencing the Jews," *PAAJR* 32 (1964): 91, note B.14, and in Hava Lazarus-Yafeh, *Intertwined Worlds: Medieval Islam and Bible Criticism* (Princeton, N.J.: Princeton University Press, 1992), 17, in the context of Jewish responses to the doctrine of *iʿjāz al-Qurʾān*. Neither work of research acknowledges that Halevi derived this claim from Sherira's *Epistle*.

8. The Mishna was ascribed a status of unique sanctity among kabbalistic thinkers of the fifteenth and sixteenth centuries. Might these conceptions have been indirectly indebted to Sherira's paean to Mishna in the *Epistle*, by way of Judah Halevi's *Kuzari*? On Mishna in *Sefer ha-kanah*, see Talya Fishman, "A Kabbalistic Perspective on Gender-Specific Commandments: On the Interplay Between Symbol and Society," *Association for Jewish Studies Review* 17.2 (1992): 199–245; on Mishna in the thought of Rabbi Joseph Karo, see R. J. Zwi Werblowsky, *Joseph Karo: Lawyer and Mystic* (Philadelphia: Jewish Publication Society, 1977), 17–18, 109–11. On Mishna in the praxis of Rabbi Hayyim Vital, see Lawrence Fine, "Recitation of Mishnah as a Vehicle for Mystical Inspiration: A Contemplative Technique Taught by Hayyim Vital," *Revue des Études Juives* 141 (1982): 183–99; on Mishna study in the pedagogy of the kabbalist R. Judah Loeb ben Bezalel, see Aharon Fritz Kleinberger, *Ha-maḥashavah ha-pedagogit shel ha-MaHaRaL* (Jerusalem: Magnes Press, 1962).

9. Overt disparagements of Mishna appear in medieval sources that invoke the (tannaitic) phrase "the tannaim bring destruction to the world" (bSot. 22a).

10. On the relative neglect of Mishna in the face of the Talmud's growing prominence, see Joel H. Zaiman, "The Traditional Study of the Mishnah," in *The Modern Study of the Mishnah*, ed. Jacob Neusner (Leiden: Brill, 1973), 1–12; Yaʿakov Sussman, "*Kitvei yad u-mesorot nusaḥ shel ha-Mishna*," *Seventh World Congress of Jewish Studies, 1977* (Jerusalem, 1980), 3:215–50, esp. 234–41. See also Joseph Davis, *Yom-Tov Lipmann Heller: Portrait of a Seventeenth-Century Rabbi* (Oxford: Littman Library, 2005), 67–69; Ronit Meroz, "*Ḥaburat R' Moshe ben Makhir*," *Peʿamim* 31 (1987): 45–47; and Elhanan Reiner, "*Temurot be-yeshivot Polin ve-Ashkenaz be-meʾot ha-16-ha-17 ve-ha-vikkuʿaḥ ʿal ha-pilpul*," in *Ke-minhag Ashkenaz u-Polin: Sefer yovel le-Chone Shmeruk, qoveẓ maʾamarim be-tarbut yehudit*, ed. Israel Bartal, Chava Turniansky, and Ezra Mendelsson (Jerusalem: Merkaz Shazar, 1993), 9–80.

11. See, e.g., Hava Lazarus-Yafeh, Mark R. Cohen, Sasson Somekh, and Sidney H. Griffith, eds., *The Majlis: Interreligious Encounters in Medieval Islam* (Wiesbaden: Harrassowitz, 1999); Joel Kraemer, *Humanism in the Renaissance of Islam: The Cultural Revival During the Buyid Age* (Leiden: Brill, 1986); David Sklare, *Samuel ben Ḥofni Gaon and His Cultural World: Texts and Studies* (Leiden: Brill, 1996), 99–141; and especially Sklare, "Responses to Islamic Polemics by Jewish Mutakallimun in the Tenth Century," in *The Majlis*, ed. Lazarus-Yafeh et al., 137–61.

12. Lewin, *Iggeret*, 21. The quote is from bGit. 59a. The term "grandeur" refers to the Patriarch's political might and is connected with his easy access to the Roman powers of the time.

13. Lewin, *Iggeret*, 21. The friendly conversations between Emperor Antoninus and Rabbi Judah concerned, among other matters, the relationship of body and soul, the evil inclination, and governmental affairs. See, e.g., bSan. 91a–b; yMeg. 3:2.

14. Lewin, *Iggeret*, 22.

15. In place of *ḥiluf*, I have translated the "French" variant, *ḥiluq*.

16. Lewin, *Iggeret*, 22.

17. Cf. Deut. 28:46; Isa. 20:3. These catchwords are indicative of a miracle.

18. Lewin, *Iggeret*, 23.

19. I have opted for the "French" variant *it'aqqerin*, which is the dominant locution in the "Sephardi" version.

20. Lewin, *Iggeret*, 36.

21. Ibid., 29.

22. See Richard C. Martin, "Inimitability," in *Encyclopaedia of the Qur'ān*, ed. J. D. McAuliffe (Leiden: Brill, 2001–6), 2:526; and R. C. Martin, "The Role of the Basrah Mu'tazilah in Formulating the Doctrine of the Apologetic Miracle," *Journal of Near Eastern Studies* 39 (1980): 175–89. Cf. Abdul Aleem, "*I'jāzu-l-Qur'ān*," *Islamic Culture* 7 (1933): 64–82, 215–33.

23. Qur'an 52:33–34, 11:13, 10:38, 17:88, 2:23–24.

24. On the articulation of this theory by al-Naẓẓām (d. 845/6), al-Fuwatī (d. 833), Ibn Sulaymān (d. ninth century), and al-Rummānī (d. 994/6), see Issa Boullata, "The Rhetorical Interpretation of the Qur'an: *I'jaz* and Related Topics," in *Approaches to the History of the Interpretation of the Qur'an*, ed. Andrew Rippin (Oxford: Clarendon; New York: Oxford University Press, 1988), 141–42.

25. Yusuf Rahman, "The Miraculous Nature of Muslim Scripture: A Study of Abd al-Jabbār's *I'jaz al-Qur'ān*," *Islamic Studies* 35 (1996): 415.

26. A useful overview of this topic is found in Rahman, "The Miraculous Nature of Muslim Scripture."

27. Gustave E. von Grunebaum, *A Tenth-Century Document of Arabic Literary Theory and Criticism: The Sections on Poetry of al-Bāqillānī's "I'jāz al-Qur'ān"* (Chicago: University of Chicago Press, 1950), xvii. Cf. G. J. H. Van Gelder, *Beyond the Line: Classical Arabic Literary Crirtics on the Coherence and Unity of the Poem* (Leiden: Brill, 1982), 5.

28. Al-Rummānī lists the ten elements of *bālagha* as: conciseness, simile, metaphor, harmony, periodic rhyme and assonance, paranomasia, variation, implication, hyperbole, and beautiful rendition. In Boullata, "Rhetorical Interpretation," 143, and (in slightly different translation) von Grunebaum, *Tenth-Century Document*, 118.

29. Al-Rummānī was responsible for the constriction of the term *i'jāz*. Van Gelder, *Beyond the Line*, 97. See also G. Van Gelder, "Brevity: The Long and Short of It in Classical Arabic Literary Theory," in *Proceedings of the Ninth Congress of the U.E.A.I., Amsterdam 1978* (Leiden: Brill, 1981), 78–88.

30. On the close connection between these themes, see Robert Brunschvig, "Un theologien Musulman contre le Judaisme," in *Homenaje a Millás-Vallicrosa* (Barcelona: Consejo Superior de Investigaciones Científicas, 1954), 232. Sklare mentions Ibn Khallād (d. mid-tenth century) and his pupil, Abū 'Abd Allāh al-Baṣrī (d. 980), as two figures who linked these ideas in "Responses to Islamic Polemics," 150.

31. Thus, 'Abd al-Jabbār mentions in volume 16 of *Al-mughnī* that "some Jew[s] who resorted to falsehood in this matter and denied the challenge, meaning actually that this

challenge could not have occurred." Cited in Haggai Ben Shammai, "The Attitude of Some Early Karaites Toward Islam," in *Studies in Medieval Jewish History and Literature,* ed. Isadore Twersky (Cambridge, Mass.: Harvard University Press, 1984), 2:34n132.

32. On Samuel b. Ḥofni's debate with the Muslim theologian Abū ʿAbd Allāh al-Baṣrī (d. 980), see Sklare, "Responses to Islamic Polemics," 148.

33. On Samuel b. Ḥofni's *Kitāb Naskh al-Sharʿ* (Treatise on Abrogation of the Law), see Sklare, "Responses to Islamic Polemics," 146, 150. Sklare infers from the relatively large number of extant manuscripts in the Geniza that this work was widely read.

34. David al-Mukammaṣ is named as one of the Jews who refuted the dogma of *iʿjāz al-Qurʾān* in Moses Ibn Ezra's *Kitāb al-muḥāḍara wa-ʾl-mudhākara*, ed. A. S. Halkin (Jerusalem: Meqits Nirdamim, 1975), 38–39.

35. In Yaʿqūb al-Qirqisānī, *Kitāb al-anwār wa-ʾl-marāqib: Code of Karaite Law*, ed. Leon Nemoy (New York: Alexander Kohut Memorial Foundation, 1939–45), 2:298–301. Cited in Ben Shammai, "The Attitude of Some Early Karaites," 34–37; Sklare, "Responses to Islamic Polemics," 155.

36. Sklare, "Responses to Islamic Polemics," 153–61. Sklare stresses that Karaites and Rabbanites responded similarly to the provocations of Muslim polemic

37. There is a rich secondary literature on this phenomenon. See, e.g., Franz Rosenthal, "A Jewish Philosopher of the Tenth Century," *HUCA* 21 (1948): 157; Abraham Halkin, "Medieval Attitudes Toward Hebrew," in *Biblical and Other Studies*, ed. A. Altmann (Cambridge, Mass.: Harvard University Press, 1963), 233–48; Dan Pagis, *Ḥidush u-masoret be-shirat ha-ḥol ha-ʿIvrit: Sepharad ve-Italia* (Jerusalem: Keter, 1976), 56–58; Nehemiah Allony, *Sefer ha-egron le-Rav Saʿadya Gaon* (Jerusalem: Ha-Aḳademyah la-Lashon ha-ʿIvrit, 1969), 30–31, 156–57; Allony, "*Sefer ha-egron haʾIvri ke-negged ha-ʿArabiyya*," in *Zer le-gevurot, Mugash le-R. Zalman Shazar*, ed. B. Z. Luria (Jerusalem: Kiryat Sefer, 1973), 464–74; Allony, "*Teguvat Rav Moshe Ibn Ezra la-ʿArabiyya be-Sefer ha-diyyunim ve-ha-siḥot*," *Tarbiẓ* 42 (1973): 97–112; Rina Drory, *Reshit ha-maggaʿim shel ha-sifrut ha-Yehudit ʿim ha-sifrut ha-ʿAravit ba-meʾah ha-ʿasirit* (Tel Aviv: Ha-Kibbuts ha-Meʾuḥad, 1988), 85; Ross Brann, *The Compunctious Poet: Cultural Ambiguity and Hebrew Poetry in Muslim Spain* (Baltimore: Johns Hopkins University Press, 1990), 80; Adele Berlin, *Biblical Poetry Through Medieval Jewish Eyes* (Bloomington: University of Indiana Press, 1991), 22–25; and Joseph Sadan, "Identity and Inimitability: Contexts of Inter-religious Polemics and Solidarity in Medieval Spain in the Light of Two Passages by Moše Ibn ʿEzra and Yaʿaqov ben Elʿazar," *Israel Oriental Studies* 14 (1994): 325–47.

38. See, e.g., al-Bāqillānī's reaction to the claim of *iʿjāz* for the Torah and Gospels in Rosenthal, "Jewish Philosopher," 156–57.

39. "*U-devareha meḥubarim ḥibur yafeh.*" The poet is described as a mnemotechnician who preserves "the useful by binding it in verse" in J. A. Notopoulos, "Mnemosyne in Oral Literature," *Transactions of the American Philological Association* 66 (1938): 469.

40. Lewin, *Iggeret*, 30.

41. Cf. Rashi, on bGit. 67a, "*otsar balum*," where Rabbi Akiva is described as having repeated traditions in recitation until they were arranged in his mouth.

42. Lewin, *Iggeret*, 28–29. Though the *Epistle* as a whole is written in geonic Aramaic, the paean to R. Meir's formulation is written in Hebrew and may preserve older traditions.

43. Lewin, *Iggeret*, 41–42. In this sense, Mishna was quite different from *midrash halakha*.

44. The term *beraita* refers to a unit of tannaitic tradition that was not incorporated into the Mishna.

45. Lewin, *Iggeret*, 30.

46. Salmon ben Yerūḥīm, *Book of the Wars of the Lord*, in *Karaite Anthology*, ed. Leon Nemoy (New Haven, Conn.: Yale University Press, 1952), 74.

47. I.e., "*mitsvat anashim melumadah.*" See, e.g., Daniel Frank, *Search Scripture Well: Karaite Exegetes and the Origins of Jewish Bible Commentary in the Islamic East* (Leiden: Brill, 2004), 57.

48. Menahem Ben Sasson sees no evidence for this. See "The Jewish Community of Medieval North Africa: Society and Leadership, Qayrawan 800–1057" (Ph.D. diss., Hebrew University, 1983), 31.

49. On the sacralization of Oral Torah in Ashkenaz, see Talya Fishman, "The Rhineland Pietists' Sacralization of Oral Torah," *Jewish Quarterly Review* 96 (2006): 9–16. On the sacralization of Oral Torah in Sepharad, see Gerson D. Cohen, *Abraham Ibn Daud's Book of Tradition* (Philadelphia: Jewish Publication Society, 1967), 56; and Fishman, *Becoming the People*, chapter 2.

50. Ignaz Goldziher, "Disputes over the Status of Ḥadīth in Islam," in *Ḥadīth: Origins and Developments*, ed. Harald Motzki (Aldershot: Ashgate, 2004), 59–60; Goldziher, "Aus der Theologie des Fachr al-Dīn al-Rāzī," *Der Islam* 3 (1912): 211–47; Joseph Schacht, *Origins of Muhammadan Jurisprudence* (Oxford: Oxford University Press, 1950), 57; Moshe Zucker, "Qetaʿim mi-Kitāb taḥẓīl al-sharīʿa al-samīʿa," *Tarbiẓ* 41 (1972): 373–410; Nabia Abbott, *Studies in Arabic Literary Papyri* (Chicago: University of Chicago Press, 1957), 2:8; Michael Cook, "ʿAnan and Islam: The Origins of Karaite Scripturalism," *Jerusalem Studies in Arabic and Islam* 9 (1987): 161–82; Cook, "The Opponents of the Writing of Tradition in Early Islam," *Arabica* 44 (1997): 437–512; Gregor Schoeler, "Oral Torah and Ḥadīṯ: Transmission, Prohibition of Writing, Redaction," in *The Oral and the Written in Early Islam* (London: Routledge, 2006), 111–41; Aisha Musa, *Ḥadīth as Scripture* (New York: Palgrave Macmillan, 2008).

51. Musa, *Ḥadīth as Scripture,* 56–59.

52. Al-Shāfiʿī claims that the Prophetic *sunna*, in the form of *ḥadīth*, constitute a second form of divine revelation that is critical to proper understanding and implementation of Qurʾan. Drawing on an earlier claim, al-Shāfiʿī asserted that the repeated references to "the Book and the Wisdom" in several *sūra*s designated the Qurʾan and *ḥadīth*, respectively. See Christopher Melchert, "Traditionist-Jurisprudents and the Framing of Islamic Law," *Islamic Law and Society* 8 (2001): 403–4; Musa, *Ḥadīth as Scripture*, 33–35.

53. Two later works that address problematic content of specific *ḥadīth* are *Bayān mushkil al-aḥādīth* by Abū Jaʿfar al-Ṭaḥāwī (d. 933) and *Bayān mushkil al-ḥadīth* by Ibn Fūrak (d. 1015).

54. The *mutakallim* Ḥasan al-Baṣrī (d. 728) is said to have claimed that the Qurʾan is the only source of doctrine, though this remark appears in a document of questioned authenticity, al-Baṣrī's defense of free will. Al-Naẓẓām, a mid-ninth-century Muʿtazilite

theologian, also expounded at length on the epistemological unreliability of *ḥadīth*. See Cook, "ʿAnan and Islam," 166, 168–69, and notes.

55. Tenth-century Arabic heresiographies by al-Nāshiʾ al-Akbar (d. 906), al-Ashʿarī (d. 936), and al-Malaṭī (d. 988) identify a number of other groups that refused to base their religious practice on the *sunna*, i.e., the behaviors instituted by the Prophet Muḥammad. See Cook, "ʿAnan and Islam," 170; and Musa, *Ḥadīth as Scripture*, 38.

56. The jurist al-Shāfiʿī summarized the debates he held with deniers of *ḥadīth*'s authority in his *Kitāb jimāʿ al-ʿilm*, and Ibn Qutayba (d. 889) did the same in his *Taʾwīl mukhtalif al-ḥadīth*. In the preface of this work, he addresses a correspondent who had described the disparagement of *ḥadīth* by rationalist theologians, i.e., *mutakallimūn*, and declares that this was provoking serious division in the Muslim community: "You have written to inform me of what you have encountered of *ahl al-kalām*'s contemptuous criticism of *ahl al-ḥadīth*, their long-winded diatribes in books criticizing them, and their hurling of so many accusations of deceit and contradictory narratives that disagreement has occurred, sects have multiplied, ties have been severed and Muslims have become enemies, accusing each other of disbelief." Cited in Musa, *Ḥadīth as Scripture,* 64.

57. Musa, *Ḥadīth as Scripture,* 60. Indeed, the first chapter of the second section of al-Baghdādī's *Taqyīd al-ʿilm* is called "Fear of Devotion to Something Other than the Qurʾan" (Musa, *Ḥadīth as Scripture*, 73). Reports in *Taqyīd al-ʿilm* transmitted on the authority of Abū Hurayra (d. 678) are variants of a single story: Abū Hurayra reports that the Prophet came across some Companions while they were writing *ḥadīth* and asked what they were writing. They answered, "the Prophet's *ḥadīth*." Abū Hurayra quotes the Prophet as saying, "Is it a book other than the Book of God that you want? The two communities before you went astray only because they wrote some books for themselves along with the Book of God" (Musa, *Ḥadīth as Scripture*, 76). Reports in *Taqyīd al-ʿilm* about Abū Saʿīd al-Khudrī are also variants of the same story: When Abū Saʿīd is asked to write down *ḥadīth* that he has transmitted, he refuses, saying, "I will not write it for you and I will not make it a Qurʾān" (Musa, *Ḥadīth as Scripture*, 76).

58. Musa, *Ḥadīth as Scripture*, 60–61.

59. On the scripturalism of the Kharijites, see G. R. Hawting, "The Significance of the Slogan *lā ḥukma illā lillāh* and the References to the *ḥudūd* in the Traditions About the Fitna and the Murder of ʿUthmān," *Bulletin of the School of Oriental and African Studies* 41 (1978): 460n37.

60. On Rabīʿ b. Ḥabīb's *Musnad*, see Cook, "ʿAnan and Islam," 171–72.

61. This letter, cited in the *Kitāb al-jawāhir* of al-Barrādī, is said to have been written in 695 by the Kharijite ʿAbd Allāh ibn Ibāḍ to Caliph ʿAbd al-Malik. It is discussed in Michael Cook, *Early Muslim Dogma* (Cambridge: Cambridge University Press, 1981), chapters 3 and 8; and in Musa, *Ḥadīth as Scripture*, 38.

62. Tadeusz Lewicki, "Les subdivisions de l'Ibāḍiyya," *Studia Islamica* 9 (1958): 71–82; "al-Ibāḍiyya," *Encyclopaedia of Islam*, 2nd ed., 3:648.

63. Gregor Schoeler, "Weiteres zur Frage der schriftlichen oder mündlichen Überlieferung," *Der Islam* 66 (1989): 38–67; Schoeler, "Oral Torah and Ḥadīṯ"; Menahem J. Kister, "*Lā taqraʾu l-qurʾāna* . . . Some Notes on the Transmission of *Ḥadīth*," *Jerusalem Studies in*

Arabic and Islam 22 (1998): 127–62; Cook, "Opponents." On the similarities and differences between Jewish and Muslim motives for preserving oral modes of transmission, see Talya Fishman, "Guarding Oral Transmission: Within and Between Cultures," *Oral Tradition* 25.1 (2010): 41–56.

64. On the opposition to *ḥadīth* inscription among scholars of Basra and Kufa, see Gregor Schoeler, "Mündliche Thora und Ḥadīth," *Der Islam* 66 (1989): 219, 235; and Cook, "Opponents," 489.

65. On the problems of ascribing the *Ṭabaqāt al-kubrā* to Ibn Saʿd, see Christopher Melchert, "How Ḥanafism Came to Originate in Kufa and Traditionalism in Medina," *Islamic Law and Society* 6 (1999): 324–26.

66. Musa, who cites this passage, points out that its chain of tradents is weak—there is no link between al-Zuhrī, who died in 741–42, and ʿUmar, who died in 644. It was nonetheless accepted by Ibn Saʿd, because the individuals named were known to have been particularly trustworthy. (Al-Shāfiʿī and Ibn Qutayba also regarded the named tradents as reliable.) See Musa, *Ḥadīth as Scripture*, 23. Interestingly, al-Zuhrī himself was renowned for having inscribed traditions on skins and writings tablets that he carried with him. He was closely linked with the Umayyad dynasty and facilitated *ḥadīth* dictation sessions for state functionaries and later for scholars. His justification for making multiple copies of *ḥadīth* was that Iraqis in the East (Abbasids) were tampering with versions that had been sent to them. See Michael Lecker, "Al-Zuhrī, Ibn Shihāb," in *Encyclopaedia of Islam*, 2nd ed., 11:565.

67. This is reported on the authority of Abū Hurayah (d. 678) in Ibn Saʿd, *Kitāb al-ṭabaqāt al-kubrā*, vol. 3, pt. 1, ed. Eduard Sachau (Leiden: Brill, 1904), 206, cited in Goldziher, "Disputes," 59–60; Musa, *Ḥadīth as Scripture,* 23.

68. Ibn Saʿd, *Kitāb al-ṭabaqāt al-kubrā*, ed. Eduard Sachau (Leiden: Brill, 1904), 5:140, quoted in Goldziher, "Disputes," 59–60; Judith Romney Wegner, "Islamic and Talmudic Jurisprudence: The Four Roots of Islamic Law and Their Talmudic Counterparts," *American Journal of Legal History* 26 (1982): 34; Cook, "Opponents," 502; Musa, *Ḥadīth as Scripture,* 23–24.

69. Goldziher, "Disputes," 59–60.

70. J. W. Fück, "Ibn Saʿd," in *Encyclopaedia of Islam*, 2nd ed., 3:922. One recension was made by Ibn Saʿd's pupil, al-Ḥusayn ibn Fahm (d. 289/902); another by Ḥārith b. Abī Usāma (d. 282/895); a third, by Ibn Abī al-Dunyā (Baghdad 823–94), who was the tutor to boys who later became Abbasid princes. I do not know whether the fourth recension, by Ibn Ḥayyawayh (d. 381/991), was written before or after Sherira's composition of the *Epistle.*

71. Fück, "Ibn Saʿd." Like *ḥadīth*, Ibn Saʿd's reports contain an *isnād* and a *matn*. See also Musa, *Ḥadīth as Scripture*, 23.

72. See Marc Saperstein, *Decoding the Rabbis: A Thirteenth Century Commentary on the Aggadah* (Cambridge, Mass.: Harvard University Press, 1980), chapter 1.

73. See Yaacov Elbaum, *Le-havin divre ḥakhamim: Mivḥar divre mavo la-agadah ve-la-midrash mi-shel ḥakhme yeme ha-benayyim* (Jerusalem: Mosad Bialik, 2000).

74. Tsemaḥ bar Ḥayyim, Gaon of Sura, had also referred to the precision of Mishna's language, even when compared with the language of the Scriptures, "which are fixed in writing." Noted in Sussman, "*Torah she-be-ʿal peh,*" 234n26.

75. Lewin, *Iggeret*, 52, and elsewhere. On Abraham Weiss's observation that Sherira's *Epistle* makes no reference to the final editing of Talmud, see Meyer Feldblum, "Professor Abraham Weiss: His Approach and Contribution to Talmudic Scholarship," in *The Abraham Weiss Jubilee Volume* (New York: Shulsinger Brothers, 1964), 47. Thanks to Professor Judah Galinsky for bringing this article to my attention.

76. According to contemporary scholars of geonica, Talmud continued to be transmitted in a lexically fluid state in the Babylonian academies through the end of the geonic period. See Yeraḥmiel Brody, "*Sifrut ha-Geonim ve-ha-teqst ha-Talmudi*," *Meḥqere Talmud* 1 (1990): 279n172, 238–40; Sussman, "*Torah she-be-ʿal peh*," 278, 304, 319, 342n57, 344n61; and Naḥman Danzig, "*Mi-Talmud ʿal peh le-Talmud bi-khtav*," *Sefer ha-shana Bar Ilan* 30–31 (2006): 49–112.

77. Lewin, *Iggeret*, 18.

78. Saʿadya Gaon, introduction to *Perush le-Sefer Yetsira*, ed. Yosef Kafih (Jerusalem: Ha-Vaʿad le-Hotsaʾat Sifre Rasag, 1973), 33.

79. This is also not addressed in the introduction to his Commentary on Proverbs, where Saʿadya writes that *mitsvot* heard from Moses were transmitted orally "and were not fixed in a book until the time that Mishna was written and the time that Talmud was written." (*Targum u-ferush ha-Gaon le-Sefer Mishle*, ed. Yosef Kafih [Jerusalem: Ha-Vaʿad Li-Hotsaʾat Sifre Rasag, 1975], 194.) Saʿadya Gaon had also offered a chronology of the transmission of Oral Torah in chapter 2 of *Sefer ha-galui*, of which only fragments are extant. In the descriptive table of contents to that work, he refers to a time in which "the collection of Mishna was finished" (*nigmar qibuts ha-Mishna*) and a later time in which "Talmud was finished" (*nigmar ha-Talmud*). See Abraham E. Harkavy, *Ha-sarid ve-ha-palit mi-Sefer ha-egron ve-Sefer ha-galui* (St. Petersburg: Studien und Mittheilungen aus der kaiserlichen Offentlichen zu St. Petersburg, 1892), 152. Cf. Saul Lieberman, "The Publication of the Mishnah," in *Hellenism in Jewish Palestine* (New York: Jewish Theological Seminary of America Press, 1962), 83–99.

80. On Rabbi Judah the Patriarch's continued transmission of Mishna in oral form, even after fixing its language, see Fishman, *Becoming the People*, chapter 1.

81. On the significance of *lafẓ* in Islamic theology, see Josef van Ess, "Lafẓ," in *Encyclopaedia of Islam*, 2nd ed., 12:545. On the significance of *maʿnā* in philosophy, see O. N. H. Leaman, "Maʿnā," in *Encyclopaedia of Islam*, 2nd ed., 6:346. According to one scholar, "most, if not all, of the history of Arabic literary theory may be described in terms of the dialectic between these two dimensions of verbal expression," i.e., between wording (*lafẓ*) and meaning (*maʿnā*). Margaret M. Larkin, "The Inimitability of the Qurʾan: Two Perspectives," *Religion and Literature* 20 (1988): 47n14.

82. Van Gelder, *Beyond the Line*, 98.

83. Von Grunebaum, *Tenth-Century Document*, xiii–xiv.

84. Larkin, "Inimitability," 33–34; J. Bouman, "The Doctrine of Abd al-Djabbār on the Qurʾān as the Created Word of Allāh," *Verbum: Essays on Some Aspect of the Religious Function of Words, Dedicated to Dr. H. W. Obbink* (Utrecht: Kemink, 1964), 80; J. R. T. M. Peters, *God's Created Speech* (Leiden: Brill, 1976), 332.

85. Rahman, "Miraculous Nature of Muslim Scripture," 416–17.

86. See, e.g., Sarah Stroumsa, "Saadya and Jewish '*Kalam*,'" in *The Cambridge Companion to Medieval Jewish Philosophy*, ed. Daniel H. Frank and Oliver Leaman (Cambridge:

Cambridge University Press, 2003), 71–90; Colette Sirat, *A History of Jewish Philosophy in the Middle Ages* (Cambridge: Cambridge University Press, 1985), 15–56; and Harry A. Wolfson, *Repercussions of the Kalam in Jewish Philosophy* (Cambridge, Mass.: Harvard University Press, 1979).

87. See Ben Shammai, "The Attitude of Some Early Karaites," 24. On the discussion of the Christian doctrine of the preexistent Word in al-Qirqisānī's *Kitāb al-anwār wa-ʾl-marāqib*, see Leon Nemoy, "A Tenth Century Criticism of the Doctrine of the Logos," *Journal of Biblical Literature* 64 (1945): 515–29.

88. Scholars of rabbinic literature have identified other arenas in which the reliability of the *Epistle*'s historical claims may have been compromised by Sherira's engagement in contemporary debates. On tendentious strains in Sherira's *Epistle*, see David Goodblatt, *Rabbinic Instruction in Sassanian Babylonia* (Leiden: Brill, 1975), 38, 44; Harry Fox, "Neusner's *The Bavli and Its Sources*: A Review Essay," *Jewish Quarterly Review* 80 (1990): 355; and the bibliographic overview provided by Avinoam Cohen in *Ravina ve-ḥakhmei doro* (Ramat Gan: Bar-Ilan University Press, 2001), 181–82.

CHAPTER 6. MAIMONIDES AND THE ARABIC ARISTOTELIAN TRADITION OF EPISTEMOLOGY

My thanks to Josef Stern and the editors of this volume for their helpful comments.

1. See, e.g., Shlomo Pines, "The Limitations of Human Knowledge According to Al-Farabi, Ibn Bajja, and Maimonides," in *Studies in Medieval Jewish History and Literature*, ed. Isadore Twersky (Cambridge, Mass.: Harvard University Press, 1979), 82–109; Alexander Altmann, "Maimonides on the Intellect and the Scope of Metaphysics," in *Von der mittelalterlichen zur modernen Aufklärung* (Tübingen: Mohr, 1987), 60–129; Herbert A. Davidson, "Maimonides on Metaphysical Knowledge," *Maimonidean Studies* 3 (1992–93): 49–99; Abraham Nuriel, "Remarks on Maimonides' Epistemology," in *Maimonides and Philosophy*, ed. Shlomo Pines and Yirmiyahu Yovel (Dordrecht: M. Nijhoff, 1986), 26–51; and Josef Stern, "Maimonides' Epistemology," in *The Cambridge Companion to Maimonides*, ed. Kenneth M. Seeskin (Cambridge: Cambridge University Press, 2005), 105–33. Some other studies will be mentioned in the notes below.

2. I am referring primarily to the Arabic epistemological tradition stemming from the *Posterior Analytics* and the *Topics*.

3. See, e.g., Sarah Stroumsa, *Maimonides in His World* (Princeton, N.J.: Princeton University Press, 2009), 53–82 (Almohad influence); and Alfred L. Ivry, "Ismāʿīlī Theology and Maimonides' Philosophy," in *The Jews of Medieval Islam: Community, Society and Identity*, ed. Daniel Frank (Leiden: Brill, 1995), 271–99 (Ismāʿīlī influence).

4. *Mishnah ʿim perush Moshe ben Maymon: Neziqin*, ed. Yosef Kafih (Jerusalem: Mosad ha-Rav Kook, 1976), 372.

5. See "Translator's Introduction: The Philosophic Sources of the *Guide of the Perplexed*," in the *Guide of the Perplexed*, trans. Shlomo Pines (Chicago: University of Chicago Press, 1963), lxvii–lxi.

6. See Herbert A. Davidson, *Moses Maimonides: The Man and His Works* (Oxford: Oxford University Press, 2005), 98, 100, 105, 113–15.

7. *Moreh nevukhim le-Rabbenu Moshe ben Maimon*, trans. Michael Schwarz (Tel Aviv: Tel Aviv University Press, 2002), 114n16.

8. *Guide* 1.50, trans. Pines, 111. (Subsequent page references are to this translation, which I have modified at times.)

9. Or: "confirms."

10. *Guide* 1.50, 111.

11. Here I would like to correct what I said in "Belief, Certainty, and Divine Attributes in the *Guide of the Perplexed*," *Maimonidean Studies* 1 (Fall 1990): 117–41, 128, that conditions (3) and (4) on their own restrict certainty to beliefs acquired through philosophical speculation.

12. *Guide* 1.71, 181.

13. *Guide* 1.59, 138. Job went from knowing God only on the basis of tradition, which is not true knowledge, to knowing God with complete certainty, but it is not clear to me whether it was demonstration that led him to certainty. See ibid., 3.23, 492.

14. Ibid., 3.51, 619.

15. Ibid., 2.19, 303.

16. Ibid., 3.50, 615–16.

17. Ibid., 2.5, 259.

18. Ibid., 3.24, 501.

19. See Israel Efros, "Maimonides' Arabic Treatise on Logic," *Proceedings of the American Academy for Jewish Research* 34 (1966): 155–60 (English), 9–42 (Arabic), especially p. 22 line 17 of the Arabic section.

20. "All that is seen by a prophet in a vision of prophecy is, *in the opinion of the prophet*, a certain truth, that the prophet has no doubts in any way concerning anything in it, and that *in his opinion* its status is the same as that of all existent things that are apprehended through the senses or through the intellect" (*Guide* 3.24, 501). The subjective reading of certainty is advanced by Josef Stern, who generously showed me a chapter of his forthcoming book on Maimonides.

21. *Guide* 1.Int, 6.

22. Cf. Abraham Heschel, "The Quest for Certainty in Saadia's Philosophy," in *Saadia Studies*, ed. Abraham Neuman and Solomon Zeitlin (Philadelphia: Dropsie College, 1943), 157–206.

23. Cf. Maimonides' discussion of the loss of special providence consequent upon the breaking of the bond in *Guide* 3.51, 624–26.

24. Deborah Black, "Knowledge (*'Ilm*) and Certitude (*Yaqīn*) in Al-Farabi's Epistemology," *Arabic Sciences and Philosophy* 16 (2006): 11–45.

25. See Alfarabi, *Kitāb al-burhān wa-Kitāb sharā'iṭ al-yaqīn*, ed. Mājid Fakhry (Beirut: Dar al-Mashriq, 1987), 98. For a partial French translation of the *Conditions of Certainty*, see Georges Vajda, "Autour de la théorie de la connaisance chez Saadia," *Revue des Études Juives* 126 (1967): 135–89, 377–97, on 393–97.

26. Alfarabi, *Kitāb al-burhān*, 20.

27. Black, "Knowledge," 37.

28. Alfarabi, *Kitāb al-burhān*, 101.

29. Black, "Knowledge," 42.

30. See Themistius, *In Aristotelis Metaphysicorum librum [lambda] paraphrasis hebraice et latine*, ed. Samuel Landauer (Berlin: Reimer, 1903), 11 [Hebrew].

31. Avicenna, *Logic: Demonstration (al-Burhān)*, ed. A. ʿAfifi (Cairo: Ministry of Education, 1956), 134, my translation.

32. See Herbert A. Davidson, *Proofs for Eternity, Creation, and the Existence of God in Medieval Islamic and Jewish Philosophy* (New York: Oxford University Press, 1987), 298; and Michael E. Marmura, ed. and trans., *The Metaphysics of "The Healing"* (Provo, Utah: Brigham Young University Press, 2004).

33. See ibid., 277, 282.

34. Book 8, chapter 4, 415n10, 11; Book 8, chapter 5, 415n4. Cf. Michael Marmura, "Avicenna's Proof from Contingency for God's Existence in the *Metaphysics* of the *Shifā*," in *Probing in Islamic Philosophy: Studies in the Philosophies of Ibn Sīnā, al-Ghazālī and Other Major Muslim Thinkers* (Binghamton, N.Y.: Binghamton University Press, 2005), 131–48.

35. The passage in the *ʿUyūn al-masāʾil* (a work traditionally attributed to Alfarabi but recently—and not uncontroversially—to Avicenna or a student of Avicenna) reads in George Hourani's translation as follows: "there is no demonstration of it [the Necessary Existent]." See "Avicenna on Necessary and Possible Existence," *Philosophical Forum* 4 (1973): 74–86, esp. 76. This passage has led Josef Stern to claim that "Avicenna . . . argued that only a demonstration *propter quid* is a real demonstration" ("Maimonides' Epistemology," 120). In fact, as we have just seen in the section on Demonstration in the *Shifā*, Avicenna considers factual demonstrations to be true demonstrations that produce certainty, and he refers to the certain knowledge of God. But, in any event, the passage on which Stern rests his claim is problematic for the following reason. Hourani points out (85n9) that in the Latin translation of the work the author claims that God's existence cannot be demonstrated *ex causa* ("from a cause"), i.e., through an explanatory demonstration. The same addition (*me-ʿila*) appears in Hebrew in all four of the manuscripts of Todros Todrosi's translation of the *ʿUyūn*, entitled *ʿEin mishpat ha-derushim*. Since there is no connection between the Latin and the Hebrew translations, this suggests that the Arabic words *min ʿilāh* were in some manuscript traditions of the Arabic. The author's point, then, would not be that only explanatory demonstrations are true demonstrations, and hence there are no true demonstrations of God's existence, but rather that there are no *explanatory* demonstrations of God's existence, a point easily accepted by Alfarabi and Avicenna (and Maimonides). This point of course does not affect Avicenna's claim that factual demonstrations provide certain knowledge of God's existence.

36. *Guide* 1.71, 181. The point is made about the impossibility of definition rather than of demonstration, but both are ruled out by God's not having causes/explanations.

37. *Sharāʾiṭ al-yaqīn*, 99, trans. Black, "Knowledge and Certitude," 22.

38. The claim is implicit in much of Josef Stern's work on the subject. This and the following two passages are a response to some of his arguments in "Maimonides' Demonstrations: Principles and Practice," *Medieval Philosophy and Theology* 10 (2001): 47–84.

39. By which I mean the sort of knowledge that binds humans to the divine and enables their minds' survival after death.

40. To *burhān* as demonstration in the formal sense one should add *bayān* and its cognates, which is often used in the sense of demonstration among Arab peripatetics and Maimonides. Admitting *bayān* enlarges considerably the scope of things that Maimonides considers to have been demonstrated.

41. The phrase *burhān qaṭiʿ* appears seven times in the *Guide*: (1) (1.56, 131) Maimonides demonstrates cogently that qualitative attributes, if predicated of God, must be predicated with complete equivocation. It is difficult to believe that any demonstration concerning God and attributes predicated of him is considered an explanatory demonstration. (2), (3), and (4) (1.71, 180; 2.15, 290 [twice]) These refer to Aristotle lacking "cogent demonstration" for the eternity of the world. According to Maimonides, the problem with Aristotle's demonstrations is not that they fail to *explain* the thesis but that they fail to *necessitate* it; they are mere opinions, subject to grave doubts. (5) (2.2, 252) Maimonides provides a "cogent demonstration" for the existence of God, the Necessary Existent who has no cause. This demonstration is a factual, not an explanatory one. (6) (2.11, 273) The demonstrations of the form and numbers of the spheres are not cogent because the form and number of the spheres may be other than what has been demonstrated—and not because the form and number are unexplained. (7) (2.16, 293) The philosophers have not provided cogent demonstrations for the eternity of the world but rather arguments subject to doubts. Once gain, the issue is not that they fail to explain but that they fail to necessitate.

Marwan Rashed has claimed recently that Alfarabi's physical demonstration of the eternity of the world is a factual, not explanatory, one. See Marwan Rashed, "Alfarabi's Lost Treatise on Changing Beings and the Possibility of a Demonstration of the Eternity of the World," *Arabic Sciences and Philosophy* 18 (2008): 19–58, esp. 44–45. Rashed also suggests that the two demonstrations for eternity cited by Maimonides in *Guide* 2.1, the physical and the theological, reflect the difference between factual and explanatory demonstrations, the former moving from effect to cause, the latter vice versa. Yet the theological proof (the "third philosophical demonstration") still does not qualify as an explanatory demonstration, no more than Avicenna's metaphysical demonstration qualifies as explanatory, since necessary existence does not *define* God and God's unknowable essence cannot be the explanans.

42. When Maimonides writes in *Guide* 2.2 that the "existence of the deity . . . is proved by cogent and certain demonstrations," Efodi comments, "He means to say that in truth there is no cogent demonstration since God has no prior causes, but rather God is proved through a demonstration of a sign (*mofet re'ayah*), which is taken from the things posterior" (in *Sefer Moreh Nevukhim* [Warsaw: Goldman, 1872], 2.17a). This complete reversal of Maimonides' meaning is a common feature of the fourteenth-century commentators, who attempt to harmonize Maimonides with their understanding of the Arabic tradition, especially Averroes. Moses of Narbonne (Narboni) considers the *mofet ḥotekh* mentioned in 1.71 to refer to an explanatory demonstration, but he does not consider the phrase to mean "explanatory demonstration," as can be seen from his commentary to 2.16, ed. Goldenthal (Vienna, 1852), 32a, where he interprets the phrase either as a conditional demonstration or as an absolute (i.e., explanatory) demonstration.

43. *Guide* 1.33, 72.

44. In *Guide* 3.Int, 416, Maimonides claims that although he has been led by "prophetic books and the dicta of the sages, together with the speculative premises that I possess" to interpretations of the Account of the Chariot that are "indubitable," he concedes that the matter may be otherwise, i.e., that his interpretations may not be correct. In his forthcoming book, Josef Stern infers from this passage that, according to Maimonides, certainty may be of something that is false. Yet even if this sort of indubitability is identical with some sort of certainty, it is not the same thing as *demonstrative* certainty, and the context is not one of demonstration but of exegesis of the ancient tradition of the Account of the Chariot. Not all sorts of certainty fulfill all the conditions of absolute certainty, as we noted above. Stern then argues, based on his interpretation of Maimonides' view of the Akedah, that a prophet can be certain of something that is false. Whether this interpretation is correct I leave for elsewhere; here it is sufficient to note that Samuel Ibn Tibbon translates *yaqīna* in 1.50 as *(emunah) amitit*, "true belief," and *ʿilm yaqīnī* in 3.23 as *yediʿa amitit*, "true knowledge." See *Sefer moreh ha-nevukhim*, ed. Yehuda Even-Shmuel (Jerusalem: Mosad ha-Rav Kook, 2000), 94 and 450, respectively. (This follows the practice of his father, Judah Ibn Tibbon; cf. his translation of *yaqīna* as *emet* in *Sefer emunot ve-deʿot* [Leipzig: Fischel, 1859], 1.)

45. For Alexander's influence on Maimonides via the Arabic translations of his work, see the reference in note 5 above. Two Arabic versions of the treatise, no longer extant in Greek, are edited and translated by Charles Genequand in *Alexander of Aphrodisias on the Cosmos* (Leiden: Brill, 2001), 42–143.

46. *Guide* 2.24, 322: "Do not criticize me for having set out the doubts that attach to this opinion [of eternity]. You may say: Can doubts disprove an opinion or establish its contrary as true? Surely this is not so.... The student of this Treatise should not engage in criticism because of my using this rhetorical mode of speech."

47. See Arthur Hyman, "Demonstrative, Dialectical and Sophistic Arguments in the Philosophy of Moses Maimonides," in *Moses Maimonides and His Time*, ed. Eric L. Ormsby (Washington, D.C.: Catholic University of America Press, 1989), 35–52; and Joel Kraemer, "Maimonides' Use of (Aristotelian) Dialectic," in *Maimonides and the Sciences*, ed. Robert S. Cohen and Hillel Levine (Dordrecht: Kluwer, 2000), 111–30.

48. Cf. George Vajda's translation of Alfarabi's *Treatise on the Topics*: "Les penseurs qui recherchent la vérité par de telles méthodes en viendront nécessairement soit à se contredire, soit à varier dans leurs opinions, soit à demeurer dans la perplexité," in "Autour de la théorie de la connaisance chez Saadia," 385.

49. *Guide* 1.51, 114.

50. Ibid., 2.25, 330.

51. One should caution against reading the modal condition of premises epistemically. It is not the case for the Aristotelians that an argument becomes dialectical if at least one of the premises is "likely" to be true, i.e., if the proponent has good grounds for believing it to be true. Rather, the connection between the subject and the predicate has to be a possible one. See Joep Lameer, *Al-Fārābī and the Syllogism: Theory and Practice of Aristotelian Syllogistics in the Works of Abū Naṣr Al-Fārābī (D. 950/951 A.D.)* (Leiden: Brill, 1992), xvii.

52. *Guide* 2.22, 320.

53. Charles Genequand, *Alexander of Aphrodisias on the Cosmos* (Leiden: Brill, 2001), 42 (Arabic), 44 (English translation).

54. Ibid., 122, 124 (Arabic), 123, 125 (English).

55. Ibid., 124 (Arabic), 125 (English).

56. *Guide* 2.3, 254; 2.23, 321; cf. 2.15, 290.

57. Ibn Tibbon often translates these terms by the same Hebrew term *safeq*, and *ishkāl* can also be translated as "dubiosity."

58. Ibid., 1.Int., 6.

59. Ibid., 1.Int., 15.

60. Ibid., 1.35, 70.

61. Ibid., 1.72, 193.

62. Ibid., 1.71, 80.

63. See Charles H. Manekin, *On Maimonides* (Belmont, Calif.: Wadsworth, 2005), 45.

64. Ibid., 2.17, 295.

65. Ibid., 2.23, 322.

66. Ibid., 2.19, 307.

67. Ibid., 2.19, 302; 2.22, 320.

68. Ibid., 2.14, 288–89.

69. Cf. Ibid., 2.19, 309, 2.22, 319.

CHAPTER 7. IBRĀHĪM IBN AL-FAKHKHĀR AL-YAHŪDĪ

1. Shihāb al-Dīn al-Maqqarī, *Nafḥ al-ṭīb min ghusn al-andalus al-raṭīb wa-dhikr wazīriha Lisān al-Dīn Ibn al-Khaṭīb*, ed. Iḥsān ʿAbbās (Beirut: Dār Ṣādir, 1968), 3:522–30.

2. Ibid., 3:528. I have translated the entire section on Ibn al-Fakhkhār in the appendix to this article.

3. References in chronological order: Fürchtegott Lebrecht, "Juden als Arabische Dichter," *Der Orient* 2.17 (1841): 244–54 (al-Fakhkhār on 250); Moritz Steinschneider, "Introduction to the Arabic Literature of the Jews," *Jewish Quarterly Review* 11 (1899): 585–625 (al-Fakhkhār on 590); Steinschneider, *Die Arabische Literatur der Juden* (Frankfurt am Main: J. Kauffmann, 1902), 158; A. S. Yahuda, "Shirat Yisraʾel bi-sefat Yishmaʿel be-ereṣ sefarad," *Ha-mizraḥ*, ed. Zeʾev Jawitz 1 (1903): 171ff., repr. in A. S. Yahuda, *ʿEver va-ʿarav* (New York: Ogen, 1946); Tzvi Graetz, *Divrei yemei Yisraʾel*, Hebrew trans. Shaul Rabinovitz (Warsaw: Aḥisefer, 1916), 244–45; Ḥayyim Brody, "Shirim u-mikhtavim me-rabi Meʾir Halevi Abulʿafiya," *Yediʿot ha-makhon le-ḥeqer ha-shirah ha-ʿivrit* 2 (1936): 1–90 (al-Fakhkhār mentioned on 12–13, 23–25, 41–42); José Millas Vallicrosa, *La poesía sagrada Hebraicoespañola*, 2nd ed. (Madrid-Barcelona: Consejo Superior de Investigaciones Científicas, 1948), 45; Henri Pérès, *La poésie Andalouse en Arabe Classique* (Paris: Adrien-Maisonneuve, 1953); Ambrosio Huici Miranda, *Historia política del Imperio Almohade* (Tetuán: Editora Marroqui, 1957), 401; Pilar Leon Tello, *Judios de Toledo* (Madrid: Consejo Superior de Investigaciones Científicas, 1979), 1:45; Zvi Avneri, "Ibn Alfakhar," *Encyclopedia Judaica*, 1st ed.,

8:1153–54; Bernard Septimus, *Hispano-Jewish Culture in Transition: The Career and Controversies of Ramah* (Cambridge, Mass.: Harvard University Press, 1982), 17–18 and elsewhere; Matti Huss, "'Minḥat Yehudah,' 'Ezrat ha-nashim,' ve-'ʿEin mishpaṭ'—mahadurot madaʿiyot bi-leviyat mavoʾ, ḥilufei girsaʾot, meqorot u-ferushim" (Ph.D. diss., Hebrew University of Jerusalem, 1991), 263–73; Yehudah Ratzaby, "Shirah ʿaravit be-fi yehudim be-Andalusiya," *Sefer Yisraʾel Levin,* ed. Reuven Tzur and Tova Rosen (Tel Aviv: Makhon Katz, 1994), 329–50 (al-Fakhkhār on 338–40); Joshua Blau and Joseph Yahalom, *Masʿei Yehudah: Ḥamishah pirqei masaʿ meḥurazim le-al-Ḥarizi* (Jerusalem: Ben-Zvi Institute, 2002), 39–40; M. J. Cano Pérez, "Ibn al-Fajjār al-Yahūdī, Ibrāhīm," in *Bibloteca de al-Andalus*, ed. Jorge Lirola Delgado and José Miguel Puerta Vílchez (Almería: Fundación Ibn Tufayl de Estudios Árabes, 2004), 94–95.

4. Other sources are mentioned by Yahuda in "Shirat Yisraʾel bi-sefat Yishmaʿel." Yahuda left no source citations and only the vaguest references; moreover, in a note (*ʿEver va-ʿarav,* 106n2) he apologizes to the reader that he did not have many of the Arabic sources in front of him when he wrote the article. Given these difficulties, I have only been able to locate some of the sources mentioned by Yahuda. Most tantalizing is a collection of Ibn Fakhkhār's epistles and poems compiled by a certain Ṣalāḥ al-Hamadhānī; as of now, I have not been able to locate this source.

5. Lit., "their mouths are shut tight."

6. See Huss, "Minḥat Yehudah," 32. For a partial English translation of the narrative by Raymond Scheindlin, see "The Misogynist," in *Rabbinic Fantasies,* ed. David Stern and Mark Jay Mirsky (Philadelphia: Jewish Publication Society, 1990), 269–94. The translation here is my own.

7. Judah al-Ḥarizi, *Taḥkemoni*, ed. Y. Toporovsky (Tel Aviv: Mosad ha-Rav Kook, 1952), 346.

8. Blau and Yahalom, *Masʿei Yehudah,* 40.

9. Brody, "Shirim u-mikhtavim me-rabi Meʾir Halevi Abulʿafiya."

10. A sign of suffering in Isaiah 51:17, 22.

11. Cf. Psalm 80:11.

12. Cf. Isaiah 17:13.

13. I.e., ink.

14. Cf. Job 38:11.

15. Cf. Psalm 39:6. The poem appears in Brody, "Shirim u-mikhtavim me-rabi Meʾir Halevi Abulʿafiya," 41–42. In a note, Brody also includes fragments of two more lines at the end of the elegy.

16. Lebrecht, "Juden als Arabische Dichter"; Yahuda, "Shirat Yisraʾel bi-sefat Yishmaʿel"; S. M. Stern, "Arabic Poems by Spanish-Hebrew Poets," in *Romanica et Occidentalia: Études dédiées á la mémoire de Hiram Peri*, ed. Moshe Lazar (Jerusalem: Magnes Press, 1963); Ratzaby, "Shirah ʿaravit be-fi yehudim be-Andalusiya"; James M. Nichols, "The Arabic Verses of Qasmūna bint Ismāʿīl Ibn Bagdāla," *International Journal of Middle East Studies* 13.2 (1981): 155–58; James A. Bellamy, "Qasmūna bint Ismāʿīl: Who Was She?" *Journal of the American Oriental Society* 103.2 (1983): 423–24. Ibn Sahl was a famous convert to Islam; see Shmuel Moreh, "Ibrahīm Ibn Sahl al-Andalusī al-Israʾīlī," *Encyclopaedia Judaica,*

2nd ed., 9:701. There are, of course, other Jewish poets who wrote in Arabic, beginning with the pre-Islamic period, known from numerous places. For an interesting if somewhat fanciful survey, see Murad Faraj, *Al-shuʿarā al-yahūd al-ʿarab* (Alexandria: Maṭbaʿat Ṣalāḥ al-Dīn, 1939).

17. Lit., "you do not rest where you stand and sit?"

18. See Jefim Schirmann, "The Ephebe in Medieval Hebrew Poetry," *Sefarad* 15 (1955): 55–68.

19. Assuming that Ibn Saʿīd was at least a teenager at the time of the meeting in Seville, it is clear that al-Fakhkhār continued to enjoy prestige years after Alfonso's death.

20. Hayyim Schirmann, *Toledot ha-shirah ha-ʿivrit bi-Sefarad ha-notsrit u-be-derom Tsarfat*, ed., supp., and annot. Ezra Fleischer (Jerusalem: Magnes Press, 1997), 376–77.

21. On the history and usage of the term *convivencia* in scholarship, see Thomas F. Glick and Oriol Pi-Sunyer, "Acculturation as an Explanatory Concept in Spanish History," *Comparative Studies in Society and History* 11.2 (1969): 136–54.

22. Homi Bhabha, *The Location of Culture* (New York: Routledge, 2004), esp. the essay "Signs Taken for Wonders."

23. María Judith Feliciano and Leyla Rouhi, "Introduction: Interrogating Iberian Frontiers," *Medieval Encounters* 12.3 (2006): 317–28 (quotation on 325).

24. The same verse is used as the concluding line in other anecdotes. See, e.g., ʿAbd al-Malik al-Thaʿālibī, *Al-iqtibās min al-Qurʾān al-karīm* (al-Manṣūra, Egypt: Dār al-Wafāʾ, 1992), 1:60.

25. Ross Brann, *Power in the Portrayal: Representations of Jews and Muslims in Eleventh- and Twelfth-Century Islamic Spain* (Princeton, N.J.: Princeton University Press, 2002), 113–14.

26. For examples, see Moses Ibn Ezra, *Kitāb al-muḥāḍara wa-ʾl-mudhākara*, ed. A. S. Halkin (Jerusalem: Mekitse Nirdamim, 1975), 92 (line 7), 108 (line 76), 112 (line 12), 116 (line 57).

27. See Hava Lazarus-Yafeh, "ʿAl yediʿat ha-Qurʾān be-qerev ha-yehudim ve-ʿal yaḥasam elav," *ʿOlamot shezurim: Biqoret ha-miqra ha-muslemit bi-yemei ha-beinayim* (Jerusalem: Mosad Bialik, 1998), 156–72. See also Jonathan Decter, "The Rendering of Qurʾanic Quotations in Hebrew Translations of Islamic Texts," *Jewish Quarterly Review* 96.3 (2006): 336–58.

28. See Lazarus-Yafeh, "ʿAl yediʿat ha-Qurʾān be-qerev ha-yehudim"; and Decter, "The Rendering of Qurʾanic Quotations."

29. Brann, *Power in the Portrayal.*

30. Saʿīd Ibn Luyūn al-Tujībī, *Lamḥ al-siḥr min rūḥ al-shʿir wa-rawḥ al-shiḥr*, ed. Saʿīd Ibn al-Aḥrash (Abū Dabi: Al-Mujammaʿ al-Thaqāfī, 2005), 336–37. Published in 1372, the book is an abridgment of the *Rūḥ al-shiʿr* of Muḥammad Ibn al-Jalāb.

31. I have not been able to identify this individual with certainty, but it is likely that he was a member of the family of Abū ʿAbd Allah al-Bayyāsī. The city of Bayyās (Baeza) was taken from the Almohads by Alfonso VIII in 1213–14, which would explain the contempt for Alfonso and his Jewish *wazīr*. It seems less likely that the target of the poem was the anonymous Jewish *wazīr* of Alfonso VI, with whom al-Fakhkhār has been confused

sometimes in scholarship. This anonymous *wazīr* is mentioned in Muḥammad ibn ʿAbd Allāh al-Ḥimyarī, *Kitāb al-rawḍ al-miʿtār fī khabr al-aqṭār* (Beirut: Maktabat Lubnān, 1975), 83–84.

32. Technically, the verse does not violate the Qurʾānic position that the Jews did not actually crucify Jesus but only that it appeared so (Qurʾān 4:157–59).

33. Lit., "fire, burning."

34. "fī dhikr tawaqqud al-adhhān al-andalusiyya wa-ḥubb al-andalusiyyīn li-ʾl-maʿrifa wa-barāʿatihim fī ʾl-ajwiba wa-ghair dhālika mimā yadullu ʿala faḍlihim."

35. Lit., "you do not rest where you stand and sit."

CHAPTER 8. THE IMPACT OF INTERRELIGIOUS POLEMIC ON MEDIEVAL PHILOSOPHY

1. This trend goes back at least to Moritz Steinschneider in his notes to Aaron ben Elijah, *ʿEts Ḥayyim: Ahron ben Elia's aus Nikomedien des Karäers System der Religionsphilosophie*, ed. Franz Delitzsch with notes and indices by Moritz Steinschneider (Leipzig: Johann Ambrosius Barth, 1841). Other classic examples are Solomon Munk, *Mélanges de philosophie juive et arabe* (Paris: A. Franck, 1857); and Shlomo Pines, "Translator's Introduction," Moses ben Maimon, *The Guide of the Perplexed*, trans. Shlomo Pines (Chicago: University of Chicago Press, 1963), lvii–cxxxiv. See also my "Study of Jewish Philosophy in Relation to the Philosophy of Other Religions—Reflections" [Hebrew], *Daʿat* 50–52 (2003): 61–71.

2. Shlomo Pines, "Shîʿite Terms and Conceptions in Judah Halevi's *Kuzari*," *Jerusalem Studies in Arabic and Islam* 2 (1980): 165–251; Ehud Krinis, "The Idea of the Chosen People in al-Kitāb al-Khazarī and Its Origins in Shīʿī Imām Doctrine" [Hebrew] (Ph.D. diss., Ben-Gurion University, 2008); Alfred L. Ivry, "Ismāʿīlī Theology and Maimonides' Philosophy," in *The Jews of Medieval Islam: Community, Society and Identity*, ed. Daniel Frank (Leiden: Brill, 1995), 271–99.

3. See, e.g., Elliot R. Wolfson, "Merkavah Traditions in Philosophical Garb: Judah Halevi Reconsidered," *Proceedings of the American Academy for Jewish Research* 57 (1991): 179–242.

4. A favorite topic is Maimonides' influence on Thomas Aquinas; see, e.g., the collection of articles in Jacob I. Dienstag, *Studies in Maimonides and St. Thomas Aquinas* (New York: Ktav, 1975). For Maimonides' influence on Meister Eckhart, see Yossef Schwartz, *"To Thee Is Silence Praise": Meister Eckhart's Reading in Maimonides' Guide of the Perplexed* [Hebrew] (Tel Aviv: ʿAm ʿOved, 2002).

5. Diana Lobel, *A Sufi-Jewish Dialogue: Philosophy and Mysticism in Baḥya ibn Paqūda's "Duties of the Heart"* (Philadelphia: University of Pennsylvania Press, 2007).

6. Ibid., 66–116.

7. Note that even though the first Jewish writings on these subjects seem to have been preserved better than the parallel Islamic ones, the Jews lagged behind members of the other two religions by 100 to 150 years, a common phenomenon in most cultural and intellectual pursuits in the classical period of Judaeo-Arabic culture (ninth to twelfth centuries).

8. Sarah Stroumsa, "The Signs of Prophecy: The Emergence and Early Development of a Theme in Arabic Theological Literature," *Harvard Theological Review* 78 (1985): 101–14 (revised in Stroumsa, *Freethinkers of Medieval Islam* [Leiden: Brill, 1999], 21–36).

9. The Kalām was the earliest type of Islamic theology that stressed the unity and justice of God. Many Kalām treatises begin with an epistemological discussion laying out the correct method of achieving the truth. See, e.g., Harry A. Wolfson, *The Philosophy of the Kalam* (Cambridge, Mass.: Harvard University Press, 1976). The Kalām's dialectical and polemical origins are discussed in Sarah Stroumsa, "The Beginnings of the Muʿtazila Reconsidered," *Jerusalem Studies in Arabic and Islam* 13 (1990): 265–93.

10. Saadia Gaon (Rabbenu Saʿadiah ben Yosef al-Fayyūmī), *Kitāb al-mukhtār fī al-ʾamānāt wa-ʾl-iʿtiqādāt (Sefer ha-nivḥar ba-ʾemunot u-va-deʿot)*, ed. and trans. Yosef Kafih (New York: Sura, 1970), 23–29; Saadia ben Joseph Gaon, *The Book of Beliefs and Opinions*, trans. Samuel Rosenblatt (New Haven, Conn.: Yale University Press, 1948), 26–33. For a discussion of Saadia's epistemology, see Georges Vajda, "Autour de la théorie de la connaissance chez Saadia," *Revue des Études Juives* 126 (1967): 375–97.

11. Saadia discusses signs of prophecy in *Amānāt*, 124–31 (3:4–6); *Beliefs and Opinions*, 147–57.

12. Saadia, *Amānāt*, 136–37 (3:8); *Beliefs and Opinions*, 163–64.

13. Moses Mendelssohn, *Jerusalem and Other Jewish Writings*, trans. Alfred Jospe (New York: Schocken Books, 1969), 124; cf. 130–32.

14. *Kuzari*, part 1, sections 8, 25, 48, 84–88; see Judah Halevi, *Kitāb al-radd wa ʾl-dalīl fī ʾl-dīn al-dhalīl (al-Kitāb al-Khazarī)*, ed. David H. Baneth, prepared for publication by Haggai Ben-Shammai (Jerusalem: Magnes Press, 1977), 9, 11–12, 14, 23–24. This argument has its background in the Islamic notion of *tawātur*; see, e.g., Bernard Weiss, "Knowledge of the Past: The Theory of *Tawâtur* According to Ghazâlî," *Studia Islamica* 61 (1985): 81–105.

15. Discussions of prophecy and its epistemological value did not cease, of course, with Halevi. Maimonides, for instance, discusses prophecy at length; see Howard T. Kreisel, *Prophecy: The History of an Idea in Medieval Jewish Philosophy* (Dordrecht: Kluwer, 2001), 148–315. For a late medieval Jewish discussion of signs of prophecy and their validation, see Joseph Albo, *Sefer ha-ʿiqqarim (Book of Principles)*, ed. and trans. Isaac Husik, 4 vols. (Philadelphia: Jewish Publication Society, 1946), 1:153–65.

In the Islamic world, Ashʿarite theologians could use neither rationality of the message, assuming that one can even determine how rational the message is, nor the righteousness of the messenger as signs of prophecy since they believed that God is not bound by any restrictions in His actions (thus, an authentic prophet could be one who was immoral and whose message was irrational). Some also questioned the reliability of reports about miracles since humans are incapable of distinguishing between miracles and sorcery; see Frank Griffel, "Al-Ġazālī's Concept of Prophecy: The Introduction of Avicennan Psychology into Ašʿarite Theology," *Arabic Sciences and Philosophy* 14 (2004): 101–44. I thank Professor Griffel for his comments on this essay.

16. See Alexander Altmann, "Saadya's Theory of Revelation: Its Origin and Background," *Studies in Religious Philosophy and Mysticism* (London: Routledge and Kegan

Paul, 1969), 140–60 (originally published in Erwin I. J. Rosenthal, ed., *Saadya Studies* [Manchester: Manchester University Press, 1943], 4–25).

17. Leon Nemoy, "A Tenth-Century Criticism of the Doctrine of the Logos (John 1, 1)," *Journal of Biblical Literature* 64 (1945): 515–29, discusses Qirqisānī's refutation of the eternity of God's word, argumentation that is more likely directed against the Islamic view of the Qur'ān than the Christian doctrine of the Logos.

18. In his discussion of Maimonides' view and its possible impact and anticipation of the Scholastic doctrine of ordinary and absolute divine power, Aviezer Ravitzky has argued that Maimonides was a pioneer since he was the first to frame the issue of possibility and impossibility in physical terms. According to Ravitzky, kalāmic analyses of God's power revolved around moral issues (for instance, whether God can do evil) rather than physical ones (*Maimonidean Essays* [Hebrew] [Jerusalem: Schocken, 2006], 157–80; see my review in *Zion* 73 [2008]: 217–22). Saadia Gaon does, however, raise the issue of natural possibility and impossibility in a framework that is clearly polemical. He cites the questions of certain heretics (*mulḥidūn*) who had asked whether God can cause five to be more than ten without adding anything to the five or taking away anything from the ten; whether God can put the world through the hollow of a ring without making the world narrower or the ring wider; or whether God can bring back yesterday. Saadia argues that these are not possibilities even though God is omnipotent. God's omnipotence means that God can do "everything" (*kull shay*), but the examples cited are "nothing" (*laysa huwa shay*) and do not fall within God's power (*Amānāt*, 114 [2:13]; *Beliefs and Opinions*, 134). In similar fashion, Judah Halevi denies God the possibility of doing the impossible in terms of creation or revelation, or in his language: "God forbid that God do something against reason" (*Kuzari* 1:67, 89; *Al-Khazarī*, 18, 25).

19. Judah Halevi does argue that Christian beliefs contradict logical analogy (*qiyās*); *Kuzari* 1:5; *Al-Khazarī*, 8.

20. See Daniel J. Lasker, "Averroistic Trends in Jewish-Christian Polemics in the Late Middle Ages," *Speculum* 55.2 (1980): 294–304.

21. See Daniel J. Lasker, *Jewish Philosophical Polemics Against Christianity in the Middle Ages* (New York: Ktav, 1977; 2nd ed., Oxford: Littman, 2007).

22. Christianity is mentioned in Baḥya's discussion of divine attributes in *Duties of the Heart*, 1, 7, 10; see Rabenu Baḥya ibn Paqūda, *Sefer torat ḥovot ha-levavot*, ed. Yosef Kafih (Jerusalem: Ha-Va'ad ha-Kelali li-Yehudei Teman bi-Yerushalayyim, 1973), 66, 91. In standard editions of Judah ibn Tibbon's translation, these references to Christians are omitted. It is perhaps this lack of explicit connection between Baḥya's discussion and the Jewish critique of Christianity that caused Diana Lobel to ignore the polemical background. For Baḥya's influence on subsequent anti-trinitarian arguments, see Gad Freudenthal's contribution to this volume.

23. See Daniel J. Lasker, "Definitions of 'One' and Divine Unity," in *Studies in Jewish Thought* [Hebrew], ed. Sarah O. Heller Wilenski and Moshe Idel (Jerusalem: Magnes Press, 1989), 51–61.

24. Wolfson, *Kalam*, 112–234; Wolfson, *Repercussions of the Kalam in Jewish Philosophy* (Cambridge, Mass.: Harvard University Press, 1979), 1–74.

25. See David Thomas, *Anti-Christian Polemic in Early Islam* (Cambridge: Cambridge University Press, 1992).

26. Lasker, *Jewish Philosophical Polemics*, 63–76.

27. This particular issue prompts consideration of a fourth party in the Islamic realm, namely, "freethinkers" who questioned many of the basic assumptions of revealed religion and stimulated philosophical discussions; see Stroumsa, *Freethinkers*. Saadia's thought, for instance, may have been partially shaped by his response to the Persian heretic Hayyoy al-Balkhī.

28. Saadia, *Amānāt*, 148–49; *Beliefs and Opinions*, 179.

29. Halevi, *Kuzari* 1:112–15; *Al-Khazarī*, 38–40; cf. also 4:21–23/171–73.

30. The issue of contradictions between Crescas's philosophical and polemical works is discussed in my introduction to *The Refutation of the Christian Principles by Hasdai Crescas* (Albany: State University of New York Press, 1992).

31. See the extensive discussion in Ryan W. Szpiech, "From *Testimonia* to Testimony: Thirteenth-Century Anti-Jewish Polemic and the *Monstrador de justicia* of Abner of Burgos/Alfonso de Valladolid" (Ph.D. diss., Yale University, 2006), 56–146.

CHAPTER 9. ARABIC INTO HEBREW

This is the somewhat revised text of a lecture given at the Center for Advanced Judaic Studies (CAJS), University of Pennsylvania, on November 15, 2006, in the framework of the research group "Jewish, Christian, and Muslim Life Under Caliphs and Sultans." It is a preliminary, exploratory statement of a few ideas I hope to treat more fully in the future. I express my gratitude to CAJS for the kind invitation, to its fellows for their feedback, and to the editors of the volume as well as to an anonymous referee for their helpful observations.

1. Binjamin Zeev Benedikt, *Merkaz ha-Torah bi-Provans* (Jerusalem: Mosad ha-Rav Kook, 1985).

2. Drawing on Moritz Steinschneider's monumental *Die Hebraeischen Übersetzungen des Mittelalters und die Juden als Dolmetscher* (Berlin, 1893; repr., Graz: Akademische Druck- u. Verlagsanstalt, 1956), I described this process in "Les sciences dans les communautés juives médiévales de Provence: Leur appropriation, leur rôle," *Revue des Études Juives* 152 (1993): 29–136, and "Science in the Medieval Jewish Culture of Southern France," *History of Science* 33 (1995): 23–58; the latter is reprinted in *Science in the Medieval Hebrew and Arabic Traditions* (Aldershot: Ashgate, 2005). See also Y. Tzvi Langermann, *The Jews and the Sciences in the Middle Ages* (Aldershot: Ashgate, 1999).

3. Isadore Twersky, "Aspects of the Social and Cultural History of Provençal Jewry," *Journal of World History* 11.1–2 (1968): 185–207, on 190–91.

4. For a historical overview and bibliography, see, e.g., Jacob J. Schacter, ed., *Judaism's Encounter with Other Cultures: Rejection or Integration?* (Northvale, N.J.: Jason Aronson, 1997).

5. *She'elot u-teshuvot le-ha-rav Rabenu Asher z.l.* (Jerusalem: n.p., 1981), § 55, p. 53[va].

6. See my "Causes and Reasons for the Emergence of the Twelfth-Century Translation Movement in Lunel: Judah Ibn Tibbon and His Patrons R. Meshullam b. Jacob and R. Asher b. Meshullam," in *Ta-Shma: Studies in Judaica in Memory of Israel M. Ta-Shma* [Hebrew], ed. R. Reiner et al. (Alon-Shevut: Tevunot Publishing, 2011), 651–72; "The Introduction of Non-Rabbinic Learning into Provence in the Middle of the Twelfth Century: Two Sociological Patterns (Abraham Ibn Ezra and Judah Ibn Tibbon)," in *Exchange and Transmission Across Cultural Boundaries: Philosophy, Mysticism and Science in the Mediterranean World*, ed. Sarah Stroumsa and Haggai Ben-Shammai (Jerusalem: Israel Academy of Science and Humanities, forthcoming); "A Twelfth-Century Provençal Amateur of Neoplatonic Philosophy in Hebrew: R. Asher b. Meshullam of Lunel," *Chora* 3–4 (2005–6): 155–82.

7. I refer to the scientific-philosophical culture; the case of medicine is rather different. See my "Arabic and Latin Cultures as Resources for the Hebrew Translation Movement: Comparative Considerations, Both Quantitative and Qualitative," in *Science in Medieval Jewish Cultures*, ed. Gad Freudenthal (New York: Cambridge University Press, 2011), 74–105.

8. See "Arabic and Latin Cultures as Resources for the Hebrew Translation Movement."

9. See the classic work by Ephraim E. Urbach, *Baʿaley ha-tosafot* (Jerusalem: Mosad Bialik, 1986).

10. On the attitudes to science and philosophy in Ashkenaz and Tsarfat, see Gad Freudenthal, ed., *Science and Philosophy in Ashkenazi Culture: Rejection, Toleration, and Accommodation*, in *Simon Dubnow Institute Yearbook* (Leipzig: Vandenhoeck and Ruprecht, 2009), 8:13–315.

11. There is no recent comprehensive study of philosophy and science in Italy during the Middle Ages. Very useful are still M. Güdemann, *Geschichte des Erziehungswesen und der Cultur der Juden in Italien während des Mittelalters* (Vienna: Alfred Hölder, 1884; repr., Amsterdam: Philo Press, 1964); and Hermann Vogelstein and Paul Ringer, *Geschichte der Juden in Rom* (Berlin: Mayer and Müller, 1896). The singularities of the Italian situation are also reviewed in my "Arabic and Latin Cultures."

12. Amos Funkenstein, "Changes in the Patterns of Christian Anti-Jewish Polemics in the Twelfth Century" [Hebrew], *Zion* 33 (1965): 125–44; updated English version in Funkenstein, *Perceptions of Jewish History* (Berkeley: University of California Press, 1993), 172–201. Funkenstein's theses have been criticized by some scholars, but the areas of their disagreements are not of immediate concern in the present context. See Daniel J. Lasker, "Jewish-Christian Polemics at the Turning Point: Jewish Evidence from the Twelfth Century," *Harvard Theological Review* 89 (1996): 161–73, at 161–64.

13. English translation in Petrus Alfonsi, *Dialogue Against the Jews*, trans. Irven M. Resnick, (Washington, D.C.: Catholic University of America Press, 2006). See Daniel J. Lasker, "Mission, Conversion, and Polemic: The Revisionist View," *Jewish Quarterly Review* 100 (2010): 706–11. On Petrus Alfonsi as a translator, see Charles Burnett, "The Works of Petrus Alfonsi: Questions of Authenticity," *Medium Aevum* 66 (1997): 42–79; and Burnett, "Postscript (2007)," *Aleph* 10 (2010): 166–68.

14. See the insightful characterization of Alfonsi in Manfred Kniewasser, "Die antijüdische Polemik des Petrus Alphonsi (getauft 1106) und des Abtes Petrus Venerabilis von Cluny (+ 1156)," *Kairos* 22 (1980): 34–76. On Alfonsi's use of science, see Barbara P. Hurwitz,

"*Fidei Causa et Tui Amore*: The Role of Petrus Alphonsi's Dialogues in the History of Jewish-Christian Debate" (Ph.D. diss., Yale University, 1983), esp. chapter 3, "Philosophy and Science in Alphonsi's Dialogues."

15. Jacob b. Reuven, *Milḥamot ha-Shem*, ed. Judah Rosenthal (Jerusalem: Mosad ha-Rav Kook, 1963). Regarding date and location of composition, see pp. viii–x. Other historians believe that the book was written in Huesca in the northern Iberian Peninsula. See, e.g., Carlos del Valle, "Jacob ben Rubén de Huesca. Polemista: Su patria y su época," in *Polemica Judeo-Cristiana: Estudios*, ed. Carlos del Valle Rodriguez (Madrid: Aben Ezra, 1992), 59–65.

16. On the Sefardi sources of *Milḥamot ha-Shem*, see Daniel J. Lasker, "Ha-pulmus ha-yehudi-noṣeri u-meqorotav be-arṣot ha-islam," *Peʿamim* 57 (1993): 4–16.

17. *Milḥamot ha-Shem*, ed. Rosenthal, 141: "How can the tormented stand up against the tormenter? . . . God knows that I did not want to mention any of this Gate [the eleventh, containing refutations of Christian theology grounded in the New Testament], but my friends compelled me. . . . And I did not reveal a tenth of a tenth, for I am afraid."

18. E.g., *Milḥamot ha-Shem*, ed. Rosenthal, 86, 137.

19. David Berger, "Gilbert Crispin, Alan of Lille, and Jacob ben Reuben," *Speculum* 49 (1974): 34–47, reprinted in his *Persecution, Polemic, and Dialogue: Essays in Jewish-Christian Relations* (Boston: Academic Studies Press, 2010), 227–44.

20. *Milḥamot ha-Shem*, ed. Rosenthal, 9 (with n. 7), similarly, p. 42. Judah Ibn Tibbon's philosophical terminology is used by Jacob throughout his book; this aspect of the work deserves a special study.

21. On which see the literature in n. 6 above.

22. *Milḥamot ha-Shem*, ed. Rosenthal, 157–64. Saadya is also cited and at times named on pp. 45, 48, 121, 122. Certain of his views are opposed on pp. 165ff.

23. See the editor's observation in *Milḥamot ha-Shem*, ed. Rosenthal, 157n1; see also the notes to the following pages. It remains to be checked whether Jacob b. Reuben knew the paraphrastic version directly or through quotations in Berakhiah b. Natronnay ha-Naqdan. On the paraphrastic translation, see Ronald C. Kiener, "The Hebrew Paraphrase of Saadiah Gaon's *Kitāb al-amānāt waʾl-iʿtiqādāt*," *AJS Review* 11 (1986): 1–25.

24. *Milḥamot ha-Shem*, ed. Rosenthal, 45.

25. Ibid., 177. Jacob b. Reuben probably used a Hebrew treatise by Ibn Zabara now no longer extant; see Joseph ben Meir Zabara, *Sepher Shaashuim*, ed. Israel Davidson (New York: Jewish Theological Seminary of America Press, 1914), xcviii–xcix. Jacob quotes from this work at great length.

26. *Milḥamot ha-Shem*, ed. Rosenthal, 32.

27. Daniel J. Lasker and Sarah Stroumsa, *The Polemic of Nestor the Priest* [Hebrew] (Jerusalem: Ben-Zvi Institute, 1996). The circumstances of the Hebrew translation of this work unfortunately are unknown. For the use of this work by Jacob b. Reuben, see Lasker, "Jewish-Christian Polemics at the Turning Point," 166.

28. *Milḥamot ha-Shem*, ed. Rosenthal, 164. Jacob b. Reuben says elsewhere that he used the biblical exegesis by Isaac Israeli, who "has interpreted the said verses the same way as we did" (p. 176). In all likelihood, this is a reference to Israeli's lost *Maʾamar yishretsu*

ha-mayim, his only exegetical writing. See the editor's introduction to *Das Buch über die Elemente . . . von Isaak b. Salomon Israeli*, ed. Salomon Fried (Frankfurt a.M.: J. Kauffmann, 1900), 49. This work by Israeli was known to Provençal scholars such as David Qimḥi (less than one generation after Jacob b. Reuben) and Yedaʿyah ha-Penini (mid-fourteenth century); see Fried, "Introduction," 46, 49.

29. Text: *Sefer ha-berit u-vikkuḥey Radaq ʿim ha-natsrut*, ed. Ephraim Talmage (Jerusalem: Mosad Bialik, 1974). The title inappropriately refers to Radaq as the author, but the text is by Joseph Qimḥi. English translation: *The Book of the Covenant of Joseph Kimhi*, trans. Frank Talmage (Toronto: Pontifical Institute of Mediaeval Studies, 1972).

30. *Sefer ha-berit*, 21; *The Book of the Covenant*, 28. On numerous occasions, the protagonist for Judaism appeals to what the "intellect" admits or considers as unacceptable. See Talmage, introduction to *The Book of the Covenant*, 21.

31. Talmage, introduction, 21.

32. *Sefer ha-berit*, 21; *The Book of the Covenant*, 28.

33. *Sefer ha-berit*, 21; *The Book of the Covenant*, 20, 28.

34. *Sefer ha-berit*, 21; *The Book of the Covenant*, 28 (modified).

35. *Sefer ha-berit*, 33 (with n. 38), 34–35; *The Book of the Covenant*, 41 (with nn. 29, 29a, 30), 43 (with n. 30a). See also Daniel J. Lasker, *Jewish Philosophical Polemics Against Christianity in the Middle Ages* (1977; Oxford: Littman Library of Jewish Civilization, 2007), 62, 203n137.

36. On *Sefer milḥamot ha-Shem* and *Sefer ha-berit*, see also the characterizations in Robert Chazan, *Fashioning Jewish Identity in Medieval Western Christendom* (Cambridge: Cambridge University Press, 2004), 94–103.

37. The use of philosophical arguments in religious polemics has been extensively and expertly studied in numerous publications by Prof. Daniel J. Lasker. His general aim is not to examine the polemics in a historical perspective but to trace the genealogy of philosophical ideas used in polemical literature. See Lasker's own characterization of his project in the introduction to the 2007 reedition of his *Jewish Philosophical Polemics Against Christianity in the Middle Ages*. His article "The Impact of Interreligious Polemic on Medieval Philosophy" (in this volume), too, aims to present "only a few examples of how recourse to the polemical literature and awareness of the polemical impulses behind certain philosophical discussions can enrich our understanding of the medieval philosophical enterprise" (this volume, p. 123). However, in his study "Natsrut, pilosofiah u-pulmus bi-provans ha-yehudit," *Zion* 68 (1993): 313–33, Lasker moved toward a historical analysis. Although he intimates that there is a connection between religious polemics and the rise of Jewish philosophy in the Midi, he remains uncommitted on possible causal relationships. He states that "the interest in philosophy and the polemical drive emerged among Provençal Jews together and remained bound together for centuries" (315); that there was "a strong connection between Jewish interest in philosophy and the Jewish inclination to anti-Christian polemics (329–30); and that "It seems that it can be concluded that between the 12th and the 14th centuries, philosophy and the interest in Christianity went hand in hand in Provence" (333). These statements deliberately avoid positing a causal relationship between the two phenomena. The closest Professor Lasker comes to positing such a causal relationship is in the following statements:

"The attempts of Jewish thinkers who emigrated to Provence and of their descendents and students to introduce philosophical learning into the Jewish community in Provence produced a philosophical-scientific inter-religious discussion" (330); "One can perhaps generalize and say that the introduction of philosophy into Jewish communities in Christendom during the Middle Ages was accompanied by anti-Christian polemics. Not all the polemicists in Christian lands were philosophers and there were also other causes for the Jewish-Christian polemics in Provence and elsewhere at that period. But those who were interested in philosophy, in Provence, in Ashkenaz and in Italy, were quite strongly involved in the Jewish-Christian polemics" (330). The causal relationship implied here is that a Jewish proficiency in philosophy generated the philosophically grounded interreligious polemics, so that that proficiency was one of the "causes for the Jewish-Christian polemics in Provence." This is the inverse of the causal relationship that I try to point out.

38. Judah Rosenthal, ed., *Sefer Yosef ha-meqanne' le-R. Yosef b.R. Nathan Official* (Jerusalem: Mekitse Nirdamim, 1970), introduction, 15–18 (Hebrew pagination).

39. Daniel J. Lasker, "Jewish Philosophical Polemics in Ashkenaz," in Ora Limor and Guy G. Stroumsa, *Contra Judaeos: Ancient and Medieval Polemics Between Christians and Jews* (Tübingen: Mohr, 1996), 195–213, on p. 199.

40. Lasker, "Jewish Philosophical Polemics," 211. Even when the author of *Sefer niṣṣaḥon yashan* had in front of him a short philosophical passage he refrained from copying it. See Berger, *The Jewish-Christian Debate*, 368–69; and Lasker, "Jewish Philosophical Polemics," 211–12.

41. *Sefer Yosef ha-meqanne'*, 33, where the notes identify the sources. The expression "the ones in disarray [*ha-mevohalim*]" seems to refer to converts and near-converts, who are largely the addressees of the book (see pp. 3, 6, 15).

42. "In what does he resemble Him? In the image of dominion and the likeness of rulership, for just as the Holy One, blessed be He, rules over all, so does man rule.... Here image and likeness are not to be taken literally but metaphorically." His strong philosophical commitment comes to the fore even more clearly in the following consideration: "What is the matter with you? On the basis of one obscure passage you deny His unity?" *Sefer ha-berit*, 32; *The Book of the Covenant*, 40–41. Qimḥi also argued that scriptural references to the deity's "limbs" are to be taken metaphorically (pp. 34, 42–43, respectively).

43. See Eleazar Touitou, *"Ha-peshaṭot ha-mitḥadeshim be-khol yom": 'Iyyunim be-perusho shel Rashbam la-Torah* (Ramat Gan: Bar-Ilan University Press, 2003); and Sarah Kamin, "Affinities Between Jewish and Christian Exegesis in Twelfth-Century Northern France," *Proceedings of the Ninth World Congress of Jewish Studies* (Jerusalem: World Union of Jewish Studies, 1985), 141–55. The issue touched upon here is obviously related to a wider one that has been much discussed in recent years: Were medieval Jews in Ashkenaz aware of the majority religious culture and are some Jewish religious rituals a reaction to them? Ivan Marcus has argued for a positive answer, suggesting that as a result of contact with the environment, Ashkenazi Judaism underwent a kind of acculturation quite distinct from that found in Sefarad. According to this argument, Jews were aware of religious practices of their Christian neighbors and instituted parallel, Jewish versions of some of them; acculturation here passed via the emulation of rituals rather than via the adoption of doctrinal contents.

See Ivan G. Marcus, *Rituals of Childhood: Jewish Acculturation in Medieval Europe* (New Haven, Conn.: Yale University Press, 1996). The difficulty facing this thesis is that the contemporary sources themselves give no evidence of an awareness that the Jewish rituals were in any way a reaction to the Christian ones: the question therefore arises whether the posited connection is not merely a construction of the modern historian. See Israel Ta-Shma, "Ṭeqes ha-ḥanikhah be-Yisrael, meqorotav, toldotav, semalav ve-darkhey hitpateḥuto," *Tarbiẓ* 68.4 (1999): 587–98. A more comprehensive discussion of the cultural specificity of northern Judaism will have to take into account this dimension, too.

44. David Berger, "Mission to Jews and Jewish-Christian Contacts in the Polemical Literature of the High Middle Ages," *American Historical Review* 91 (1986): 576–591, on 590, reprinted in *Persecution, Polemic, and Dialogue*, 177–98, on 197.

45. Thus Gilbert Dahan writes, with reference notably to the north: "La controverse s'est-elle enfin haussée à un niveau philosophique? Son histoire est assez curieuse à cet égard: jusqu'au XIIIe siècle, les polémistes chrétiens s'efforcent de situer leur démarche sur un plan rationnel; il n'y parviennent pas et se heurtent à une fin de non recevoir de la part des juifs." Gilbert Dahan, *La polémique chrétienne contre le judaïsme au moyen âge* (Paris: Albin Michel, 1991), 120–21.

46. Ta-Shma, *Ha-sifrut ha-parshanit la-Talmud*, vol. 1, *1000–1200* (Jerusalem: Magnes Press, 1999), 96–117 (113–14 on the absence of science from yeshivah curricula). See also Ta-Shma, *Ha-sifrut ha-parshanit la-Talmud*, vol. 2, *1200–1400* (Jerusalem, Magnes Press, 2000), 99–101.

47. Mark R. Cohen, *Under Crescent and Cross: The Jews in the Middle Ages* (Princeton, N.J.: Princeton University Press, 1994); Cohen, "Anti-Jewish Violence and the Place of the Jews in Christendom and in Islam: A Paradigm," in *Religious Violence Between Christians and Jews: Medieval Roots, Modern Perspectives*, ed. Anna Sapir Abulafia (Houndsmills, Hampshire: Palgrave, 2002), 107–37. This important article now appears (in revised form) in an enlarged edition of *Under Crescent and Cross* (Princeton, N.J.: Princeton University Press, 2008), 271–86.

48. Cohen, "Anti-Jewish Violence," 124.

49. Ibid., 125.

50. See my "Arabic and Latin Cultures."

51. See, e.g., Dahan, *La polémique chrétienne contre le judaïsme*, 35–42, 63. See also the concise observations in Talmage, introduction, 16–17, 20–21.

52. Berger, "Mission to Jews": "The polemical works that I have examined do more than reveal the absence of a missionary ideology; they also make assertions about frequent discussions between Jews and Christians at and especially below the level of the upper clergy" (585 [*Persecution, Polemic, and Dialogue*, 190]); "These exchanges . . . were real and frequent" (586 [191]); "These were not formal disputations [but rather] for the most part informal discussions that took place in the course of everyday life" (588 [194]). Similarly Dahan, *La polémique chrétienne contre le judaïsme*, 69–86.

53. E.g., Talmage, introduction, 23.

54. *Sefer ha-berit*, 21; *The Book of the Covenant*, 27 (with n. 1); see also pp. 21 and 28, respectively.

55. David Berger, *The Jewish-Christian Debate in the High Middle Ages: A Critical Edition of Niẓẓaḥon Vetus with an Introduction, Translation, and Commentary* (Philadelphia: Jewish Publication Society of America, 1979), 20–21.

56. See now the studies collected in Freudenthal, *Science and Philosophy in Ashkenazi Culture.*

57. See my "Arabic and Latin Cultures."

CHAPTER 10. FUSION COOKING IN AN ISLAMIC MILIEU

1. Isadore Twersky, *Introduction to the Code of Maimonides* (New Haven, Conn.: Yale University Press, 1980), 60.

2. Sarah Stroumsa, "The Muslim Context of Medieval Jewish Philosophy," in *Cambridge History of Jewish Philosophy: From Antiquity Through the Seventeenth Century*, ed. Steven Nadler and T. M. Rudavsky (Cambridge: Cambridge University Press, 2009), 55.

3. For a more extensive study of such restrictions, see David M. Freidenreich, *Foreigners and Their Food: Constructing Otherness in Jewish, Christian, and Islamic Law* (Berkeley: University of California Press, 2011).

4. William Ewald, "Comparative Jurisprudence (I): What Was It Like to Try a Rat?" *University of Pennsylvania Law Review* 143 (1995): 1940.

5. Ibid., 1991ff.

6. On Barhebraeus, see Hidemi Takahashi, *Barhebraeus: A Bio-Bibliography* (Piscataway, N.J.: Gorgias Press, 2005).

7. Carlo Alfonso Nallino, "Il diritto musulmano nel Nomocanone siriaco cristiano di Barhebreo," *Rivista degli Studi Orientali* 9 (1921–23): 512–80, reprinted in *Raccolta di scritti editi e inediti*, vol. 4, *diritto musulmano, Dirittio orientali cristiani* (Rome: Istituto per l'Oriente, 1942), 214–90; citations below refer to the original pagination. Familiarity with Islamic law was commonplace among medieval Christian scholars active within the Islamic world; see David M. Freidenreich, "Muslims in Eastern Canon Law, 1000–1500," in *Christian-Muslim Relations: A Bibliographical History*, vol. 5, ed. David Thomas et al. (Leiden: Brill, forthcoming), and the works cited there.

8. See, e.g., Arthur Vööbus, *Syrische Kanonessammlungen: Ein Beitrag zur Quellenkunde* (Louvain: Secrétariat du Corpus SCO, 1970), 2:551–52; Herman G. B. Teule, "Barhebraeus' Ethicon, al-Ghazzālī, and Ibn Sīnā," *Islamochristiana* 18 (1992): 74; and Takahashi, *Barhebraeus*, 67.

9. Hanna Khadra, "Le Nomocanon de Bar Hebraeus: Son importance juridique entre les sources chrétiennes et les sources musulmanes" (Ph.D. diss., Pontificia Università Lateranense, Rome, 2005). The titles of Ghazālī's three codes, *al-Wajīz*, *al-Wasīṭ*, and *al-Basīṭ*, literally express their relative sizes.

10. Gregorius Barhebraeus, *Nomocanon*, ed. Paul Bedjan (Paris: Harrassowitz, 1898), 458–67 (chapter 35). This chapter of the *Ktābā d-Hudāye*, which appears in the context of chapters related to civil law, contains "the only systematic presentation of

canon law in matters of diet that we possess from the Syrian churches," according to Michael Cook, "Early Islamic Dietary Law," *Jerusalem Studies in Arabic and Islam* 7 (1986): 264.

11. Barhebraeus, *Nomocanon*, 458. All translations in this essay are original.

12. See al-Ghazālī's *Kitāb al-wajīz*, in ʿAbd al-Karīm b. Muḥammad al-Rāfiʿī, *Kitāb al-ʿazīz: sharḥ al-wajīz* (Beirut: Dār al-Kutub al-ʿIlmiyya, 1997), 12:3; and Muḥammad b. Muḥammad al-Ghazālī, *Kitāb al-wasīṭ fī al-madhāhib* (Cairo: Dār al-Salām, 1997), 7:101–2.

13. Nallino, "Diritto musulmano," 567. The classic studies of Christian dietary regulations remain Karl Böckenhoff, *Das apostolische Speisegesetz in den ersten fünf Jahrhunderten* (Paderborn: Ferdinand Schöningh, 1903); and Böckenhoff, *Speisesatzungen mosaicher Art* (Münster: Aschendorffschen Buchhandlung, 1907).

14. Arthur Vööbus, ed., *The Synodicon in the West Syrian Tradition*, CSCO, Scriptores Syri, vols. 161–64 (Louvain: Secrétariat du Corpus SCO, 1975); see Canons of the Testament of Our Lord, c. 38 (161:45, 162:61), and Canons of the Synod of Ancyra, cc. 4, 6 (161:94–96, 162:102–3). Khadra, "Le Nomocanon," 189–91, and Walter Selb, *Orientalisches Kirchenrecht, band II: Die Geschichte des Kirchenrechts der Westsyrer (von den Anfängen bis zur Mongolenzeit)* (Vienna: Verlag der Österreichischen Akademie der Wissenschaften, 1989), 155, identify the *Synodicon* as one of the sources familiar to Barhebraeus. Herman G. B. Teule, "Juridical Texts in the *Ethicon* of Barhebraeus," *Oriens Christianus* 79 (1995): 23–45, however, argues that the latter work displays no familiarity with the *Synodicon*.

15. Jacob of Edessa, Responsum 17 to John the Stylite, in Vööbus, *Synodicon*, 161:254 (English trans. 162:232); Jacob cites 1 Cor. 10:25. Khadra, "Le Nomocanon," 183n642, states that Jacob is the most frequently cited authority in the *Ktābā d-Hudāye*, although this claim appears to rest solely on a study of the first eight chapters of the work, which address distinctly ecclesiastical matters.

16. Responsum 3 to Thomas the Recluse, in Vööbus, *Synodicon*, 161:257–58 (English trans. 162:235). Jacob declares that those who eat such food "shall be cast out from the Church of God and from association with the faithful as one who is impure and despised and abominable, and they shall be numbered among the Jews until they purify themselves through repentance." (This translation is my own.)

17. In doing so, al-Ghazālī glosses over extensive discussions within Sunni legal literature of such questions as whether one may purchase meat prohibited under Jewish law from a Jewish butcher and whether one may purchase meat that a Christian slaughters in the name of Christ. See Freidenreich, *Foreigners and Their Food*; Freidenreich, "Five Questions About Non-Muslim Meat: Toward a New Appreciation of Ibn Qayyim al-Ǧawziyyah's Contribution to Islamic Law," in *A Scholar in the Shadow: Essays in the Legal and Theological Thought of Ibn Qayyim al-Ǧawziyyah*, ed. Caterina Bori and Livnat Holtzman, *Oriente Moderno* 90.1 (2010): 43–64.

18. See David M. Freidenreich, "Muslims in Canon Law, ca. 650–1000," in *Christian-Muslim Relations*, vol. 1, ed. Thomas et al. (Leiden: Brill, 2009), 99–114. Christians also regularly equated Jews and pagans. For example, canon 25 of the Council of ʿIshoyahb I, held in Ctesiphon in 585, condemns Christians who "celebrate festivals with Jews, heretics,

and pagans or accept something sent by them from the festivals of other religions"; see J. B. Chabot, *Synodicon Orientale* (Paris: C. Klincksieck, 1902), 157–58 (French trans. 417–18). More broadly, see Averil Cameron, "Jews and Heretics—A Category Error," in *The Ways That Never Parted: Jews and Christians in Late Antiquity and the Early Middle Ages*, ed. Adam H. Becker and Annette Yoshiko Reed (Tübingen: Mohr Siebeck, 2003), 345–60. Whereas Barhebraeus compares Jews unfavorably to Muslims, Jacob of Edessa would apparently have compared Jews unfavorably to pagans (Muslim or otherwise); see Jacob's responsa on pagan and Jewish foodstuffs, cited above.

19. See, e.g., the reference to "pagans" in the canon cited in the previous note, convened in the capital of the Sasanid Persian Empire.

20. I am unaware of earlier Syrian Orthodox regulations governing the mental competency of butchers, but this does not prove that Christians were unfamiliar with such a rule before they encountered it in Islamic legal literature. The principle that madmen and unqualified minors are unfit to perform the act of animal slaughter, already attested in early Rabbinic literature (Mishnah *Ḥullin* 1.1, Tosefta *Ḥul.* 1.3), may well have been widespread in Near Eastern cultures.

21. Khadra, "Le Nomocanon," 198–99, echoing Nallino, "Diritto musulmano," 526. On the influence of al-Ghazālī on Barhebraeus's oeuvre, see Teule, "Barhebraeus' *Ethicon*."

22. For a brief introduction to Maimonides and his work, see *Encyclopaedia Judaica*, 2nd ed., 13:381–97. On the *Mishneh Torah*, see especially Twersky, *Introduction*.

23. On the sources Maimonides employs in the *Mishneh Torah*, see Twersky, *Introduction*, 49–61; Twersky's summary remark about the importance of attention to these sources is the epigraph to this essay. Twersky refers briefly to "non-Jewish sources: medical literature, works on astronomy, mathematics, and geometry, and the whole range of classical philosophy" (59) but not to aspects of strictly Islamic thought. Gerald J. Blidstein, "Where Do We Stand in the Study of Maimonidean Halakhah?" in *Studies in Maimonides*, ed. Isadore Twersky (Cambridge, Mass.: Harvard University Press, 1990), 27–29, identifies the relationship between Maimonidean law and Islamic law as a desideratum for future scholarship; one such study, which focuses on aspects of civil law, is Gideon Libson, "Parallels Between Maimonides and Islamic Law," in *The Thought of Moses Maimonides: Philosophical and Legal Studies*, ed. Ira Robinson, Lawrence Kaplan, and Julien Bauer (Lewiston, N.Y.: Edwin Mellen, 1990), 209–48.

24. For an examination of the ways in which Ibn Adret reinterprets texts produced in an Islamic milieu in light of the Christian environment in which he lived, see Martin Jacobs, "Interreligious Polemics in Medieval Spain: Biblical Interpretation Between Ibn Ḥazm, Shlomoh ibn Adret, and Shimʿon ben Ṣemaḥ Duran," *Jerusalem Studies in Jewish Thought* 21 (2007): 35*–57*.

25. Moses Maimonides, *Mishneh Torah* (Jerusalem: Shabse Frankel, 1975), *Hilkhot maʾakhalot asurot* 11.1, 4. Many earlier editions of the *Mishneh Torah* preserve the censored European text, which omits or alters Maimonides' statements regarding Christians.

26. Maimonides addresses the latter set of prohibitions in *Hil. maʾakhalot asurot* 17.9, where he clarifies that the prohibition of drinking with gentiles applies "even in a place where there is no concern regarding wine offered in idolatrous libation."

27. *Hil. ma'akhalot asurot* 11.7; Maimonides' definition of the resident alien (*ger toshav*) appears in *Hil. ʿavodah zarah* 10.6. Among other discussions of this passage and its relationship to Maimonidean attitudes regarding Islam, see David Novak, "The Treatment of Islam and Muslims in the Legal Writings of Maimonides," in *Studies in Islamic and Judaic Traditions*, ed. William M. Brinner and Stephen D. Ricks (Atlanta: Scholars Press, 1986), 236–37; and Eliezer Schlossberg, "Yaḥaso shel ha-Rambam el ha-Islam," *Peʿamim* 42 (1990): 42–45.

28. Solomon Ibn Adret, *Torat ha-bayit ha-arokh* 5.1, in *Torat ha-bayit ha-arokh ve-ha-qaṣar*, ed. Moshe ha-Kohen Baron (Jerusalem: Mosad ha-Rav Kook, 1995), 2:401–2.

29. This responsum is preserved in Abraham b. Isaac of Narbonne, *Sefer ha-eshkol*, ed. Chanokh Albeck and Shalom Albeck (Jerusalem: Reuven Mass, 1934–38), 2:74.

30. See *Halakhot pesuqot min ha-Geonim*, ed. Joel Miller (1893; New York: Menorah, 1957), 22, §25.

31. *Sefer ha-eshkol*, 2:78. See also the responsum cited in the previous note.

32. Responsum 269, in Joshua Blau, ed., *Teshuvot ha-Rambam* (Jerusalem: Meqitse Nirdamim, 1957), 515–16. Maimonides indicates that the newborn analogy was cited by the petitioner; in his reply, Maimonides does not address the rationale for leniency with respect to wine made by Muslims but rather emphasizes that consumption of such wine remains prohibited.

33. Responsum 448, in Blau, *Teshuvot ha-Rambam*, 726.

34. "Know that the Christians, who in their various sects espouse false claims regarding the messiah, are all idolaters . . . and one should interact with them in accordance with all laws governing interaction with idolaters." Maimonides, *Commentary on the Mishnah*, *ʿAvodah Zarah* 1.3, in Deror Fiqsler, *Masekhet ʿAvodah Zarah ʿim perush ha-Rambam: Mahadurah mevoʾeret* (Jerusalem: Maʿaliyot, 2002), 8; cf. *Mishneh Torah, Hil. ʿavodah zarah* 9.4.

35. As R. Jacob of Ramerupt observes (bAZ 57b, s.v. *le-apoqei*), adults act with intention when touching containers of wine, even if that intention has nothing to do with idolatrous motives; newborns, in contrast, do not act with intention at all. On this distinction and the circumstances that compelled it, see Haym Soloveitchik, *Yeinam: Saḥar be-yeinam shel goyim ʿal gilgulah shel halakhah be-ʿolam ha-maʿaseh* (Tel Aviv: ʿAlma, 2003), 122–24.

36. Alternatively, it is possible that Ibn Adret willfully misinterprets Maimonides' opinion on this subject, rejecting it as a deviation from the Rabbinic legal tradition. An example of this response to the *Mishneh Torah* among later interpreters and codifiers is discussed by Isadore Twersky, "Some Non-Halakic Aspects of the Mishneh Torah," in *Jewish Medieval and Renaissance Studies*, ed. Alexander Altmann (Cambridge, Mass.: Harvard University Press, 1967), 118, reprinted in *Studies in Jewish Law and Philosophy* (New York: KTAV, 1982), 75.

37. This rationalist conception of monotheism, highlighted by Ibn Khaldūn in his history of the Berbers, finds especially clear expression in Muḥammad Ibn Ṭufayl's *Risālat Ḥayy ibn Yaqẓān*, whose Andalusian author (d. 1185) served as personal physician to the Almohad caliph Yūsuf Abū Yaʿqūb.

38. Madeleine Fletcher, "The Almohad Tawhīd: Theology Which Relies on Logic," *Numen* 38 (1991): 110–27.

39. Sarah Stroumsa, *Maimonides in His World: Portrait of a Mediterranean Thinker* (Princeton, N.J.: Princeton University Press, 2008), 53–83.

40. Daniel Boyarin, *Border Lines: The Partition of Judaeo-Christianity* (Philadelphia: University of Pennsylvania Press, 2004).

41. Ivan G. Marcus, *Rituals of Childhood: Jewish Acculturation in Medieval Europe* (New Haven, Conn.: Yale University Press, 1996), 12. Marcus highlights the ways in which Ashkenazic Jews "assimilated reworked aspects of Christian culture, in the form of a social polemical denial, into their Judaism." The present study suggests that the phenomenon of "inward acculturation" Marcus describes manifests itself in non-polemical contexts as well.

42. See David M. Freidenreich, "Christians in Early and Classical Islamic Law," in *Christian-Muslim Relations*, vol. 1, ed. Thomas et al. (Leiden: Brill, 2009), 83–98.

43. On the specifically Islamic origins of this concept, see Guy G. Stroumsa, "Early Christianity—A Religion of the Book?" in *Homer, the Bible, and Beyond: Literary and Religious Canons in the Ancient World*, ed. Margalit Finkelberg and Guy G. Stroumsa (Leiden: Brill, 1993), 153–55.

44. *Hil. ma'akhalot asurot* 17.9. In this passage, Maimonides emphasizes the need to avoid social interaction with gentiles as a means of preventing intermarriage. In responsum 269 (Blau) and *Ma'akhalot asurot* 11.10, however, Maimonides offers a simple expedient to enable Jews to drink with Muslims without contravening the law. He provides similar loopholes with respect to the prohibition of Muslim bread in *Ma'akhalot asurot* 17.12–13 on the grounds that symbolic acknowledgment of the prohibition is sufficient to prevent intermarriage.

45. *Hil. yesodei ha-Torah* 1.

46. On scriptural disputation with Muslims and with Christians, see responsum 149 in Blau, *Teshuvot ha-Rambam*, 284–85.

47. Barhebraeus was presumably unaware of the fact that twelfth- and thirteenth-century canon law commentators in Latin Europe also justified traditional Christian prohibitions against Jewish food and commensality with Jews by reference to Jewish abuse of scripture and the associated risk that Jews might "deceive" Christians. See David M. Freidenreich, "Sharing Meals with Non-Christians in Canon Law Commentaries, circa 1160–1260: A Case Study in Legal Development," *Medieval Encounters* 14 (2008): 41–77. On Barhebraeus's contact with Latin Christians and their thought, see the discussion and bibliography in Takahashi, *Barhebraeus*, 35–37.

48. See Ze'ev Maghen, *After Hardship Cometh Ease: The Jews as Backdrop for Muslim Moderation* (Berlin: Walter de Gruyter, 2006).

INDEX

Vajda, Georges, 16
Vulgate, 181n8

Wahb b. Munabbih, 23, 24, 166n56
al-Warrāq, Abū ʿĪsā, 120
Wasserstein, David J.: "The Muslims and the Golden Age," 179n24, 179n26
al-Wāthiq, 35
Weiss, Abraham, 191n75
Wolfson, Harry A.: *The Philosophy of the Kalam*, 120; *Repercussions of the Kalam*, 120

Yaḥyā ibn ʿAdī, 116, 120
Yannai, 18–19, 166n48
Yūsuf al-Baṣīr, 68
Yūsuf ibn Dhāsī, 38

Zoroastrians, 2, 148, 149, 150, 152, 161n3
al-Zuhrī, Ibn Shihāb, 72, 190n66

ACKNOWLEDGMENTS

The essays in this volume are the fruits of research, seminars, and casual discussions over lunch or in a hallway at the University of Pennsylvania's Katz Center for Advanced Judaic Studies. The volume's contributors all participated in the 2006–7 research group "Jews, Christians, and Muslims Under Caliphs and Sultans." On behalf of all the members of this research group, we extend our gratitude to the staff and supporters of the Center for fostering an especially conducive atmosphere for scholarship and collegiality.

The process of transforming a year's worth of research into a coherent volume is one that involves considerable effort and collaboration. We are grateful to the contributors for the time they spent preparing these essays and responding to countless requests for revisions. David Ruderman, Director of the Katz Center, has provided valuable assistance throughout the process.